The Empress of Ireland

Also by Christopher Robbins

Assassin

Air America

The Ravens

The Test of Courage

The Empress of Ireland

Chronicle of an Unusual Friendship

CHRISTOPHER ROBBINS

Scribner

First published in Great Britain by Scribner in 2004
An imprint of Simon & Schuster UK Ltd
A Viacom company

1 3 5 7 9 10 8 6 4 2

Simon & Schuster UK Ltd
Africa House
64–78 Kingsway
London WC2B 6AH

Simon & Schuster Australia
Sydney

www.simonsays.co.uk

A CIP catalogue for this book is available
from the British Library.

ISBN: 0-7432-2071-4

Typeset by M Rules
Printed and bound in Great Britain by Mackays of Chatham plc

PICTURE CREDITS
pp. 2, 8, 19, 54, 99, 124, 152, 189, 248, 260, 280, 322, 326, 351, 372: Private collection
pp. 110, 115: Evening Gazette, Lytham
pp. 11, 290, 300, 309: Roland Grant Archive
pp. 38, 46, 146, 234, 254, 285: Camera Press
p. 296: Popperfoto
p. 330: Retna

For Mary Agnes,
and in memory of John, my big brother.

CONTENTS

PROLOGUE

'Fucking old queen!'

It was mid-morning in the Turk's Head, Belgravia, the quiet hour before the arrival of the lunchtime clientele, when only the idle and the alcoholic are about, and the smell of polish and air-freshener briefly dominates the fug of stale beer and stubbed cigarettes. The pub was empty except for a row of three muddy labourers at the bar, skiving off work from a building site around the corner. They wore identical blue donkey jackets and were crouched monkey-like over pints of Guinness.

Brian Desmond Hurst affected not to have heard the insult that accompanied his entrance. He was a tall, distinguished man in his early eighties, with pale blue, ageless eyes, a shock of flowing white hair and thick, bushy eyebrows. He wore a Savile Row jacket with the cut of another era, grey flannels, suede shoes of chocolate brown, and an emerald green tie that shone against a white shirt. Unperturbed and aloof, he made his stately progress across the room carrying a single orange cupped in his left hand.

'Morning, Bri.' The publican polished glasses with exaggerated concentration, also pretending not to have heard the sniggered abuse. He picked up the orange that Brian placed before him and cut it in half. The publican squeezed the juice into a champagne flute, and turned to take a half-bottle of Bollinger from the fridge. Brian watched and waited as the orange juice was topped up with champagne, then lifted the glass to his mouth and swallowed its contents in two large gulps. He gave a sigh of satisfaction: '*Breakfast!*'

As the publican squeezed the juice from the other half of the orange into the glass, and prepared once again to fill it with champagne, Brian nodded in the direction of the labourers. 'Please ask those three gentlemen if they would like a drink.'

The publican draped the dishcloth over his arm and moved purposefully along the bar, a man charged with a sensitive mission. As mine host in a pub in an exclusive part of London, his ear was tuned to the background hum of happy drinkers as is a sea captain's to the throb of his ship's engines, and he reacted strongly against anything that disturbed lucrative good cheer. This morning, public house etiquette had been violated by outsiders who had insulted a regular without provocation, and now pub lore was further strained by the offer of a drink from the defamed party. A delicate situation.

'Mr Desmond Hurst wonders if you *gentlemen* would care for a drink?' As the publican waited for a reply, he lowered his eyes and wiped the spotless mahogany bar with his dishcloth. The men shifted uncomfortably on their stools, without looking at one another, and there was a moment of tension and embarrassment. One by one they mumbled orders for fresh sleevers of Guinness. The pints were drawn in silence and placed on the bar, and as each man lifted his drink to his lips he gave up a shamed murmur of thanks: 'Cheers, mate!' . . . 'Cheers!'

'Your very good health,' Brian said, raising his glass of champagne in the trio's direction. 'And by the way, gentlemen, I am *not* an old queen.' He paused, forcing the men to look at him. '*I am the Empress of Ireland!*'

PART I

London

Brian Desmond Hurst

It was lunchtime on a dark, drizzling winter's day in the early 1970s when I first entered the magical world of Brian Desmond Hurst. This was headquartered at the north end of Kinnerton Street, Belgravia, where he lived alone in a large Georgian house leased from the Duke of Westminster for three pounds a week. The front door was situated beneath an arch formed by a bedroom built across an alley off the street, and was opened by a tall, gloomy individual in a tweed jacket. He glared at me.

'Yeah?'

'I've come to see Mr Desmond Hurst. He's expecting me.'

The man turned and walked away without a word, leaving the door open. I crossed the threshold uncertainly, and made my way along the hallway in the direction of voices. I stepped into a drawing room where a dozen or so men stood holding drinks. Half spoke in drawling, upper-class accents, and the other half in barrow-boy Cockney. The room was grandly shabby, furnished with a mixture of antiques, threadbare chairs and sagging sofas. The walls were hung with oil paintings – one of which was six feet long and unframed, with a corner crudely hacked off to make it fit around a door. Over the mantel hung a portrait of St Bridget, painted in the style of Modigliani. An illegal log fire burned in the grate.

In the far corner, by the leaded front window looking on to the street, I saw an elderly man enthroned in a wing-backed chair with a brightly coloured Afghan kilim rug thrown over it. A group was gathered around him, and one young man sat at his feet. An arm snaked around my shoulders, and an enthusiastic American voice called out, 'You made it! Come and meet Bri!'

Apart from his name and address, I knew very little about Brian Desmond Hurst, except that he was a film producer in search of a scriptwriter. And I was about to be proposed to this stranger as a suitable candidate by an American acquaintance I scarcely knew, despite the fact that at the time I was only twenty-seven years old and had never even read a screenplay. 'You're gonna love Bri! Believe me!'

My sponsor in this introduction was himself an enigma. I had met Billy the previous summer, when I had spent several months in Spain, where he added colour to the local scene with his psychedelic shirts, purple velvet trousers, cowboy boots and black felt hat wrapped in a garish bandanna. All I knew of his background was gleaned from the harrowing stories he told of hallucinogenic experiences on the west coast of America, where Billy had dropped LSD with the same abandon that the holiday crowd on the Costa Blanca ordered lunchtime jugs of sangria. 'I was into acid in San Francisco so early on, man, it was still *legal*! Owsley's Sunshine! Best damned shit on God's earth. I dropped a tab every morning to set me up for the day.'

After I first met Billy in Spain, he seemed to show up everywhere. Whatever beach, house, party, restaurant or club was momentarily in favour, he would be there. And he never found it too much trouble to drive newly-made acquaintances wherever they wanted to go, any time of the day or night, obligingly materialising in a black Cadillac convertible with California plates, upholstered in soft crimson leather. As he drove along the coast road in southern Spain, eyes dancing with dangerous drugs, he liked to hum a demented version of 'Happy Trails' by the Grateful Dead.

It came as a surprise to bump into this creature of the sun in a Soho pub that winter, hair coiffed and teased, and dressed in a three-piece pin-striped suit. The abrupt change from ingratiating druggie to conservative businessman was not altogether convincing, and lacked attention to detail. Billy clung to a couple of the props of his previous personality: a pair of mirrored dark glasses was pushed back on his head, and he was shod in snakeskin cowboy boots. He asked me how things were going and I replied that I was trying to claw my way out of debt by writing pieces for Fleet Street. A number of articles were about to appear in the *Observer* magazine. 'What are you up to?'

'Just putting some people together.'

This, I came to understand, was what Billy did. I never discovered how he made any money doing it, as he seemed to ask for nothing in return, but was forever introducing the most unlikely people to one another. 'Give me your card, I might be able to get you some writing work,' he said. 'I'll give you a ring.'

As I did not have a card, I wrote my number on the back of a beer mat. Billy, however, was furnished with exquisite visiting cards which he kept in a small tortoiseshell box. They were engraved by Smythson's of Bond Street, and printed on expensive ebony-coloured board, each one separated from the other by a small square of tissue paper. The card disclosed that Billy had changed more than his haircut and colourful summer clothes since I last saw him. Count Wilhelm Wissen von Platz, the elegant spidery script read, Argyll Street, Kensington.

I fingered the card and maintained a diplomatic silence, trying not to laugh.

'Drop by for a drink some night, old cock,' the count said. 'Check out the pad. Five thousand square feet of fully furnished, double-fronted, white-stuccoed, Queen Anne luxury, man. It's a blast – top-hole!'

In the months that Billy had been in London, he had also developed a curious patois. This magpie mixture of slang, regional accents and bizarre turns of phrase was culled from encounters with people from all classes and walks of life, and further enriched by foreign shopkeepers and immigrant waiters. The core vocabulary, however, seemed to be gleaned from dated Gor-Blimey Cockney and old English films of the stiff-upper-lip variety. There was also the uncomfortable coupling of San Francisco acid-head with continental aristocrat, further enriching the verbal stew. The clanging uproar of this linguistic cacophony failed to register upon Billy's tin ear.

The social metamorphosis from American hipster into Prussian Junker was as shameless as it was rapid. I was eager to hear about the count's recent elevation, but he seemed to sense I was about to ask awkward questions. 'Later,' Billy said, turning away. '*Ciao,* me old china!'

I did not expect to hear from the bogus count again, but underestimated his drive for putting people together. This was not the acquired habit of a hustler, but fundamental to his nature, an instinctive need, like food, sleep or sex. The promised call came within a couple of days. 'Oil up the Underwood, baby – gotta big-time movie producer who needs a screenwriter!'

I explained that I was a journalist, not a screenwriter.

'Hey man, it's all words!' He rattled off an address. 'Big bucks! Be there for lunch at one tomorrow! Pip, pip.'

And so it was that I made my way to 83 Kinnerton Street and the drawing room of Brian Desmond Hurst. Although the day was dreary and wet, Billy continued to sport the unlikely aristocratic accessories of cowboy boots and dark glasses – pushed back on his head as before. He led me across the room to the imposing presence in the winged chair. There was an aura surrounding Brian Desmond Hurst that suggested it might be appropriate to drop on one knee and kiss his hand.

'Here he is,' Billy said, like an impresario promoting some dim starlet. 'Christopher Robbins – the *Observer*'s hottest new writer.'

'Ah, the *Observer*.' Brian sighed and gave an appreciative

nod. 'The paper of the arts. *Always* gave me good reviews. Well, *almost* always. Wilhelm, fetch Christopher a Great Big Glass of Wine.'

The voice was rich but soft, cultivated but unaffected, with just a touch of Ireland purring in the background. It was an instrument of perfect pitch, I would come to appreciate, keenly honed and effortlessly paced, as finely tuned for the anecdote and well-turned phrase as it was for the dirty joke and outrageous aside.

Lunch was served with surly resentment by the gloomy man who had opened the front door. It consisted of over-cooked scrambled eggs dolloped on to uneven wedges of doorstep toast, eaten from a collection of chipped, unmatched plates balanced on the knees. There seemed to be limitless wine, no two bottles of which were the same. Brian held court with gossip, anecdotes and jokes while the count circled, a bottle in each hand, replenishing glasses. The booze-fuelled babble of conversation became a roar. One of the Cockneys turned to me and voiced the opinion that the Old Bill was *way out of order* in London these days and was taking *diabolical liberties* with the citizenry. 'And they wonder why people carry sawn-offs!' An upper-class voice enquired whether I gave any credence to the story that Wallis Simpson, wife of the Duke of Windsor, was a man.

Suddenly, from across the room, I heard myself addressed. 'Christopher, what do you consider the single most important thing affecting our lives today?'

I was caught off-guard. Along with everybody else I was half-tight, and enjoying myself so much that I had almost forgotten why I had been invited. As Brian knew I was a journalist, I thought he might expect me to comment on current world events. The oil crisis obsessed the press at the time, so I plumped for that, trying to sound well-informed and serious-minded. 'Well, I suppose you could say that one area of considerable global concern is the price of oil!'

'Don't talk to me about the price of petrol,' the Cockney said. '*Diabolical!*'

'Frightful!' an upper-class voice chimed in. 'I *shudder* to tell you what it costs to fill the Rolls.'

A look of irritation and mild contempt flashed across Brian's face. '*The most important thing in our lives today*,' he said in a weary tone, 'the most important thing, in fact, in the past two thousand years of *all* human life – is the birth of Christ.'

'I'm sorry,' I said weakly, 'I thought you meant . . .'

Billy appeared at Brian's elbow and refilled his glass as he talked over me, raising his voice to be heard above the swell of conversation. 'I have been making films for fifty years – comedies, tragedies, classics, adventure stories, documentaries – even musicals, would you believe? But now I want to make my masterpiece. A Great Big Religious Picture. To tell the most important story of all.'

'The birth of Christ,' I said in a small, hopeless voice, directing a desperate look at Billy who snapped his sun-glasses into place like a visor.

'*The events leading up to* the birth of Christ,' Brian said in triumph. He smiled and gave me a look that said: *What do you think of that?*

'Gotta go!' Billy said suddenly. 'Important meeting with some Arabs at the Dorchester.' He leaned forward and, much to my surprise, kissed Brian full on the lips. 'Hope you guys can work it out. Fare thee well!'

As Billy's cowboy-booted heels clopped through the door, Brian turned to me. 'Wilhelm told me you met in Spain when he was putting together some multi-million-pound film fund?'

'We met in Spain, yes. Where did you meet . . . *Wilhelm*?'

'Nag's Head,' Brian said, jerking his head in the direction of the pub a few doors along the street. 'They do good bangers and mash at lunchtime.' The thought seemed to distract him momentarily from the birth of Christ, and there was a pause before he returned to the subject. 'I need a young writer with fire in his belly – not some hack in it for the money. I want somebody inspired – somebody talented and fresh. Someone with passion.'

He was interrupted by a guest who came across to say goodbye. 'Don't go away,' Brian said to me. 'Wait until we're on our own and we'll talk.'

A film about the events leading up to the birth of Christ! I had gone to lunch not knowing what to expect – with no expectations at all, really. I was a broke freelance writer drawn to the words 'big bucks' like a salmon to the sea, but I had no screenwriting skills whatsoever and had never considered acquiring any. I nursed a vague notion on the way over that I might be able to contribute a story idea for a thriller or do some research for a historical drama – but a religious picture! I was spectacularly ill-suited for such a venture, lacking both knowledge and faith, and was certainly not the inspired writer with fire in his belly called for in the job description.

The gloomy man stuck his head round the door. 'I'm off, Bri, unless there's something else you want.'

'Not this afternoon, Josephine.'

As the last of the guests departed and I was left to face Brian alone, I suffered feelings of mild panic. The 'hot young writer' was about to be exposed as unschooled, Grub Street chancer and Godless, opportunistic fraud.

'Make us a cup of coffee, will you?' Brian said. 'Milk, no sugar for me. Kitchen's downstairs. At least, I *think* that's where it is.'

I descended into the basement kitchen and searched for mugs and Nescafé. As I waited for the kettle to boil I mulled over the situation. Brian was much older than I had expected, maybe something of a religious nut . . . possibly even queer. There were no women at the lunch party, I had noticed, and his exuberant guests were a decidedly unusual social mix. And

Billy had kissed Brian on the lips, which was odd. All that apart, the project itself was out of the question for the hard-boiled, cynical investigative reporter I then imagined myself to be. I cursed the phoney count for landing me in such an absurd situation and rehearsed excuses and suitable exit lines. 'Honoured and flattered to be considered, etc. etc., not really the right man for the job, pressure of work, blah blah blah . . .'

I went back upstairs with the mugs of coffee. The log fire had burned down and it was beginning to get dark outside. It had been a long lunch. 'Turn on the electric fire,' Brian said. 'It's bloody freezing in here.'

I moved to switch on the fire. 'The thing is . . .' I began.

'Both bars, that's it – let's go mad!' Brian drank some coffee. 'You make a nice cup of instant, Christopher. Just how I like it.' He put the cup down beside him. 'Yes, the events leading up to the birth of Christ. *Quite a story!* I want to shoot the film in Malta and Morocco. Maybe Libya. I made *Black Tent* there, you know. Of course, King Idris was alive then, but I think I might be able to get around this Gaddafi. I'm sure he's not as bad as they make out. The Holy Land is just not possible these days with all those Jews and Arabs driving tanks around everywhere shooting one another. Do you know Morocco?'

'I'm afraid not.'

'We'd better get down there and look it over for locations. I have a house in Tangier. Beautiful place high up in the Kasbah. We can stay there. Not that Tangier has much to do with the Holy Land' – Brian winked – 'but an hour's drive away up into the mountains there's Chechouen. You step back thousands of years. Not to mention an abundant supply of cheap extras – all of them dressed in easily removed *djellabas*. Ever been to Malta?'

'Never.'

'We can do studio stuff there – and some exteriors. Shot *Malta Story* on the island with Alec Guinness and Jack

Brian with Siobhan McKenna in the drawing room at Kinnerton Street

Hawkins. Naturally, the islanders consider me something of a national treasure. I do dislike London in the bleak midwinter, so let's get off to Morocco fast. How are you fixed at the moment?'

'Well, the thing is . . .'

Before I had a chance to make my excuses, Brian leaned forward and pulled open the drawer of a small table beside his chair. He groped inside, fished out a large Coutts chequebook and flapped it in my direction. 'Let's get the business out of the way. Shall we say,' he glanced around him for inspiration, 'six thousand pounds?'

Six thousand pounds in those far-off days was a decent fee for anyone, but six thousand pounds to me was wealth beyond the dreams of avarice. It was rent paid, bank overdraft cleared . . . wine, women and song. Suddenly the events leading up to the birth of Christ seemed more promising as the plot for a movie. There were all sorts of dramatic possibilities, what with the wise men trekking across the desert and Herod killing the children. It was quite interesting, really. True, I knew nothing about screenwriting, but I rationalised that everybody had to start somewhere. Cutting-edge or not as a cinematic theme, there was six thousand quid in the birth of Christ for me.

'Larry Olivier and Michael Redgrave have already agreed to be in the film,' Brian continued. 'Larry as Augustus, Michael as Herod. Vanessa could play Mariamne, perhaps. The subject allows for – no, the subject *demands* – a stellar cast. The Duke of Westminster has expressed interest in financing the picture. Believe me, this will be a Box Office Blockbuster! *Guaranteed!*' As he spoke, the chequebook disappeared back inside the drawer.

'Let's have a whisky. There's Scotch and Irish in those decanters on the sideboard.'

It was dark when I stepped back out into Kinnerton Street. I was tipsy on wine and whisky, famous names and exotic places – and the prospect of adventure. Sitting on top of the double-decker bus home, I marvelled at life's twists and turns, and wondered vaguely who Mariamne might be. Suddenly and unexpectedly, I was launched upon a career as a well-paid screenwriter. Writing parts for Lord Olivier and Sir Michael Redgrave, no less. With a billionaire duke as a backer. And lots of foreign travel in the offing with this splendid character Brian Desmond Hurst. Wonderful, heady, exciting stuff. As the bus took me towards my shoebox flat in Bloomsbury, I pondered the dramatic problems of adapting the events leading up to the birth of Christ for the big screen, and wondered how soon it would be appropriate to ask for an advance.

One of the first things I did in the days following our meeting was research Brian's film career. It was impressive, and I felt inappropriately privileged to have been chosen as the man to write his masterpiece. Brian Desmond Hurst was – and remains – Ireland's most prolific film director, with more than thirty movies to his credit, including *Scrooge* (also known as *A Christmas Carol*), *Tom Brown's Schooldays*, *Dangerous Moonlight*, *Theirs Is the Glory*, *Malta Story*, *Simba* and *Playboy of the Western World*. He had worked with all of the leading British stars of his day including Lord Olivier, Sir Alec Guinness, Sir Ralph Richardson and Sir Michael Redgrave. He gave many actors their first film roles – among them Vanessa Redgrave, Siobhan McKenna and Roger Moore – and promoted the careers of a legion of directors and writers. Indeed, his career was so impressive that the question I should have been asking, of course, was, 'Why me?'

Brian seemed to be considered a bit of a maverick within the film community. As one film directory I dipped into put it, 'This director's work has covered an almost bewildering range of themes: his last half-dozen pictures have been a comedy with music, a Dickens adaptation, two war stories, a Mau Mau drama and a costume romance; and his subjects before that were equally varied. Such versatility makes it difficult to pin down any one aspect of a shifting talent.' As far as I could make out, he had not directed a film for a decade, since *Playboy of the Western World*, although he sat on the board of an Irish movie company with Lord Killanin.

I had loved *Scrooge*, and been moved to tears by its unashamed sentimentality. *Tom Brown's Schooldays* had terrified me as a twelve-year-old when it had been shown at my preparatory school in the final week of term before I went up into the senior school. Although I had been a boarder from the age of seven and was no stranger to institutional misery, I dreaded the legendary brutality and bullying of the big school, and the film reinforced my fears. Throughout the holidays, before I went up, I suffered nightmares, and when I was finally driven to school my father had to stop the car while I was sick by the side of the road.

Alastair Sim as Scrooge in the film of the same name – Brian's most famous movie

My research also confirmed my original suspicions about Brian's sexual orientation. I mentioned his name to a gossip columnist at the bar of El Vino's, in Fleet Street, and it was overheard by an old-fashioned journalist famous for his bibulous and reactionary views. 'Desmond Hurst! A *notorious* bugger! A homosexualist corrupter of the most blatant sort! A *shameless* pervert!'

This posed potential difficulties. After all, the homosexualist corrupter and shameless pervert was fifty years my senior. It had crossed my mind that Billy might be gay, and that Brian had therefore assumed I was. However, invited for drinks at the count's fully furnished Queen Anne luxury pad a week later, I was confronted by evidence that suggested his sexual proclivities were extravagantly heterosexual.

Billy lived with a beautiful young woman named Sarah, who clung to his arm and whose eyes never left him. A number of his *louche* friends were draped over sofas and chairs, drinking champagne and listening to music. A man sat cross-legged on the floor, skilfully constructing a joint the size of a Cuban cigar out of hash, tobacco and a half-dozen cigarette papers.

'We'll go eat later, honey,' Billy said, disentangling himself from his disciple. 'Go get ready. Tally-ho.'

Sarah reluctantly peeled herself from Billy's side and gave him a sad, sexy *moue* through parted lips as she sashayed across the room, rhythmically moving her rump to the music. The count watched her progress with naked lust. 'What's not to like? Some fine filly, what?'

Billy led me into the study and closed the door behind us. He collapsed into a large armchair and began to roll a slender joint of Californian grass, explaining that he did not understand the crass London habit of constructing clumsy, carrot-like spliffs of black hash that reduced the smoker to dribbling incoherence. 'Sober, stoned or fried, I like to keep an edge.' He lit up, inhaling deeply. 'So what do you think, squire?'

'A beautiful girl.'

'Some pair, huh?' Billy gave a girlish squeal of laughter, an endearing giggle that was part of his personality and helped soften the provocation of his more outlandish affectations. 'Intelligent too. But it hasn't spoilt her. For years I stayed away from these hoity-toity English chicks because I believed all that shit about them being frigid. I found out it's propaganda put out by English guys to scare off the competition. Frigid my arse! I've never met such obliging perverts. And I'm talking as somebody who's been around the music business.' Billy was overcome by erotic nostalgia as he took a stretch limousine down memory lane. 'I've been tied up and teased by gorgeous blondes in San Francisco and had my brains fucked out by beautiful black chicks in Chicago. I've been blown in the back of a limo in New York by under-age nympho twins – but I had to come to Kensington to hit pay-dirt.'

My mind raced.

Billy pulled himself up in his chair and lowered his voice as he described one of Sarah's more original sexual practices.

'Christ!'

Billy squealed. 'Do you believe that shit! Just so long as it doesn't frighten the horses, old man, what?'

I steered the conversation towards Brian and the movie, and explained that I had been hired as a screenwriter for six thousand pounds. 'You should have held out for ten – but what the hell, you got the gig. Bully for you.' I clumsily offered to pay a fee for the introduction. 'Thanks, but that's not the way I operate. Make the movie. Get rich. There'll be room for Billy somewhere down the line.'

I fidgeted in my chair, and discreetly voiced my suspicion that Brian might be homosexual. Billy squealed. 'You are one perceptive *hombre*, Chris – I have to hand it to you. The old poof just couldn't hide it from you, could he?' He squealed again. 'My advice is: don't go round the house naked in a fur hat. Otherwise you'll be okay.'

'Naked in a fur hat?'

'What are those things on the redcoats' heads outside Buckingham Palace?'

'You mean the busbies worn by the Brigade of Guards?'

'Whatever. Don't dance naked around Kinnerton Street in one of those.'

'Thank you for the advice.'

'Bri likes Guardsmen. Big, butch, muscular guys over six feet tall.'

'You mean, I'm not his type.'

'You got it! No offence.'

'One other thing – I'm still trying to get to grips with the subject of the film.'

'Remind me.'

'The events leading up to the birth of Christ.'

'Oh yeah.'

'A bit old-fashioned, maybe?'

'Not everybody's cup of Rosie Lee. But who knows what the public will want in a year's time? They sure as shit don't. They might want a love story, hardcore porn or something violent and fast. Maybe a tea-and-crumpets costume drama hits the spot, or some French existential crap. Why not a Jesus picture? You'll be the only guys at the Cannes Film Festival pushing a God movie, you can bet on that!'

'I suppose that's true.'

Over the next two hours Billy progressed from marijuana to long lines of cocaine, which he chopped meticulously with a razor and then snorted through a tightly rolled hundred-dollar bill from a large Venetian mirror laid upon the study desk. In between lines of coke he threw back shot glasses of tequila.

I had finished a bottle of champagne and was halfway through a second, when Billy announced some time after midnight that we should all go out for dinner. I found myself among a dozen people grouped around a large, circular table at Tramp, the nightclub in Jermyn Street. Nobody seemed to know one another, but everybody knew Billy. On my right sat a pretty, serious-minded young Russian princess, said to live with her mother in a council house in South London. She spoke of her work for the Red Cross and various encounters with ghosts. An opinionated redhead sat on my left, braying from time to time like an excited mare. Her boyfriend, a pale, skinny melancholic who worked for a record company, seemed to have developed the same dislike from intimate knowledge that I formed on first acquaintance. A very fat, very drunk English lord – said also to be *very* rich – sat next to a beautiful blonde model of stunning stupidity. I failed to recognise a man with a distinctive, electrified-chicken hairdo, whom I later learned was Ronnie Wood, guitarist then for the Faces and Rod Stewart, and later the Rolling Stones.

Billy dominated the conversation around the table, letting rip with energetic bursts of staccato monologue, the length and intensity of which were punctuated by squeals of giggling that acted as pauses or full-stops. He seemed unaffected by his prodigious intake of drugs and hard liquor, and ordered plates of giant prawns to be brought to the table, along with bottles of Roederer Cristal champagne and a bottle of tequila.

I engaged in the first of many strange conversations that any mention of the movie's subject-matter always seemed to generate. In the course of the evening, I told the pale music executive that I was writing a script for a film. 'What's it called?'

'The working title is *Born to be King*.'

'What's it about?'

'The events leading up to the birth of Christ.'

'Blimey!'

The subject provoked instant outrage in the redhead. '*Events leading up to the birth of Christ!* You are *joking*!'

'No. Quite serious. Three wise men, massacre of the innocents – that sort of thing.'

'They'll be crawling over one another to see that one – *I don't think!*'

'What do you know about it, you silly tart?' her boyfriend snarled. 'You couldn't write nothing! You can't even write out a cheque to Harrods without spelling it wrong.'

'What's Harrods got to do with it? I just happen to think the events leading up to the birth of Christ is a crap idea for a movie.'

'You're just not spiritual,' Sarah said from across the table. 'Obviously, you've got to be Christian and not just interested in shopping.'

'You, a Christian?' the redhead brayed. 'That's a joke!'

'I am a Christian, actually,' Sarah said, sounding cross. 'And other spiritual stuff besides.'

'I'm as Christian as you are any day – *Mother Teresa!*'

'I suppose you don't believe in anything?'

'Fuck you,' the girl said, rising abruptly from the table.

She made her way from the restaurant into the discotheque, and as she went through the doorway lifted her dress to expose her naked bottom.

Billy had not contributed to the religious debate swirling about him, but now moved quickly around the table to sit beside me in the chair left vacant by the redhead. A fanatical gleam had entered his eyes. 'Know what you've got with this movie?'

I shook my head.

'*Controversy!*' He smacked the table with the palm of his hand. 'This birth of Christ stuff divides people into camps. They get steamed up. They talk about it, argue about it. It brings out strong feelings and emotion.'

'So it seems.'

'Man, that's what it's all about! You're really on to something. *Events leading up to the birth of Christ*. It sounds like corny shit at first, but what's really happening is that you're pulling the pin out of a grenade and quietly rolling it under the seats of the audience. *Whammo!* You've got something with this movie, man. Christians are gonna reach for their guns.'

'I never thought of it like that.'

'Studios *kill* to be controversial. Controversy's a public relations slam dunk – an advertising man's wet dream. And you've stumbled into it without trying.' Billy saluted me. 'Congratulations, Carruthers!'

Billy was so used to promoting obscure and untalented groups, so practised in the dynamics of selling half-baked concepts and far-fetched schemes, that in the late-night grip of pot, coke and booze, the film had acquired the certainty of a slam-dunk success. The force of his own argument had overwhelmed him. Billy had pitched the movie to himself, and he was sold. 'It's going to happen, baby. I'm going to *make* it happen! This is going to be very, *very* big!'

*

A few days later I returned to Kinnerton Street and sat with Brian beside the electric fire in the drawing room. 'I must say, you seem to have greatly interested Wilhelm in our little project. He telephoned and sounded *most* excited. Said he had somebody in the City who might be good for half the budget. Somebody he wanted to "put me together with" – strange phrase, but there you are.'

'What *is* the budget?'

'A major picture like this will cost *many* millions. But first things first – you write the script, and I give it to my old assistant director Bluey for a breakdown. I do not intend to stint. But not *too* many armies of a hundred thousand men, please.'

I smiled obligingly.

'Wilhelm mentioned that in view of the size and importance of the picture, your fee should be at least ten thousand pounds, with a bonus in proportion to the final budget.'

'I had no idea he was going to ask for any such thing,' I said, flustered and embarrassed. 'I hope you don't think I authorised him to ask for more money. I agreed to a sum and that's that.'

Brian waved his hand, a grand gesture of empty munificence that I would come to recognise as part of the standard vocabulary of his body language. 'Wilhelm is quite right. Ten thousand it shall be. I don't want people saying I pay my writers slave labour rates. On certain previous pictures, it is true, I have been known to fuck the writer – but in a totally different context. And a nice big bonus. And, of course, a share of the profits.'

'That's most generous.'

Brian waved away my thanks with another imperial gesture. His voice assumed a tone of concern. 'You're not paying Wilhelm a percentage, are you?'

'I thought I should offer him an introductory fee but he absolutely refused.'

'Quite so,' Brian said, nodding approval. 'The man's an

aristocrat. Things go so much smoother when one's among gentlemen. Although, a strange thing – he always kisses me full on the lips when he says goodbye. *Very* continental. Or do you think he's *like that*?'

'Oh no. He lives with a beautiful girl in a big Kensington house. Possibly a bit kinky, though.'

'Kinky? How?'

'Well, apparently his girlfriend likes to blow cocaine through a straw into his bottom.'

'*Really?*' Brian was thoughtful. 'An imaginative and obliging young lady, no doubt, but I do not approve of all this drug-taking. I remember my old friend Gerald Hamilton telling me that the first cocaine addict he ever met was a count, in Capri after the First World War. Count Adelsward-Fersen. A rich fellow, he was a descendant of the man who drove the *berline* of the French royal family when Marie-Antoinette and Louis XVI tried to leave the country to save themselves from the guillotine. The cocaine-sniffing count was considered by the superstitious natives of Capri to be under a curse, because a local was killed working on his villa when he fell from a precipice into the sea. Curse or not, the cocaine had rendered him *most* peculiar. Although as far as I know, the count's favoured orifice of ingestion was the nostril.'

From the beginning, our meetings always followed this meandering pattern of anecdote and reminiscence. It was not that Brian went off at a tangent, or tended to digress, or was unable to keep to the subject when at work – tangential rambling and digression was *how* he worked. It was also how he thought, and pretty much how he lived. I would arrive to discuss the film, and some chance remark would remind Brian of something and he would be off. The repertoire of stories seemed limitless.

'When I first worked in Hollywood as an assistant to John Ford – who was a close friend, and called me "cousin" – he

A portrait of Brian taken during the most prolific period of his career

was making *Arrowsmith* with Ronald Colman, from the novel by Sinclair Lewis. Colman couldn't act and his scripts were combed and combed until there was nothing in them he couldn't do. In *Arrowsmith* he played a character experimenting with a serum for a disease by giving it to one group and withholding it from another. In one scene Colman had to appear drunk and throw a phial of serum against a wall with great violence. This kind of acting was beyond his capabilities. After forty takes there was a deathly silence and I said quietly, "Do you want anything printed, Mr Ford?" Jack said, "Stick your fingers into that pile of shit and take out any two – they all stink."'

Our work routine, if it could be called that, was established early on. I would arrive at Kinnerton Street at around 10.30 in the morning, and we would sit chatting for about half an hour over a cup of instant coffee. We would then walk to the greengrocer where Brian bought the orange for his champagne breakfast and proceed to the pub of choice. There were three pubs in Kinnerton Street, and we were regulars in all of them – the Turk's Head, the Nag's Head and the Wilton Arms. Sometimes we strayed further afield, down narrow alleys and cobblestoned mews, to the Naval Volunteer or the Star. But on damp winter's days, when Brian's lungs played him up, we stayed close to home.

Whatever the favoured destination, we would settle at the bar and drink at a gentle pace until lunch, usually eaten in the pub. However, if Brian was entertaining friends, we often returned to the house where I descended into the basement kitchen – a room Brian claimed never to have entered – to rustle up scrambled eggs on toast. When he was feeling expansive, we went to Wheeler's in Lowndes Square, and later, when I had been elevated to trusted *amanuensis* and crony, he would take me along to lunches and dinners in places like the Berkeley and the Connaught, where he was often invited by various grandees. Sometimes these people were gracious about having an expensive, extra mouth to feed, and sometimes they were not. When I objected to accompanying him on the genuine grounds that it made me feel uncomfortable to tag along uninvited, Brian would be either ruthless or manipulative, depending on his mood. 'Don't worry, the old bore can afford it . . .' or 'Very well, if that's the way you feel – ring him up and tell him I can't be bothered.'

I need not have troubled to make discreet enquiries about Brian's sexuality, for he made no secret of his habits. 'Some people have asked me over the years whether I'm bisexual,' he told me. 'In fact, I am trisexual. The Army, the Navy and the Household Cavalry.'

A stream of Guardsmen, usually somewhat wooden and taciturn characters, presented themselves at the house for active service. 'Exciting news,' Brian once announced, replacing the phone after a call. 'The corporal-major of the Household Cavalry telephoned to say that the colonel has just opened a new box of recruits.'

Homosexual prostitution in the Brigade of Guards is one of the less hallowed traditions of the British Army. It has a long history, I discovered, stretching back many generations. Young Guardsmen from the provinces on poor pay suddenly find themselves living in the best areas of London, as the barracks of the oldest and smartest regiments tend to have fashionable addresses. A certain percentage have always made themselves available, at a price, to the Old Queens of Belgravia – referred to by the soldiers as 'Old Twanks'.

And there have always been public houses, and cruising spots in the royal parks, where willing soldiers can be approached by the cognoscenti. In the late nineteenth century command central seems to have been a tobacconist run by a Mrs Truman, next door to the Albany Street Barracks, home of the Blues, in Regent's Park. The old lady would receive orders for soldiers and dispatch them as she might a box of cigars. In the 1930s, the recognised tariff was a couple of pints of bitter and a pound for the Foot Guards – the Horse Guards cost rather more. I have no idea what the rate was when Brian was active, but a number of Guardsmen seemed to have been rewarded with his old sports coats.

Brian's highly individualistic form of snobbery – suitable for any number of sociological doctoral theses from almost any angle – did not preclude the easy intermingling of social classes. Corporals and belted earls mixed freely, although aristocrats were always formally introduced sotto voce by their title. There was, of course, no reason why the classes should not mix in Brian's house, particularly as corporal and lord often ended up in bed together, but it did create difficulties for officers who suddenly found themselves confronted with other ranks from their own regiment. One young captain complained to Brian that he needed to be warned in advance if there were likely to be any of his soldiers in the house.

'Why, pray?' Brian asked, affronted.

'It undermines discipline.'

'Nonsense.'

'The last time I was here I ran into the lance-corporal who brings my charger from the stable every morning when I go riding in Hyde Park.'

'What of it?'

'The next morning he brought me my horse and as he handed me the reins, he looked up and said, "Have a nice gallop, darling!"'

Policemen also dropped by – Brian liked the occasional copper – but whether in uniform or not, the men to whom he was most attracted were all extremely masculine, at the peak of physical fitness, and preferably working class. 'Run out and buy a half-dozen bottles of Newcastle Brown, will you Christopher? Terry's coming round and the corporal gets *most* upset if there's only champagne to drink.' Although I would often hear Brian make his joke about being the Empress of Ireland, he was not in the least effeminate, and was not sexually interested in feminine men, to whom he referred contemptuously as pansies. His gay friends, however, to borrow a phrase of Tennessee Williams, covered the waterfront. It was, of course, a revelation to me to discover just how many 'straight' men were homosexual. (Brian sometimes subscribed to the notion that *all* men are homosexual. 'Why do you say that?' I asked, irritated. 'You *know* it isn't true.' The answer was political. 'It helps encourage some of the weaker sisters to cross the line.')

Uniformed men apart, the house was also home to an endlessly changing cast of waifs and strays who somehow made their way to Kinnerton Street. Lodgers were usually male, but not always, and drawn from a broad cross-section of humanity – anyone, really, who happened to have aroused Brian's interest, sexual or otherwise. A tall and striking Australian girl was allowed to rent the lower bedroom for a time because she made Brian laugh, but was evicted when she pulled his hair, convinced it was a wig. Young men with profound religious convictions, bound for the priesthood or the monastery, were particularly favoured, although they often found themselves in the kitchen at breakfast time competing for the toaster with feral rent-boys. Most lodgers spent their evenings down in the kitchen, huddled around the formica table, smoking earnestly and listening to the radio; right of access to the drawing room and the television was by invitation only, and subject to preposterous whim.

In the early evening a flow of fascinating people would drop by for a drink. These came from all walks of life and included theatre and film actors, directors and producers, eccentric neighbours, assorted aristocrats, sly procurers and male prostitutes. I was usually only around in the morning and afternoon, but the endless distractions and social activity meant there were never enough hours in the day to concentrate upon the screenplay. After a couple of months of this, not a word had been committed to paper. And I had not been paid a penny.

Although I was writing for numerous newspapers and magazines at the time, I was a victim of what my brother dubbed 'Micawber's Misery'. This was a condition named after the advice thriftless Mr Micawber gives David Copperfield: 'Annual income twenty pounds, annual expenditure nineteen pounds and nineteen six, result happiness. Annual income twenty pounds, annual expenditure twenty pounds ought and sixpence, result misery. The blossom is blighted, the leaf is withered, the God of day goes down upon the dreary scene and you are for ever floored.'

As might be expected, Brian's advice in this area was particularly unhelpful. His grip on what other people held to be financial reality was erratic, and he possessed none of the garden qualities that the majority of the human race is obliged to nurture to stay alive. Money was there to spend, not manage. He made fortunes in his career, but never saved a penny. Most of the objects of great value that he bought –

including paintings by Raphael, Monet, Picasso and Modigliani – were given away to friends, and sometimes impetuously to virtual strangers. The lessons learned from this prodigality were peculiar. 'Don't be like me, Christopher. Thirty-six years old before I owned my first coachbuilt Rolls Royce – *what a bore!*'

At some particularly dire point in my cash-flow crisis, as I had delicately learned to describe the consequences of my extravagance, I made an oblique appeal to Brian for money. 'The wolf,' I announced in a tone intended to convey dreadful portent, 'is at the door.'

'My advice – *don't let the bugger in!*'

'This is serious, Bri – worse than usual. Non-payment of rates. They arrest you for that.' I cleared my throat. 'I was wondering how remuneration for a script is actually structured?'

'*How remuneration for a script is actually structured,*' Brian parroted, in a mocking tone. 'You mean how and when you get paid?'

'In a nutshell.'

'As a rule, the writer gets so much at the commencement of the first draft of a script, so much when he hands it in – so much for the second draft, and so much for the polish.'

'Have I not commenced?'

'*Have I not commenced!* I hope you're not going to write like this. Don't say commence, say start. Don't say remuneration, say payment.'

'I am ready to start and receive payment.'

'That's better. I'm afraid that journalism, written in haste for cash, is a breeding ground of bad literary habits. A script should be well written but straightforward, something everybody can understand – producers, financiers, gaffers and best boys – even the bloody actors. It should not read like the high-falutin' waffle of some pseudo-intellectual attempting to hide his lack of talent and originality by disguising the commonplace with dense jargon and ten-guinea words. And it should not be sloppy or slapped together as if banged out by some drunken Fleet Street hack with a deadline to meet. It must be well structured and build dramatically, developing character and tension. The prose should be spare, the sentences lean. Favour the short Anglo-Saxon word over its flowery French synonym. Be frugal with adjectives and adverbs. Slang should be banished, neologisms shunned. Above all, be direct!'

'I need money.'

'You will be the first to be paid the moment our investors write a cheque. You have my word. And investors will be fighting over one another to put money into this hot property, I can assure you. Of course, because of my close connections with the Grosvenors, I would like the duke to be given the first opportunity. Some of the people on the boards of these new film companies these days are not in the least suitable as partners. No fun. No fun at all.'

'I need an advance on the screenplay now.'

Brian dug into his trouser pocket and took out two crumpled twenty-pound notes, which he tossed on to the bar in front of me. 'I was going to give that to the milkman, who has been making threatening noises again, but go ahead and give it to the council if you must. I'll just have to take my tea black.'

It is impossible now to recall the exact moment when I finally understood, not only that Brian was in no position to pay me anything, but also that he was practically as broke as I was. Those staples of the young writer's life, false hope and self-delusion, kept me going. I wanted to believe that backers would be found, and then there was the food, the drink, the stories and the prospect of travel. But the truth was I had been bewitched by Brian's charm and had no wish to break the spell.

We ordered lunch and carried our plates to a corner table by the fire. '*Style*,' Brian said, savouring the word as he cut into an overcooked sausage. 'Mysterious stuff. As mysterious in its way as talent. Or even soul. Some people hold that a film script does not need literary style, and judging by the lorry-loads of shit I've had to read over the years that is the prevailing opinion. I disagree. Style is the essence of all literary form, not mere embellishment. Every category of writing from poetry to screenplay must concern itself with the right use of language if it is to be effective. That is the difference between greeting-card sentiment and literature, and separates rubbish from art. Not many people care about this subject, but the few who do care very much.'

It was rare that Brian spoke about anything for long without reaching back into his long life for an illustrative anecdote. The homily on style reminded him of the English teachers in Belfast who had taught him after demobilisation at the end of the First World War. He had wanted to attend art college but the course was full, so he switched to journalism. 'We had two of the best English teachers in the world – O'Halloran and O'Callaghan. They taught us the importance of always searching for and using the right word, and gave this as an example: *The angel of death is abroad in the land, I can hear the beating of his wings*. Wouldn't it have been terrible if the writer had used *flapping*? As Mark Twain said, "The difference between the right word and the nearly right word is the difference between lightning and lightning bugs."'

The teachers also sowed the seeds of republicanism, a concept then as alien and taboo to a young Protestant Ulsterman, born in Belfast, as that of Catholicism and homosexuality. Brian was brought up a Protestant, but converted to Roman Catholicism, and embraced his adopted religion with theatrical displays of piety.

One anecdote on the search for the right word triggered another, drawn from the early 1920s when Brian was in Paris as an art student. 'There was a very beautiful *déclassée* woman called Lady Duff Twysden, the wife of an English admiral. She was remarkable for that period because she had run away to Paris to live with her lover. They were practically starving so we art students adopted them, feeding them when we could. On Duff's thirty-sixth birthday we gave a dinner party for her and managed to procure thirty-six bottles of champagne. The Irish novelist, Liam O'Flaherty, was a good friend of mine, and came to the party bringing James Joyce, already famous and regarded as a literary genius. He sang for us in his beautiful voice the lovely Irish song, 'The Lark in the Clear Air', and then fell silent for a long time. The rest of us proceeded to get very merry on the champagne. Joyce suddenly spoke: "Liam, I have been thinking about this word I need and I have found it." We all held our breath to see what this magical word about to come out of Joyce's mouth might be. We rather expected a flowing sentence like, *He loved the yellow, mellow, smellow, melons of her rump*. "Liam," Joyce said, "the word I've been searching for is, *Yes*."'*

The screenplay was at a stage when it was not so much the need to find the right words as any words at all. The film had been talked about endlessly as if it actually existed, and I had immersed myself in background reading and historical research, but the scenario remained unwritten. 'I fear we both share the powerful character trait of procrastination,' Brian said. 'It depresses me to say it, and I don't want to alarm you, but I have this terrible feeling that work is imminent.'

After lunch we made our way back to the house to decide upon a plan. Brian gave me a fiver to buy a bottle of Beaujolais, directing me through the tradesmen's entrance of

*This story is more significant than Brian understood. Joyce was greatly excited to discover that 'yes' was the word he needed to begin and end the last episode of *Ulysses*. He wrote to a friend (Valery Larbaud) in the summer of 1921: 'You asked me one time what the last word of *Ulysses* would be. Here it is: yes.' Many years later Joyce discovered with the same excitement that the final word of *Finnegans Wake* should be 'the'.

a wine shop in Knightsbridge. 'The public isn't suppose to use that door, but just give the manager my regards.'

The manager was young, overweight and without charm, and gave me a dirty look when I entered through the back door. He visibly flinched when I passed on Brian's greeting, and refused to meet my eyes throughout the purchase. 'Gave him my best, did you?' Brian said, as we sat drinking the Beaujolais back at the house.

'Yes. He didn't seem thrilled.'

'No sense of humour, that one. A couple of weeks ago I went in and he was bent over a case of claret, chubby cheeks wobbling and straining inside that massive pair of baggy pants of his. Who could resist? I pinched his bottom.'

I sighed.

'And he expects to be paid in cash. No credit. No cheques. I really don't know why I don't go elsewhere. But – to the business at hand. Do you think you could have the bones of a script put down in a couple of months, if you had peace and quiet and were plied with drink?'

'I suppose so.'

'Good. Tidy up any outstanding business here – perhaps write those half-dozen articles where deadlines are overdue, and we'll head for Morocco. You will be free of the pressure of creditors who wish to imprison you, and angry editors who have lost all patience. And from the reproaches of those girlfriends you seem to annoy so much. Morocco – flaming sunsets, golden sands, a warm and welcoming ocean, the romance of Arabia.'

'Sounds like paradise.'

'It is, *it is*! High in the Kasbah, above the narrow, labyrinthine alleys of the souk, looking out across the sea. The muse will settle beside you and guide your pen. Odalisques worthy of the Sultan's harem shall fill your nights with erotic adventure. Hurry home and pack your toothbrush.'

A date was fixed a fortnight ahead. In the interim, while I

banged out articles without any evident encouragement from the muse, I was invited to lunch at Kinnerton Street to meet the companion Brian had chosen for the trip. A tall man with black curly hair was sunk in the sofa, and regarded me with what seemed to be a calculating but amused eye. He was introduced as Dave, *formerly of Her Majesty's Welsh Guards*. 'Pleased to make your acquaintance, boyo,' Dave said, holding out his hand and struggling to rise from the sofa. It might sound clichéd to have a Welshman say *boyo*, but Dave really did – frequently, in the sing-song, lilting accent of the valleys.

Later, Brian asked: 'So what did you make of Dave?'

'He seems perfectly pleasant.'

'If Dave was "perfectly pleasant" I would not be bringing him with us to Tangier.' Brian chuckled before declaring grandly: 'He will be accompanying me in the capacity of body servant.'

'Very well.'

'You think you two will be able to rub along all right?'

'Yes. I liked him. Seemed cheerful enough.'

'Remarkably – in the circumstances.' Brian grew confidential. 'He's not had a happy life. He was quite a regular here when he was a Guardsman, then went back to Wales and got married and had three children. I like a man to have either three children or three convictions. As Dave is rather oversexed, his poor Welsh wife insisted on a vasectomy after the third child. Both agreed three was enough for anyone. *Snip, snip!* No more nippers for Dave. Now comes the sad part. His wife is taking the three children to school in the family rustbucket one morning, turns the corner and is flattened by one of those milk tankers. Everyone was killed.'

'God, that's awful!'

'It happened about six months ago. His whole life fell apart. So he needs a bit of a holiday.'

The day for departure arrived. I made my way to Kinnerton Street, suitcase in hand, and found a black taxi and a milk float parked outside the house. The front door was open and I stepped inside to the hubbub of genial voices and the pop of a champagne cork. It was a quarter to nine.

Brian stood in the front room surrounded by Dave the ex-Guardsman, Ronnie the milkman, a stranger introduced as Derek the house-sitter, and an unnamed taxi driver. The group was on its second bottle, and receiving its third or fourth anecdote: 'The front doorbell rang and I opened it to find a little man in a bowler hat and a long overcoat, and a young girl. The man turned to the girl and pointed at me: "That 'im?" The girl sniffed. "No, that ain't 'im." They just turned and walked away. I called after them: "What is all this?" The man turned and raised his hat apologetically, "Sorry to bother you, sir, but somebody using your name has made my daughter pregnant."'

There was a gurgle of worldly, masculine laughter from the assembly. Dave poured me a glass of champagne. 'This is the way to travel, eh boyo? And not even out the bloody front door yet!'

The conversation somehow swung round to Brian's service on the Gallipoli peninsula during the First World War, and how as a result he had nearly died in hospital in Egypt. 'I convalesced for a time at the Palace of Princess Zariet Fatima Hanem, and nearby was a company from the Egyptian Labour Corps. They were very fond of swearing in English to impress us, and if they saw a couple of English soldiers they would let rip and show off – *hell, damn, Jesus, bloody, fuck!* One day I was watching an Arab trying to back a mule into the shafts of a cart. He was not having any success and was getting more and more frustrated. Finally, the mule kicked and sent him flying about twenty feet. He got up, rubbing his backside, absolutely mad with fury, and screamed at the mule – *liar!*'

On finishing my second glass of champagne I murmured that maybe we should be on our way or we would miss the plane. 'Want to settle the bill?' Ronnie the milkman asked pleasantly. Brian went to the small table beside the wing chair and took out the Coutts chequebook. 'No more cheques, Bri, if you don't mind,' Ronnie said. 'Not after last time.'

Brian took a fat wodge of notes from his pocket and reluctantly separated a twenty from it. He pushed it into Ronnie's hand as if it were a tip. 'It's a bit more than twenty, Bri.'

'Take that for now, I need the cash for the trip. My entourage these days, Ronnie, may be diminished in number, but it remains *expensive*.'

'When you come back then,' Ronnie said, without protest. He was a man who accepted a world in which people like Brian lived in large houses in Belgravia, drank champagne for breakfast, and went on exotic trips accompanied by an entourage, but never seemed to have enough ready cash to pay their milk bill. Dave helped the driver take the assorted bags from the hall and load them into the taxi, while Brian gave last-minute instructions to the house-sitter. 'If Lord Maugham calls, tell him I've gone to Tangier. And that if he wants to join us he should send me a telegram. Explain there's no phone at the house. And if that troublemaker Terry comes around, tell him to fuck off!'

Outside, the taxi driver held the door open for Brian, an unprecedented courtesy from a London cabbie. The driver winked at me as I climbed in. 'He's a card, that Brian, and no mistake!'

As we drove along the Cromwell Road, Brian voiced doubts about the house-sitter. 'I do hope Derek will be responsible. Great big chap, strong as an ox, but such a fairy. Broke a plate in the kitchen last night and burst into tears!'

'Highly strung,' Dave said.

'Highly sexed, low hung, more like,' Brian said. 'But eager to please, *in that department*.' He cleared his throat and gently nudged Dave. 'Of course, we have never asked Christopher, have we Dave, what he is – *in that department*?'

Brian had not broached this question before, or even shown any curiosity during the time we had spent together, and as he was well aware that I had girlfriends I assumed he knew the answer. But then, Dave had once been married with three children, and many of the men who came round to Kinnerton Street seemed to move seamlessly from men to women and back again. And here I was, in the back of a taxi with an old queen and his body servant, on the way to queer Tangier where we were to share a house for a couple of months. It was the Moment of Truth.

'About ninety per cent to ten,' I answered.

'Ninety–ten?' Brian pondered the answer. 'Do you think, Dave, he means ninety per cent young boys and ten per cent old men?' Later, Brian snorted, '*Ninety–ten!* You only threw the ten per cent in because you were worried I'd drop you from the movie.' In truth I threw in the homosexual tithe in recognition of time served in an all-boys' boarding school, a ten-year sentence from seven to seventeen. The Classics, in the form of Latin, Greek and homosexuality, were on the curriculum, although I proved to be a disappointment in all of them. There had been the usual adolescent experiences of sexual exploration and confused emotional attachments that went with the territory in a boys' school, but on release from the prison house I found myself physically and psychologically unhinged by the nuclear force of sexual attraction exerted by women. Almost from the beginning Brian seemed to have written me off as a hopeless case *in that department*. The question was never brought up again.

History books often refer to the royal 'progress' of monarchs, as kings or queens forged their stately passage from palace to hunting lodge, accompanied by scores of servants, courtiers and soldiers. While I had read the words and formed a picture in my mind, I had never really understood the reality until I travelled with Brian Desmond Hurst. What he lacked in numbers he made up for in pomp. He comported himself like a pasha, moving beneath a cloud of banknotes, and tipping with the ostentatious vulgarity of a big winner in Las Vegas. Fivers swirled and fluttered about him, settling on porters, drivers and anyone who offered the smallest service. Dave was sent to buy a large box of expensive, handmade chocolates for the lucky employee who happened to check our bags. The woman was so pleased she stepped across the luggage scales to hug and kiss her benefactor.

'Charming woman,' Brian said loudly, as the caravan moved on.

A *frisson* of excitement accompanied our small but expensive entourage – made up of Dave, myself and assorted porters – as it progressed through the terminal with stops for champagne refreshment on the way. Immigration and customs officials were regaled with *bon mots*, policemen were told small jokes, and fellow passengers complimented on their children, luggage or clothes. 'Your hat, madam, is *exquisite*.' Heads turned as people strained to catch a glimpse of the fabulous personage at the centre of the compact energy field moving through the airport lounge with the force of a tiny tornado.

The trip to Tangier was my first with Brian, and therefore a new and exhilarating experience, but they would all be charged with the same excitement. Every journey undertaken, however insignificant, became a unique occasion promising glamour and adventure; even the deadly aspects of travel, such as hanging around airports and sitting on buses, were injected with a sense of fun. And no one enjoyed the experience more than Brian. As the taxi turned out of Kinnerton Street, at the start of each of our expeditions, he always said the same. 'Goody, goody – we're off!' He would then turn to me, blue eyes shining with boyish excitement. 'What larks, Christopher! What larks!'

PART II

Tangier

The house in Tangier, where we took up residence to begin work on the script, was reached by taking a taxi to a small square, and then climbing slowly up through the Kasbah on foot to the very top of the city. It was a charming place on three floors, covered in beautiful tiling and built around a central courtyard like many of the old Arab houses. According to Brian, it had once been part of the palace harem. There was a roof with a spectacular view of the ocean, but we were told to be discreet in our use of it. Rooftops in the Arab world were the domain of women, where they spent a large part of the day, and their privacy was to be respected.

There was some mystery surrounding who actually owned the house: Brian, the film director Terence Young, Lord Maugham or some other, unknown party. Brian insisted it was his, and that he had given it to Terence to use as he wished. However, there were signs about the place that Robin Maugham had also recently stayed there – although he was then domiciled in Majorca, before opting for pickled retirement in Brighton. It had also been used by a young friend of Brian's, who had decorated it beautifully, and the walls were hung with swatches of wool dyed in the bright blues and reds of the mountain people. It was airy and light, peaceful and quiet – the perfect place to write.

Tangier, in those days, was a strange city. It had once been in English hands when it was handed over to Charles II in 1661, together with Bombay, as part of the dowry of his Portuguese bride, Catherine of Braganza. Later, it was recovered by

The kasbah of Tangier

Morocco, and became a haven for Arab pirates. Modern pirates followed in their wake, smuggling cigarettes and booze between Spain, Morocco and Gibraltar in high-powered motor-boats when Tangier became an 'international city'.

The Fleet Street press of the 1950s and early '60s had exhausted themselves 'blowing the lid off the wickedest city in the world' in one exposé after another. In fact, Tangier was a safe, well-ordered place and its only real claim to wickedness was that it was tolerant towards the large foreign community that included writers, artists, assorted criminals and homosexuals.

Many of the older English inhabitants had created an Edwardian homosexual paradise for themselves. The houses inhabited by this smart, wealthy colony were spectacular. They were large, luxuriously furnished and decorated, and often boasted beautiful gardens. A stately formality overlaid the decadence of this particular expatriate population, which spent its time pursuing young, willing Arabs.

There was also a seamy, package-tour side to Tangier that I truly never experienced. For example, one of the gay bars hidden down an alley was known as the Scotch House. The only connection that this hot, heaving meat market had with Scotland was a large black man standing on a small platform in one corner, dressed in a mini-kilt and holding bagpipes. On the hour and the half-hour he solemnly erected his handkerchief sized tartan, to the sound of 'Scotland the Brave'. An exhausted, wheezing of the pipes accompanied the subsequent lowering.

Brian took the large bedroom on the first floor of the Kasbah house, and I was placed on the ground floor, while Dave was put on call in a room on the third floor. My office was a room used as a library, situated off the central sitting room. I set up my typewriter, opened a packet of typing paper, sharpened a box of pencils, filled my fountain pen, laid out my notes, and stacked the various research books I had brought with me, including the New Testament, relevant volumes of Josephus, a couple of biographies of King Herod, various works on the Bible as history, and . . . stared at the wall.

Over the next few days I grew intimately familiar with that wall, and could have accurately reproduced from memory a detailed drawing that would have stood up in a court of law. I knew every bump in the plasterwork, the nuances of its white finish, every crack and stain, and studied a greyish, damp spot in the right-hand corner as if it were a map for buried treasure. I resharpened the pencils, rearranged the books, thumbed through Josephus and the New Testament, reread the notes and . . . stared at the wall.

'Getting started,' Brian said kindly after the third day, 'is half the battle.'

He seemed quite calm, but I was thoroughly unnerved.

During the day Brian and Dave made their way slowly downhill, through the labyrinth of the souk, after which they crossed to the beach, where Brian entertained innumerable youths. I would be left behind in the house to work. The notes I made for the plot of the screenplay possessed all the originality and promise of a primary school's Christmas pageant. By day four I was so thoroughly deserted by the muse, I simply lay on the sumptuous pillows furnishing the salon, and read three-quarters of a thick novel. And then, sipping a glass of mint tea, I decided to go back into the torture chamber and have another go at the opening sequence. And I began to write . . .

By the time Brian and Dave returned from the beach, the script was under way. *Horsemen on symbolic white horses thunder across an open plain lit by an even more symbolic full moon. Closer and closer they ride towards the camera, until the screen is filled with the bucking heads and frothing mouths of wild-eyed stallions, mounted by riders in black, brandishing flashing sabres, to the deafening accompaniment of pounding hoofs. The horsemen approach a vast wooden door along an interior stone corridor. It flies open to reveal King Herod floundering among bed sheets. As he calls for guards, the horsemen disappear – it has all been a terrible nightmare, portent of things to come for the evil king.* Dramatic, visual, tense – stuff that would get them on the edge of their seats.

'The writer has written,' Brian said. 'Praise be! This calls for a celebration. Dave, open a bottle of champagne.'

In the days that followed, Brian treated me as if I were an *idiot savant* and was solicitous to an almost ludicrous degree, like an anxious husband with a pregnant wife, or a Soviet gymnastics instructor entrusted with one of Mother Russia's national treasures in the form of a nine-year-old acrobatic prodigy. Dave was sent up with glasses of mint tea, deposited wordlessly by my side. A strict rule of silence was imposed upon the household. Brian returned from his daily lunch on the beach with tubs of ice cream for me.

He was intrigued and pleased to learn that I used a fountain pen for the first draft of each scene – a chunky, butch Mont Blanc – later transcribing the original work on a typewriter in a rapid, jabbing, four-finger rattle. Having been condemned to various antique typewriters since my days as a cub reporter, I explained that I found it liberating to fall back on the pen. 'I am pleased to see it,' Brian said. 'The typewriter must have had a deleterious affect on literature, rarely spoken about. *Tap-tap, tap-TAP-tap, tap-tap, ting, CRASH*. An unholy, modern, urban rhythm that subconsciously dehumanises and mechanises prose. Good, possibly, for war reporting and American novels, but abrasive and harsh.'

By day seven I had the wise men moving through the desert, a tortuous journey matched with torturous dialogue conducted with sceptical Bedouin met along the way.

'Dave and I are eagerly waiting to read the golden words, aren't we?'

'It would be interesting,' Dave said diplomatically. 'When you're ready, like.'

'I'd feel much more comfortable if you'd wait a bit until I had a whole chunk.'

'*Act* is the technical term,' Brian said. 'A whole *act*. But if that is what the writer desires and needs, that is the way it must be. We dare not startle the muse – let the quill continue to fly over the parchment.'

I was surprised to find Brian so patient and trusting, especially as he had never read a word I had written. He seemed to display those rare qualities in a producer that writers forever seek and rarely find: complete confidence in the scribe of choice, non-interference, indulgence in the form of cups of tea and ice cream, and the patience of Job. A couple of days later I learned the secret of how this was achieved.

'Brian's very happy with the way things are going,' Dave said.

'I hope he won't be disappointed when he actually reads some of it.'

'So far he loves every word.'

'But he hasn't seen anything yet!'

'Don't be daft,' Dave replied. 'He's read every line. Up at dawn, he is, slipping like a cat into the room where you work, all stealthy like, for a butcher's at the day's work. Reads it all with a torch, and then sneaks back to bed while you're sound asleep.'

'But I *hide* the pages every night.'

'He said you did that. Under some books or something, but that you'd have to be more devious than that to keep it from a cunning old bastard like himself. Said he had one writer who hid his stuff in his wife's handbag. Took him a while to twig that one.'

I shook my head and muttered about invasion of privacy and lack of professionalism, although my outrage was tempered by the pleasure and relief I felt because Brian was satisfied with what had been written. 'Where's the harm?' Dave said. 'It makes him happy instead of all tense and difficult. Makes life a lot easier for me, boyo. And you know he likes what you've done. Where's the harm?'

The following evening, after yet another day's inspired work – seven action-packed pages of wise men and shepherds – I decided to leave my work in full view, but booby-trapped. I placed my fountain pen on top of the pile of pages, and made two, tiny pencil dots at each end, so that the slightest movement would be detected. The next morning I was surprised to find it still in place and the pages untouched. I told Dave that Brian was now so happy with the script that he had even stopped his nocturnal ramblings, and seemed content to wait to read it. 'Oh, no, he's read the new stuff. He loves the bit where the wise men make their entrance in a snowstorm in the mountains, even if it will be expensive to shoot.'

'It's *impossible* that he read that scene without my knowing it!' I explained the trap that I had set.

'Like he said himself, he's a devious bastard,' Dave said respectfully.

Brian's admiration for the entrance of the wise men showed taste. The words were stolen – albeit in a modified prose form – from T. S. Eliot's poem 'Journey of the Magi'. The poetic images were visually powerful and heavy with symbolism: sore-footed, bad-tempered camels collapsing in deep snow; a running stream and a water-mill beating the darkness; an old white horse in a meadow, galloping away against a low sky, with three trees on a hill in the background; sandalled feet kicking empty wineskins, as gnarled hands at a tavern door dice for pieces of silver. I had also discovered that Brian was right from the start – the events leading up to the birth of Christ made a hell of a story. I decided to have some fun and make a formal announcement that I was ready for him to read some pages.

'Are you sure? I will only read them if you are *absolutely* certain you are happy for me to do so. There is *nothing* so destructive for a writer than the feeling that somebody is peering impatiently over his shoulder. I don't want you to do *anything* that might throw you off your stride. Are you certain? *Absolutely* sure? Very well, I shall read them within the hour. Dave, put some champagne on ice.'

Brian retired to his bedroom, and when he emerged a half-hour later he had changed into a white kaftan and pointed Moroccan slippers embroidered with gold thread. He sank on to the cushions of the central salon, instructed Dave to pour him a glass of champagne, and picked up the thin sheaf of pages. I sat in a corner with a book, while Dave rolled his eyes and shook his head in disbelief at the extent to which Brian was prepared to take his subterfuge.

The reading was a bravura performance, subtle and nuanced, yet pure ham. Brian nodded, raised eyebrows, sighed with pleasure and groaned ambiguously now and again. It would have been impossible for anyone to know whether he loved or hated what he was reading. He said nothing. It was a half-hour of heartless manipulation, and if I had not known in advance what he thought, I would have suffered. When he finished, he slowly gathered the pages spread around him and placed the pile carefully on a small table. 'A glass of champagne for the master!'

Dave obediently rose and, to Brian's intense annoyance, filled his glass. 'Not me, you bloody fool – Christopher!'

He waited until champagne was given to me, and then raised his glass in a toast. 'A good beginning. You have breathed life into characters that we usually take for granted, and put novelty, surprise and tension into a story with which we are perhaps over-familiar. Bravo! My hope and faith have been well rewarded. Keep going like this and we'll have every actor in England desperate to play a part, and financiers throwing money at us. Well done!'

Brian raised his glass to me and we all drank.

'Congratulations, boyo!' Dave said.

'Right! Now you've had the praise and know what a wonderful writer I think you are, I need never say it again. From now on I wield the tyrant's whip and become the whining, bullying, prick producer. But never be disturbed personally by any criticism I may make – I am only working to improve something I already consider good.'

I thought it might be the right time to come clean about T. S. Eliot, and asked innocently whether it was all right to lift other writers' work to put in a screenplay. 'Absolutely not!' Brian said with alarming finality. Almost immediately, he asked, 'Which writers did you have in mind?' I explained that I had been inspired by a poem of Eliot, where certain symbolic images translated into visual ones. 'Interesting,' he said. 'You are the first of my writers to my knowledge to plunder poetry. But is it plagiarism to turn poetic images into camera shots? Surely not. Anyway, we can be sure that no financier will pick up on it, while actors only read Eliot's plays, not his poetry – and only their parts at that. Critics will not notice because it is not in the dialogue. It certainly works. Leave it in. I do not know the poem – perhaps you would be good enough to read it to us.'

I went into the study and fetched the book containing the plagiarised poem. I sat down beside Brian and Dave and began to read:

> *A cold coming we had of it,*
> *Just the worst time of the year*
> *For a journey, and such a long journey . . .*

'Nice poem, that,' Dave said, when I had finished. 'Very nice indeed.'

The words had cast a spell on us, and we each drifted into a separate reverie. The light was fading, making the room a calm and enchanted place. Each of us was happy in his own way: I had been praised for my work; Brian was relieved to find the script was what he wanted; while Dave was content to hold unhappiness at bay. We seemed bathed in an atmosphere of good fellowship and well-being. But there was more to it, somehow, than that. We had been touched by Brian's magic. 'A special moment,' he said. 'Do you feel it? An instant of time out of time. In this difficult world it's important to recognise these rare atoms of God-given peace. A portion of eternity.'

My routine was to stay in the house and write most days, and then go out with Brian for dinner, either to a restaurant or the home of one of his friends. La Belle Hélène was the bar and restaurant we most frequented, owned by a strangely glamorous, middle-aged French lesbian with a face of elephant hide. She was said to have bought the establishment from money earned during a long circus career as a motorcyclist on the flaming wall of death. We ate elaborately at La Belle Hélène's and drank copiously, and Brian indulged us extravagantly at lunch and dinner. Whenever he was offered a particularly fine wine or delicacy, he would murmur, '*It'll do!*' He did it often, and for some reason always seemed to be highly amused each time he uttered the phrase. 'I don't get it,' I said. 'What's funny?'

'Oh, just a private joke. The Marquess and Marchioness of Londonderry were at dinner when the marquess suddenly fell down in a fit. The marchioness called out to the maid to run down to the wine cellar and fetch a bottle of brandy. The maid came back holding a dusty old bottle with a large "N" on it – a priceless Napoleon brandy. "This is all I could find, your lady." To which the marchioness replied, "*It'll do.*"'

At table, I always encouraged Brian to tell me Tangerine stories from the old days. 'There used to be a character called Manola in the city who ran a male brothel. Whatever was demanded he could provide. To test the limits of his resources I requested a blond Spanish footballer. "Give me twenty minutes," Manola said. Twenty minutes later he returned with a beautiful athletic blond Spanish footballer. Those of us in the know, however, did not use Manola's brothel because he had spy-holes and see-through mirrors, which he used to rent out.

'I once thought I would enliven a dull dinner party by telling two extremely straitlaced American matrons about Manola's, and asking innocently if they had similar establishments in Cincinnati. They were pleasingly shocked and assured me that while they had a fine Country Club, there was no male brothel. After a while one of them said, "But when you think about it, Gracie, if men can go to places like that for women, why shouldn't women have the same opportunity? It's only fair."'

Whenever Noël Coward visited Tangier he always spent a

Brian's great friend Noël Coward

large part of his time with Brian, avoiding the socially competitive English homosexual expatriates. 'Save me, darling, from this terrible English colony desperate for my presence.' Brian and his friends hid him, lunching and dining in secret. 'Each day, the leaders of so-called Tangier Society would ring me up to make sure that Noël was eating with us. Everything was all right as long as he wasn't lunching or dining with any other member of the English colony.

'At a small private lunch on the beach Noël was talking brilliantly about the craft of playwrighting, and an obliging but dim young actor sat at his feet taking in every word as holy writ. Noël said, "There must always be a strong, last-act curtain." The actor looked up at the master and said, "Muslin's nice."'

One night Brian took Coward to a restaurant run by a White Russian, who not only made the best *boeuf Stroganoff* in the world but also had a very handsome Spanish barman. 'There were six of us and we were the only people in the downstairs bar apart from an old, drunken English woman, wearing a dirty spotted cardigan, sitting on a barstool and leaning against the wall to stop herself falling down.'

When the woman recognised Noël Coward, she heaved herself off her stool and approached the table. She slapped him heartily on the shoulder. 'Mr Coward, sing me one of your songs.' In situations like this, Coward was known for fast, eviscerating wit that left the victim gutted, and the party nervously awaited the inevitable disembowelling. Coward took a long pull at his drink, and then placed his glass carefully on the table. He mopped his lips with a clean white handkerchief and looked the woman in the eye. 'Certainly, my dear – it will be a pleasure.' He moved to an untuned, upright piano and performed his entire Las Vegas repertoire. 'Then he helped the woman off the stool, took her outside, called a taxi and pushed money into her hand. It was a very generous gesture, very moving.'

Dinner was taken upstairs in a private gallery. The blinds were drawn, Brian asked the barman to remove his clothes, and the Stroganoff was duly served by him naked. 'Despite the entertainment, Noël suddenly said to me, "Binkie has turned down my play." This was a reference to *Waiting in the Wings*, his play about a home for retired actresses. When I thought of the thousands and thousands that the producer Binkie Beaumont had made out of Noël, I knew the knife was turning in his heart.'

After dinner Brian was in the habit of taking a walk, and would usually fall behind whomever he was with to importune willing young men always described nevertheless as 'victims'. Coward turned to him on one such walk and asked, 'Dear boy, what on earth are you up to?'

'Casting,' Brian replied.

Later they visited one of the decadent bars near the docks, a rough Spanish place where the company was mixed. Coward made it clear that he was attracted to a particular young man. 'A rather dark number known around and about as *Chocolata.*' Brian arranged an introduction and organised for the young man to be smuggled into Coward's smart hotel, the Minzah, which maintained a stricter policy concerning exotic overnight guests than most establishments. The following day Coward and Brian met at the Café de Paris for a mid-morning aperitif. 'Well Noël, how was your evening?'

'Divine!' Coward crooned. 'Splendid casting, dear boy – *splendid* casting!'

It was in Tangier that Brian saw Coward for the last time, where he had gone to recuperate after a serious operation. 'I went to say goodbye to him as he was going down to Marrakech. He was sitting alone in the back of this enormous Rolls-Royce with a blanket over his legs. Too late I realised I should have jumped into the car and gone with him. There he was, Noël Coward – brilliant, witty, famous, rich, a household name the world over . . . and so utterly lonely.'

A Moroccan, whom I presumed had once been a lover of Brian's, came to the house to invite us to his home for dinner. Akbar was well-dressed in a smart suit, a slim and handsome man in his early forties, who had done well in some sort of export business. He had also married an English woman, who had brought her mother to Tangier to live with them. In the course of his visit to deliver the dinner invitation, he casually admired Brian's shoes.

'You can have them if you like.' Brian often said this when someone admired something he owned, and sometimes even acted upon it. Usually people held back, leaving the silver on the table, or the vase on the mantelpiece, or even a painting on the wall. Akbar, however, had possibly been on the non-receiving end of Brian's largesse too many times before. 'Thank you, I would love them.'

Brian took off one of his shoes and handed it to Akbar. It was obvious it would not fit. 'Here, try it for size.'

'No, no,' Akbar said. 'I do not wish to wear them. I will keep them in my room and every time I see them I will think of you – I will say to myself, "Those are the shoes of my generous friend Brian."' Dave and I exchanged a look. This Akbar was one wily Arab – Brian had been beaten at his own game.

Akbar's house was large and modern, boasting all the trappings that could be desired of the middle-class *nouveau riche*. 'I do not wish to live in shitty, smelly Kasbah,' he said. 'No thank you.' But there was something cold and sterile about the place, an emptiness. An introduction to the freeze-dried wife and mother-in-law explained the Arctic atmosphere – I had never seen people so physically desiccated by the disappointment and misery of a bad marriage. Even their small talk was vicious. The wife had once been a good-looking blonde, but no longer. Her mother, a shrunken, wrinkled version of the daughter, stood beside her as echo and prompt. Together they made a human thesaurus of major and minor put-downs of Akbar, his country and his people. They both *hated* Tangier, *hated* Morocco, *hated* the Arabs.

There were two other guests – a large, solid American from the mid-West, and his jolly, chirping wife. The man was a business associate of Akbar's, prosperous and round, and their small talk was in direct contrast to that of their hostess – they *loved* everything. 'You're an Englishman, right?'

'Yes.'

'We *love* London,' the wife said. 'We love it very, *very* much.'

'We do. We love London. My favourite city. And we've noticed over the years how words are used different.'

'Two countries separated by a common language,' I said, clever-Dick style.

'Say again?'

'I think Shaw said something like that. You know, about the cultural differences between American and English. We speak the same language but don't really understand one another. That sort of thing.'

'Well, I don't know what this Shaw fellow said, but I have noticed how you use words different. Take cookie, for instance. You say "biscuit".'

'You say lift, we say elevator,' the wife said, and laughed as if it was the damnedest thing.

'Yeah,' her husband said. 'We say candy, you say sweets.'

Brian began to sing. 'You say tom*ay*to, I say tom*ar*to, you say pot*ay*to, and I say pot*ar*to . . . let's call the bloody thing off!'

'You say pot*ar*to?' the wife said sceptically.

As we sat down to dinner the mid-Westerner found more examples of trans-Atlantic linguistic difference: 'We say faucet, you say tap.' His wife jumped in: 'We say washcloth, you say flannel.'

'Pants,' the mid-Westerner said. 'Trousers,' his wife countered. The couple had been made manic by wordplay, and it seemed there might be no end to their encyclopaedic knowledge of Anglo-American synonyms. They became frantic, batting words back and forth to one another like Chinese ping-pong players: 'Jumper . . . pullover, soda . . . pop, chemist . . . pharmacy, truck . . . lorry . . .'

'Tell me,' Brian interrupted, 'have you ever admired a woman's fanny in England?'

'Now hold on,' the mid-Westerner said pleasantly, 'I don't want my wife getting ideas that I've been looking at the tush on those English girls.'

'You'd be safer with *tush*,' Brian said. 'Fanny in England, you see, means cunt.'

There was a moment of stunned silence as trans-Atlantic communications collapsed. The mid-Western couple looked as if they had been doused with a bucket of ice-cold water. Unlike Britain, where even then filthy language had become the standard currency of street and television, the 'C' word retained real kick in North America.

'Box!' Dave said flatly, breaking the awkward silence. The table looked at him, mystified. 'I've heard Americans call a woman's whatnot that. You could get in trouble over there, like, if you didn't know.'

'Okay, we get the picture,' the mid-Westerner said, giving his wife a lopsided grin and winking at her. 'We'll shut up.' Perhaps he had a sense of humour after all. For me, the couple's good-natured rubbish was the conversational high-spot of the evening, and infinitely preferable to what came next. Sandwiched between bitter wife and acid mother-in-law, I had bile and poison poured into both ears until my brain began to curdle. My host, apparently, was the Most Evil Man in the World, peer of Hitler and Stalin, child of Satan. He was cruel, he was cheap, he was unfaithful, he was mad, he had horrible habits, and he played too much golf. The ladies said they were prisoners and slaves, kidnapped and cut off from the outside world, and there wasn't a single decent women's hairdresser in the whole town. I nodded and grunted at appropriate moments. Dave got very drunk and flirted crudely with the wife, while making extravagant promises to free them from their terrible captivity. 'You'll help, won't you, boyo?'

'Mrrgh,' I said, in a non-committal mumble I hoped could be taken either way, wondering why the wretched duo didn't drive out to the airport, buy a couple of tickets and board a plane. Just as the evening was grinding down to a dull, exhausted silence, Akbar decided to enliven things by showing us his horse. This was a beautiful black Arab yearling, a frisky creature that seemed to have some trouble on the outside steps, but was relatively well-behaved as it entered the dining room. The magnificent animal made a round of the table, snorting and whinnying impressively. 'He always does this,' the wife said venomously. 'His party piece. Bringing the fucking horse into the house.'

Apart from the older, dated Edwardian homosexual society in Tangier, there was also a set of Gilded Youths who seemed impossibly fashionable, beautiful and well-connected. One of these was a blond male model from London who had been described in *The Times* as the 'best-looking man in the world'. He was handsome in the way of a movie star or Greek god, not overly bright, but sweet-natured. One of the consequences of his good looks was an almost pathological shyness. He avoided parties, shunned the gay crowd, and spent much of his time in Tangier sitting in dingy cafés with me, drinking mint tea. 'What's it like,' I asked him enviously, 'to be the best-looking man in the world?'

'Horrible!'

'Oh, come on!'

He shook his head and looked sad. '*Everybody* wants to fuck you.'

There were few foreign girls in Tangier, for obvious reasons, and those who were attracted to the place showed a distinct lack of interest in the occasional, stray heterosexual.

Most members of this small group seemed bonded to the Gilded Youths, who offered the company and friendship of handsome men without the demands and complications that usually entailed. One of the few women attached to the Gilded Youths who Brian not only tolerated but seemed to like, was a large, crop-haired blonde in her late twenties called Penny, who had a pretty villa near the sea. A big-boned, hefty girl who was physically awkward, she nonetheless had social grace and charm, but her tragedy was impossible, unrequited love. She had lost her heart to one of the Gilded Youths who betrayed not a trace of heterosexuality, and she attended the fey object of her passion with doglike devotion.

Penny was the most well-mannered young woman I have ever met, entertained constantly, and went to enormous pains over even a simple gathering for tea. She baked small cakes and made tiny, exquisite sandwiches. She was also something of a matchmaker.

'Here on your own?' Penny asked me one day.

'Very much so.'

'You know Alexander's brother, Simon, is coming over from England next week. I think you'd really like him. Want to see a photo?'

'Alex doesn't have any sisters does he?'

'I'm frightfully sorry,' Penny stuttered, blushing furiously. 'I thought you were . . . I just assumed . . . I mean, you know, staying with Brian . . . Oh dear, what a terrible *faux pas*!'

'Think nothing of it. Happens all the time.'

We were invited to dinner at Penny's home one evening, and the food was excellent. There was plenty of wine too, although Brian and I seemed to be the only people to drink. The Gilded Youths favoured hash, a drug that did not suit Brian, whose idea of a convivial evening involved the pleasures of lively conversation and laughter rather than silence and dreamy introspection.

After dinner, the hash pipe went round. Brian refused it, and so did I. The group grew quiet and Penny put on some Moroccan music, and although the atmosphere was pleasant enough, it had a strained quality. I could tell that Brian was becoming actively bored. A rambling conversation about cherries began, punctuated by extended, awkward silences. Penny had remarked that the luscious cherries we had eaten were fresh that morning from the market. 'Weren't they wonderful?'

There was a pause. 'God, I do love cherries,' an American voice announced. A pause. 'And their colour,' somebody said. 'The redness. *Cherry* red!' A pause. 'Those cherries tasted *good,*' the American said. 'Juicy.' A pause. 'Sweet!' And so on.

'What was all that about cherries?' Brian asked in the taxi home. 'I've never been so bored in my life. The cherries were good, the cherries were red, the cherries were sweet, the cherries were fucking wonderful. I thought I'd go mad!'

'It's the local hash. Strong stuff. It tends to turn all conversation into dialogue from a Pinter play.'

'I noticed that you did not participate,' Brian said, giving me a sideways glance. 'You're *full* of surprises.'

'Doesn't go with drink. The two don't mix.'

'On the subject of drink – how about dropping off at the Café de Paris for a digestif?'

'Good idea.'

'I need a bloody great *ballon* of cognac after all that cherry talk.'

The author in the Tangier kasbah

It was late but still warm as we sat at a pavement table outside the Café de Paris, where waiters in white aprons served our drinks as they might at any café in France. 'A little French colonialism does a country's culture no end of good,' Brian said, savouring the atmosphere. 'God bless the French and their *mission civilisatrice*. Can't be beat! If only a few English seaside towns had reaped the benefits.'

His mind drifted back to his art student days in Paris during the 1920s. 'I shared a studio with a couple of other students off the rue Vercingetorix. There were no conveniences of any kind at all in the studio, just a stove, which always had a pot of stew or something on it. Outside in the street there was a lavatory at either end and two in the middle. Clatter, clatter in the morning with everybody running to them.

'We students were sent out twice a week for outdoor sketching, and I was sitting on a bench in the gardens of the Luxembourg Palace, absorbed in sketching one of the stone queens of France which are all over the place there, when someone sat on the bench beside me. I continued sketching. Then I heard this voice, speaking formal but heavily accented English. "Excuse me, sir, but by any chance are you homosexual?" I looked round to see this very good-looking Dane. "Why do you ask me such a question?" He answered: "You look up to watch the young men go by but ignore the girls." It was hard to deny, so I sort of shrugged. "I'm getting married on Friday and my friends tell me that love with a man can be quite charming and exciting."

'Methodical people, the Danes. I studied him a bit. As there was no one at the studio in the day, I took him back and we made love. After we had showered and dressed, and we sat having a glass of wine, he said, "If that's what it is, I don't like it at all. But will you come and have lunch with me tomorrow and meet my fiancée?" I agreed and we had a very pleasant lunch, and they asked me to attend their wedding at the Danish Embassy the following Friday. Sent each other Christmas cards for years.'

'People weren't openly homosexual in Paris then, were they?'

'No. But among Bohemian and student circles nobody cared. And the French have always been more broad-minded about sex than Anglo-Saxons. In those days they rather thought that people who liked boys were going through a phase and would get over it. Of course, with me it was the other way round. And if you were English they almost expected you to like boys – you know, the English vice.'

'But you're Irish!'

'Yes, but in Paris I had a blue blazer and flannels, so I passed. There was an old French nobleman who fancied me who used to come to the entrance of the art college in a carriage with four horses. I enjoyed it all immensely and so did the other students, but I didn't like him in that way and wanted to call it all off. The students said, "You can't give him up. The horses and carriage coming and all the rest of it – it's too romantic." So I continued to see him just to please them. One day we were driving through a secluded part of the Bois de Boulogne and the old nobleman ran his hand up my leg and got hold of my cock. "*Ça c'est du très bon flannel anglais.*" I finally gave this nobleman up, not because of his advances, which I always rejected, but because he invited me up to his flat and then served me champagne which hadn't been chilled. When I explained this to the art students, they said, "We understand. That is too much. You cannot be expected to make love on warm champagne."'

Brian studied in Paris for two years at L'Ecole des Beaux Arts, on the rue Bonaparte. Two evenings a week he took fast-sketching classes at the Académie de la Grande Chaumière, in Montparnasse, when only ten minutes was allowed per drawing, to encourage flexibility. As part of the students' education they were sent in small groups to the studios of painters of the stature of Fernand Léger, Juan Gris and Georges Braque, and sculptors like Ossip Zadkine, Constantin Brancusi and Auguste Rodin. 'Rodin was working in this gigantic old greenhouse on the outskirts of Paris that had previously held vines. The vines had been removed but the glass was still green from them and cast a most eerie light. Inside, two naked women moved about, and when the light fell on them as Rodin wanted, he would say, "*Arrêtez-vous là!*" And he would make a sketch. He gave us tea with lemon, and presented each student with a drawing. The art school tried to take them off us, claiming them as their property. I told them, "You're not getting mine! It was given to me personally by Monsieur Rodin."'

Brian gave the sketch to Nina Hamnet, an English painter living in Paris. 'Nina had been very kind to Modigliani's mistress, who was forever trying to kill herself, and eventually succeeded. At one stage Modigliani and Picasso had swapped paintings – Modigliani had exchanged a nude for a small, blue sketch called *The Fever Hospital*. Modigliani gave this to Nina for her kindness to his mistress, and she gave it to me. And in the fullness of time I gave it to Robin Maugham – which was bloody stupid of me.

'When Modigliani died we watched the funeral procession from Le Dôme, in Montparnasse. It was attended by many high French officials, and to see these great dignitaries in their top hats and frock coats jostling among the throng of prostitutes and dope addicts, to whom Modigliani gave most of his money, was something never to be forgotten.

'We art students were a progressive lot, and put on a revue at a theatre called L'Oeil de Paris. The curtain went up on the first act to reveal an airplane propeller painted scarlet with no visible means of support. It turned slowly to the musical accompaniment of an orchestra made up of twenty-two typewriters. In the second act, two coatstands – one wearing a male black raincoat, the other a female white raincoat –

danced together, worked from below the stage. The third act was a wild striptease by a German dancer, Valesqua Gert, who danced and gyrated naked. It was all very *avant garde* – and fucking boring.'

It was fun sitting outside the Café de Paris, whether at night taking a digestif, or in the morning with a *café crème* and a croissant. One day I saw three women standing some distance from us dressed in long black robes and masks, leaving only the eyes uncovered. I looked over at them idly and must have been staring, for one of the three returned my look with a bold, suggestive wink.

As they moved away, I told Brian what had happened. 'The clothes and mask are supposed to make them invisible to men and cut them off,' he said. 'But there are human beings inside. Modern young girls, many of them, who feel like prisoners. Imagine their frustration, their anger! A time-bomb ticking within the male fortress of Arabia. I hope you had your subversive wits about you and winked back.'

There was an English church in Tangier where Dave and I accompanied Brian one Sunday morning. I had hoped that the congregation might feature some of the more exotic plants among the city's fauna, but was disappointed to find the usual sparse and bloodless congregation the Anglican Church seems to attract the world over. We settled into a pew where Brian was conspicuous in his piety. He shot dark, threatening looks at Dave who coughed, muttered and fidgeted with impatience, except during the hymns when his bold Welsh tenor rang out gloriously above the repressed mumbling of the rest of us.

Brian took Communion as if he were being filmed by Cecil B. de Mille in long-shot, medium-shot and close-up. He walked slowly towards the altar rail, head bowed with ostentatious humility, and received the wafer and wine in slow motion – it took the priest three times as long to deal with him as anyone else. He returned with hands clasped together in prayer, head thrown back and eyes towards heaven. I am not certain that white doves fluttered above him, or that a halo shone over his head, but that is the impression he projected. The performance annoyed Dave as much as it amused me. 'Look at the wicked old bugger!' he said, in genuine disgust. 'Bloody hypocrite! Makes you sick.'

After church, Brian returned to the house while Dave and I walked on the beach. 'Brian's not *all* bad, you know,' Dave said. 'Do you a good turn if he can. Did me a turn, all right. I was married, you know.'

'Oh?' I had never mentioned that I knew anything about Dave's sad past.

'Kiddies and all. Three of them. Two girls and a boy.' Dave paused, and looked away into the sun, perhaps wondering whether to continue. 'They got creamed by a bloody lorry. Killed. Just like that.'

'I'm so sorry.'

'Yeah. I remember getting the news. It's not like on the telly or in the films. I was working on the buildings and was in this greasy spoon with the lads, about to have breakfast. Funny, I remember what was on the plate – egg, chips, tomatoes, sausage, beans, bacon and a fried slice. You can eat all that when you're on the buildings. This young copper comes in asking for me. The other blokes go quiet, thinking it's trouble. They were right there! For a moment I thought he was going to arrest me. My past's not been spotless, like. But then because he was so respectful and polite I knew it wasn't that sort of trouble. Knew it was personal – that it was *real* trouble.

'We went outside and he told me. He was a kid, this copper, out of his depth. They should have sent an older bloke, a sergeant or something. Though I don't suppose anybody rushed to volunteer. The poor sod was awkward and tongue-tied. Didn't know how to begin – then he mumbled and sort of rushed through it. Wife . . . kids . . . sorry. *Dead!* I remember thanking him and shaking his hand. Funny, that.

'Then I thought I better go home and it struck me – *you don't have a home any more – it's all over for you, boyo!*' Dave stopped, unable to make sense of the emotional avalanche that had overwhelmed him, and I could see he was trying to keep control. He turned away from me and looked out to sea. 'Tragedy's not like on the telly. Not like that at all. One moment you're looking at a plate of eggs, chips and beans, sipping a mug of strong tea, and the next – wife and kiddies gone. *Dead.*'

We continued to walk along the beach in silence. 'No, Bri was good to me then. I'd gone downhill. Didn't give a monkey's. Walked the streets for days, don't know how long, then hitch-hiked to London. Bri put me up. "Take this," he'd say when I woke up shouting in the night. Don't know what they were, but they put me out good and proper. Oblivion. I was better off unconscious. He let me stay for weeks. Never expected any hanky-panky. Gave me the odd fiver. Sort of nursed me. I tell you, if it wasn't for Bri I would have topped myself. I was mental. So when he asked me down here, I thought, "Why not go and ponce for a bit? Nothing for you at home, boyo." And Bri's good for a laugh, isn't he?'

The story of King Herod and Mariamne put life into the project which had filled me with panic before I started to write. The tragedy had first been set down by the Jewish historian, Flavius Josephus, eighteen centuries before I took up my pen. The story was a corker.

In brief, Herod is an upstart from the south who has replaced the legitimate Hasmonean Jewish king with the help of the Romans. He marries a reluctant Hasmonean princess, Mariamne, a spirited woman of remarkable beauty and wisdom. She looks down on Herod as a Roman lackey, scarcely even Jewish, who has unjustly usurped her family's throne. The family into which Herod has married immediately begins to plot against him, led by Alexandra, one of history's most evil mothers-in-law. Herod refuses to appoint Mariamne's younger brother, the beautiful eighteen-year-old Aristobulus, to the high priesthood, which puts the mother-in-law on the warpath. She appeals to Cleopatra, no less, to intercede and plans to escape into Egypt with her son, hidden in two coffins. Herod discovers the plot, and while he makes a public show of forgiving Alexandra, he secretly plans to dispose of her son, who in contrast to Herod is enormously popular among the Jews.

At a feast given by Alexandra, on a hot night, the guests retire to bathe in the ponds. Herod's men duck Aristobulus as if in sport, but hold him underwater until he drowns. Alexandra's extreme grief takes the form of a secret vow to live only in the hope of avenging herself. She complains once more to Cleopatra, and Herod is summoned to Rome by Mark Anthony. In fear of his life, he instructs a confidant that if he is killed then Mariamne is to be executed – explaining that his love for his wife is so great that he is unwilling that any man should have her after his death.

The confidant reveals the plan to Mariamne, who does not take her proposed assassination as a romantic proof of love. When Herod returns safely from Rome he is rejected by his wife with the utmost coldness. Confused by her hatred, his mood alternates between burning passion and rage. Mariamne continues to reject her husband's every advance, and reproaches him with the murder of her father and brother. Herod goes into an uncontrollable rage. It is at this moment that his sister – who hates Mariamne – sends in the king's cupbearer with a story that his wife had intended to give him a love potion – the suggestion being that this was poison. Herod immediately has Mariamne's eunuch tortured to find out the truth. The eunuch is unable to say anything about a love potion, even when in terrible pain, but reveals that Mariamne's hatred is caused by her discovery of the secret arrangement to have her killed.

Herod is now certain that the man entrusted with this secret would only have revealed it if Mariamne paid with a sexual favour. Maddened by jealousy, he has the man executed and Mariamne brought to trial. She is condemned, with the sadistic recommendation that her execution be slow and painful. The vile Alexandra turns furiously against her daughter to save her own skin, but Mariamne goes 'to her death with an unshaken firmness of mind and without changing the colour of her face'.

Herod's fury turns to terrible grief. Unable to conduct public business, he wanders through the palace calling out his dead wife's name. He orders his servants to act as if she were still alive. He becomes ill, and quite mad, and the doctors give him up for dead (he actually survives for another quarter of a century). It is at this stage in the story that I introduced the wise men into the script, who come to Herod looking for a royal son, alerted by the Star of Bethlehem. Paranoid, Herod orders the massacre of the innocents.

All I had to do was visualise this exciting story and write the dialogue. It struck me, as I wrote, how truly original and revolutionary the teachings of Christ must have been in such a savage time, advocating love and forgiveness when it was the accepted political axiom of the day to achieve power and hold on to it through terror and murder. I explained all this to Brian, and suggested a change of title from *Born to be King*. 'It's misleading. And what's a king in the end? Nothing, compared to the man whose philosophy changed the world.'

'Go on.'

'I thought – *Darkness Before Dawn*.'

'Oh, yes. Very good.'

'Not pretentious?'

'A little pretension will do the audience good. Let us not forget, Christopher, that we are making a pretentious film.'

One day we set off by car to have lunch in a small seaside town some twenty miles to the south of Tangier. Brian sat in the front with Penny, who was driving, and I sat in the back with Dave. The Gilded Youth who was the object of Penny's unrequited love had returned to London, so we saw her often and had grown fond of her. She needed balm for her bruised and aching heart, Brian said, adding practically that she also owned a car.

Penny had brought along a small pot of *majoun*, a narcotic mixture of the best hashish mixed with honey and nuts to form a paste, and said to be the sweetmeat of kings. Brian shook his head, and waved it away when he was offered some. Penny took a small spoonful and passed it to Dave, who helped himself to a generous ration, and then it was my turn. I dug the spoon into the pot, dug out a large dollop, and put it in my mouth. The *majoun* was strange-tasting, somewhat bitter at first, but made pleasant by the honey and nuts. I took a second spoonful before passing it on. Later I took a heaped third. 'Delicious!'

'Steady on,' Penny said. 'It's pretty potent, you know.'

The drug began to creep up on me as we sat down for lunch. We were in an open-air place by the sea and Brian had ordered fish and white wine. We nibbled olives and made desultory conversation for a while, but by the time the fish arrived the drug had taken hold. It was not a pleasant feeling. I became acutely self-conscious – gentle precursor of the raging paranoia to come – and lapsed into silence. I stole a glance at Dave, who was staring fixedly at the tablecloth and rocking gently to and fro. 'Oh dear,' he sighed. 'Dear, dear, dear.'

Penny had a dreamy far-away look and stared out to sea. At first Brian seemed bored, then cross. 'What's the matter with everybody? Are you all drunk?'

Penny laughed a little hysterically.

'Dear oh dear,' Dave said. 'Dear, dear!'

The first stage of the ingested high made me intensely

uncomfortable. Every remark seemed to suggest a dozen different meanings; reluctant to commit myself one way or the other in case I gave the wrong answer and drew attention to my strange state, I continued to remain silent. 'Salt?' Brian asked.

The question seemed to pose enormous problems. To say yes might suggest that the fish was not to my liking; to refuse, that my palate was somehow off-kilter. It was not a simple question at all. *Did* the fish need salt? And how much? I reflected on the fact that, apparently, some salts were saltier than others. The saltiness of salt was something to think about. Salt! How extraordinary to take such a strange substance for granted. These white crystal granules prized since the beginning of recorded time. Salt beside the salty sea. And there was the fishiness of fish . . .

'Do you want the bloody salt or not?' Brian said.

'*No!*' The word came out like a bark; Brian flinched and gave me a searching look.

It got worse. Just as I thought I was as high as it was possible to get, a new, unwelcome surge of strangeness came from the soles of my feet and made its way through my body. And this was repeated again and again, in wave after wave of unwelcome sensation. I came close to panic, and in a cry that was somewhere between a simper and a whinny, blurted: 'When does it stop?'

'When does what stop?' Brian said. Nobody else spoke, and I did not add to my cryptic utterance. Still fixated on the tablecloth, Dave had become like stone. Penny was singing a nursery rhyme, softly and nervously, like a frightened child alone in the dark.

'That is very irritating!' Brian said. 'Very irritating indeed!'

Penny shut up as if she had been slapped.

My initial state of heightened self-consciousness escalated steadily through various stages of paranoia until it reached stark terror. I became very, very frightened, and wanted to crawl from the table and lock myself in a dark room. Everything seemed unsafe, the people around me alien and threatening.

'You are behaving very oddly,' Brian said, as he finished his fish. He shook his head. 'I'm going for a walk.'

After what seemed like an age, Dave suggested that we also go for a walk, and Penny and I followed him on to the beach. A boy who could not have been much older than twelve approached me grinning, his hand held out. I almost cut and ran, but took his hand. His trigger finger scratched my palm in a gay handshake, and I jumped in alarm. 'You English?' the boy said, puzzled by my strange reaction. I nodded. 'All English very queer. You want blow job?'

'No, thank you.'

'Hand job?'

I shook my head. Unconcerned by the rejection, the boy stuck to us as we made our way down the beach, and sat beside us on the sand. He fixed Penny, who was twice his age and three times his size, with a businesslike look. He made a fist, and slowly raised his arm from the elbow. 'You want fucky?'

Penny looked panicked. 'Oh no!' she cried, before instinctively remembering her manners. '*Thank you.*'

The boy sighed, on the edge of petulance. 'All English very queer,' he repeated, as if reminding us of an accepted national characteristic we were unpatriotically ignoring. In the distance, Brian was standing by some rocks talking to a couple of young men. 'He very queer?'

'Mr Hurst is Irish,' I heard myself say. The inappropriate reply hung in the air, pompous and absurd.

'Ireesh,' the boy said. There was a long moment in which he grappled with the statement.

Dave suddenly declared: 'Mr Hurst is a great big Irish poof.'

There was an extended silence, and then simultaneously

we all burst out laughing. Dave let out a deep, rolling roar, while Penny trilled, and my laughter was a sobbing gurgle of relief. Our mutual terror dissipated. The spell had been broken. The boy smiled at us indulgently: 'You very stoned.'

When we stood we were exhausted. 'You weren't kidding when you said that stuff was potent,' I said to Penny. 'It made me completely paranoid.'

'You're only supposed to take half a teaspoonful,' Penny said defensively. 'At the most.'

'Not my cup of tea, boyo,' Dave said. 'Not my cup of tea at all. Brian thinks we've gone mad. Out of our minds, he thinks we are. I thought for a moment I'd gone loony. Very funny stuff, that *majoun* – must be the eating of it that does you in. *Intensifies* the experience, like. Not my cup of tea at all.'

We gave the boy a few dinar for the pleasure of his company, and he left us with a cheerful wave. Then we joined Brian and made our way to the car for the drive back to Tangier. We were mostly silent at first, still rendered a little sensitive by the receding effects of the hash. After about half an hour we saw in the distance a young boy standing beside the road with a tray. We slowed down and he began to run towards us in excitement.

Brian wound down the car window and looked into a tray of festering red mullet. The boy was clearly tired from a long stint by the side of the road in the blazing sun, but was now filled with hope. His eyes shone and he muttered enthusiastically in Arabic. However fresh the fish had been in the morning, they were sad and grey-looking now, a most unappetising collection. Even from inside the car the smell was sickening, and Brian made a gentle gesture of refusal with his head. The boy looked utterly crushed.

We drove on, overcome by a blanket of depression. After a while, Brian said, 'We can't buy every rotten fish in Morocco just to keep people happy.'

'He just looked so crestfallen,' I said.

'Poor little sod,' Dave said. 'I thought he was going to burst into tears.'

'Perhaps we should have bought them,' Penny said.

'You wouldn't buy a basket of rotten fish at home just to please the fishmonger, would you?' Brian said. 'We would all have died of food poisoning if we'd cooked those. And an unpleasant drive home with the stinking things too.'

There was silence again and we drove on flanked by the spectacular, flaming sunset, which only added to the leaden melancholy that had descended upon us. 'Bugger!' Brian said. 'Turn the bloody car round.'

We turned and raced back to where the boy had stood, and our spirits instantly lifted on the short journey, together with our guilty consciences. We became excited and talkative, almost festive. 'We can give him a few dinar, like,' Dave said, 'and then chuck 'em a bit further on.'

'We don't have to eat them,' Penny said. 'We can just pretend we're taking them home for supper.'

But when we arrived at the spot where the boy had stood, there was no sign of him. Abandoning all hope of a sale, he had disappeared among the rocks and the lengthening shadows cast by the setting sun.

'Somebody else might have stopped and bought his fish,' Penny said. But nobody, including herself, believed it. Brian sank into a mood of the darkest gloom, and I knew instinctively the nature of his depression – he had missed an opportunity to be generous and was overcome with remorse. We drove into Tangier in silence.

Almost from the first day I met him, Brian told stories of his great friend Gerald Hamilton, one of the first foreigners to settle in Tangier after the war. Gerald found life depressing in bombed-out London, and fled to Morocco to escape 'an age of bottled salad dressing, dyed kippers, snack bars and jeans worn in public'. He was notorious the world over as a great rogue and crook without morals or conscience, a man of unvarnished villainy. 'You, Christopher,' Brian said, 'would have liked and enjoyed Gerald enormously.'

Alas, Gerald Hamilton was already dead when I first met Brian, so I was to be neither corrupted nor conned by this dangerous creature. The return to Tangier had stirred memories of Gerald for Brian, and although the anecdotes he told of his friend were very funny in themselves, it was clear he greatly mourned the old rogue's passing. An enormous presence had disappeared from Brian's life, a giant personality of outrageous eccentricity, whose place could never be filled. The world had been left emptier, smaller, duller and less fun. 'I miss Gerald very much,' Brian said. 'His wit, his urbanity . . . his wicked originality.'

The publication of Christopher Isherwood's novel *Mr Norris Changes Trains* had turned Gerald Hamilton into an international celebrity of sorts. Mr Norris – based on Gerald – is unforgettable, a character in the pantheon of literature's minor immortals, dominating a small gem of a book. But the portrait is not a pretty one.

The reader first encounters Mr Norris dressed in mauve silk underwear, long socks and rubber abdominal belt, cringing at the feet of a hefty Berlin whore wielding a leather whip. As he crawls to clean her shoes with a brush and yellow cloth, she scolds: 'You call that clean, you swine! I'll skin you alive!'

'Gerald was amused to find himself fictionally portrayed as a man who enjoyed thrice-weekly thrashings from dominating German whores,' Brian said. 'This was far from the truth. In real life he was not a heterosexual masochist, but a tireless homosexual procurer. Gerald was extremely gifted as a pick-up artist, and very generous in passing along the fruits of this talent to his friends. When he lived in Glebe Place, in Chelsea, he had a collection of victims up and down the King's Road – Lavatory Willy, because he worked in the

The notorious and wonderfully wicked Gerald Hamilton

World's End loo, Wine-Shop Jimmy, Supermarket Freddie, and so on.'

The physical description of the fictional Mr Norris is severe: dishonest blue eyes shine from a face of chubby cheeks fresh as rosebuds, his nose is said to be soft and snout-like, and he has a chin like a concertina. His wrinkled bald head is crowned with a daring and glossy hairpiece of waved locks. Despite his porcine appearance and physique, Mr Norris displays almost surgical standards of cleanliness. He never shaves himself, but sends daily for the barber's boy to perform this chore, and comb his wig. Every morning he massages cream into his cheeks for eight minutes, then rubs ointment on his toes to avoid blisters, corns and bunions. He never neglects a lengthy gargle with mouthwash: 'Coming into daily contact, as I do, with members of the proletariat, I have to defend myself against positive onslaughts of microbes.' Three times a week he spends ten minutes thinning his eyebrows with a pair of tweezers – *thinning*, not plucking, 'A piece of effeminacy I abhor.' Once a fortnight he performs a thorough ablution of hands and wrists with depilatory lotion to banish the hated suggestion of kinship with the apes. And on grey winter days he wears pancake: 'I felt I needed a dash of colour this morning – the weather's so depressing.'

Mr Norris is said to be an amazing old crook with weak nerves and bad teeth, vulnerable to blackmail over incidents from his hideous past, yet entirely without shame. He lives in permanent and excruciating financial anxiety, but enjoys perfect digestion and an untroubled conscience. He is a police spy, user of friends, and con-man who sees the capitals of Europe as nothing more than a collection of baited traps.

The 'real' Mr Norris was all of the above and more – continental con-man, pacifist gun-runner, communist snob, reactionary monarchist lickspittle, and sexual exotic. Most men would struggle to avoid being identified in print as a flamboyant, amoral crook, but Gerald Hamilton rejoiced in it. Far from threatening Isherwood with a lawsuit for libel, he basked happily in the notoriety and wrote autobiographies on the strength of it. The second of these was actually titled *Mr Norris and I . . .*, with a prologue written by Isherwood, who remained a lifelong friend despite being conned out of hard cash himself. A third volume of memoirs, dedicated to Brian – *To my old friend, Brian Desmond Hurst, as a slight token of my affection and respect* – is subtitled 'The Definitive Autobiography of Isherwood's "Mr Norris"'. It is much the same as the first two, a regurgitation of old stories, justifications, evasions and outright lies. 'Gerald couldn't find a title,' Brian said, 'so I told him the Irish saying that my father used when we were complaining about somebody, "Ah, to be sure, that's the way it is with them." So Gerald called his book *The Way It Was With Me*.'

In person, Gerald physically matched the description of Mr Norris. Short, pink and plump, with fat, little hands white as flour, his portliness was offset by an aura of neatness and precision. The nose was large and set at a slight angle to his face, and his lower lip seemed grotesquely swollen as if recently punched. An occasional flash of gold shone from a mouthful of crooked and discoloured teeth. The wig beggared belief (and concealed two fatal doses of cyanide).

No one, not even his closest friends, could ever decode his character, which confounded the most sophisticated men. 'You took Gerald as he was, or suffered the consequences,' Brian said. 'Those who tried to evaluate him according to some moral code, or hold him to a particular standard of behaviour, found themselves flummoxed and dismayed.' Brian always maintained that Gerald's background was a mystery, and that while he claimed to be an Ulsterman, his courtly good manners and impeccable English made this highly unlikely. 'Central European, I'd say, from one of those countries you can't keep up with that are always changing their boundaries and loyalties.'

In fact, Gerald was born in Shanghai, in 1896. On the early death of his mother, he was placed by his father – a committed Orangeman from County Tyrone, in Northern Ireland – in the care of two Chinese *amahs*. He later ascribed his Eastern temperament and outlook on life, and extraordinary affection for everything Chinese, as a result of being 'suckled by Chinese breasts.' Struck down with dysentery, and on the point of death, he promised a friend that if he lived he would convert to Catholicism. The subsequent conversion provoked outrage in his father: 'You can become a Parsee or a Buddhist, or a damned Fire-Worshipper for all I care, but I will have no son of mine an RC!' Many years later Gerald realised the truth behind his conversion – it was not a positive act of faith in choosing one Church or creed, but a negative act of rebellion against his father, and the tenets of the Church of which he was such a militant supporter.

In this, Gerald was the opposite of his fellow Ulsterman, Brian, whose conversion to Catholicism was sincere, and who believed he had found the true faith (although whether he ever received instruction and formally converted – or precisely when this happened – is uncertain). Similarly, the men were opposed in their views on the obligation of an Irishman to Britain in regard to foreign wars. Gerald claimed the privilege of neutrality because of his Irish heritage: 'I was not in agreement with any fellow countryman of mine enlisting in the British Army to fight England's battles.' He was a pacifist in both wars, and although anti-Nazi, was emotionally pro-German. Brian, on the other hand, volunteered to fight with the Royal Irish Rifles in the First World War, and lived in London throughout the Blitz in the Second, when he made propaganda films for the government. And while both men became convinced Irish republicans, Brian's sympathy and respect for Ulster never diminished.

At the beginning of the First World War, Gerald had installed himself in the Savoy, from which comfortable base he intended to foment mischief on behalf of Ireland. He was promptly arrested by British Army staff officers in uniform and two plain-clothes detectives brandishing revolvers, and incarcerated in Brixton Prison. The popular papers declared him a traitor, and posters appeared throughout the country bearing the slogan, 'Hang Hamilton!' Although depressed by his internment, and loudly protesting his innocence, he seems to have enjoyed the attention.

Despite Gerald's 'rooted objection to institutions, whether educational, penal, medical or ecclesiastical', he was kept in Brixton Prison for three years. He was released on Christmas Eve, 1918, and spent the night in a Turkish bath-house, in Jermyn Street, re-acquainting himself with old habits. He returned to the continent and his interrelated pursuits of politics and crime, and was imprisoned both in France and Italy for the theft of a pearl necklace. He was placed in jails of medieval squalor, and transported between them shackled in handcuffs and chains. I asked Brian if he thought Gerald had exaggerated his prison experiences for effect. 'No. I think the opposite is true. He saw dreadful things, witnessed shocking cruelty and barbarity. As a sophisticated and cultivated man he suffered terribly and was deeply humiliated. It shook him. Gerald, despite his dishonesty, was a kindly soul. In conversation he turned the experience into interesting stories, and only went a little deeper in his books. He was loath to be a bore. But no, he did not exaggerate.'

On his release from prison, Gerald continued to pursue various rackets, each one more fantastic and elaborate than the other. He became a great friend of Aleister Crowley, the magician and Satanist tagged by his biographer as 'the Great Beast, the most evil man in the world for whom no deed was too hideous, no sin too vile.' The men shared an apartment in Berlin, a convenient and rewarding arrangement for them both, as Crowley was spying on Hamilton for MI5, and Gerald was spying on Crowley for the Germans. The communist spy Guy Burgess was also a friend for many years, before he eventually fled to live in Moscow. An old sinner like Gerald Hamilton might be expected to be generous in his judgement of others, and he remained sublimely unimpressed by wickedness as long as it was accompanied by wit and good manners.

As the Second World War approached, Gerald's politics became convoluted as a communist pro-German pacifist. He established a connection with the Vatican through the Irish Embassy, and applied for an exit visa to go to Ireland, reasoning that he could better conduct his negotiations through a neutral Catholic country. The application was refused. Undeterred, he made plans to cross the Irish Sea in secret, disguised as a nun.

A party of Irish nuns, from a convent near London, was about to make the journey, and he felt certain that a troop of holy sisters armed with prayer books and rosaries would not arouse suspicion. The sister in charge of the expedition, inculcated with anti-English sentiment stretching back to the 'Troubles', was happy to go along with the outrageous subterfuge. Suitable attire in the form of habit and hood was found in the convent, but a decoding clerk in the Irish Embassy betrayed the plan to British intelligence: 'I was arrested before I had even got my coif into place.'

Gerald was held at Scotland Yard for a week, and once again committed to Brixton Prison. He complained to the MI5 intelligence officer interrogating him that, as he was not a fascist, and no longer a communist, but merely a pacifist, he could not understand why he had been interned. 'I don't know what you are politically,' the officer said, 'but I do know you're a damn nuisance.'

He was not let out of Brixton until 1942, but was gracious enough to concede that prison life had been comparatively comfortable. He had been allowed books, clothes, food and wine from outside, but had become inconsolably distressed when an uncouth warder decanted a rare and priceless bottle of 1916 Chambertin straight into his mess tin. On his release, Gerald moved into a small house in Kinnerton Street, and became a neighbour of Brian's who then inhabited a large artist's studio in Bradbrooke House, Studio Place.

'Gerald laid out his little garden beautifully and tried to make the most of life by enjoying his superb cellar of wines,' Brian recalled. 'Gerald always decided on the wine first, then matched what he was eating to it. He displayed a lifelong, virulent prejudice against smoking solely on the grounds that it destroyed the palate for wine. At one point he posted a large notice in his sitting room – VISITORS ARE REQUESTED NOT TO SMOKE IN THIS ROOM. I had fun adapting this sign when he was out. I crossed out the SM of smoke and replaced it with a

P. Gerald did not notice for several days, much to our general amusement. The sign disappeared soon after.'

Although Gerald had been an open, if highly unlikely, communist, he developed into a die-hard Tory of the antediluvian variety after the war, and denounced the horror of modern London in comparison to the 'placid and happy place' of his youth. Reactionary political views do not seem to have affected his relationship with Brian (who believed himself to be a stalwart of Old Labour and man of the left!). The friends preferred to discuss food, drink and sex. 'Gerald was intolerant, but highly intelligent and excellent company. Shrill political debate was not his style. He was a wonderful raconteur and very funny.'

Although Gerald dismissed the post-war House of Lords as adulterated small beer – demeaned by sportsmen and actors – the old crook swooned before continental royalty. Blood royal had been a lifelong obsession, and ideologically liberated from the comrades he felt free to tell anecdotes of his various encounters with European royalty. 'As titbits of gossip, these could be amusing,' Brian said, 'but he had a tendency to become hypnotised by the recitation of magnificent titles. Royal namedropping could clog his conversation, and while he became mesmerised with the regal splendour of his acquaintanceship, his listeners grew drowsy. It was the solitary area where Gerald could be a bore.'

Edited into short form, however, his royal hobnobbing does paint a picture of an extraordinary life. He had been granted an audience with the Russian royal family, later to be slaughtered in the revolution. The Tsar of Russia had 'extraordinary melancholy in his eyes', while the Tsarina was 'much stouter than the photographs of her would have led one to suppose'. He also met Rasputin, and was impressed by his hypnotic powers – which he assured Brian (who readily believed this sort of thing), 'He was able to exert even by telegram.'

Invited to the opera by Tsar Ferdinand of Bulgaria, Gerald was delighted to find this grand personage decked out in a magnificent costume of shimmering gold material, tight black breeches, and a pancake black beret to which was pinned a gold and jewelled aigrette. On being asked what uniform this was, the Tsar solemnly declared it to be that of a Bulgarian field marshal. In Germany he was offered the hospitality of Prince Max of Baden, the last imperial Chancellor, who asked Gerald if he would care to play hockey: 'I declined the invitation politely.' And he was proud to boast acquaintance with the chief imperial eunuch of the last Dowager Empress of China – the man who had carried the empress's little dog Moo-tan in front of the imperial bier at her funeral.

But the crowning moment in a lifetime of courtier-like devotion to royalty came at the wedding of the eldest son of the Crown Prince of Sweden and Princess Sybilla of Coborg. One hundred and fifty guests were formally announced in strict order of protocol, an endless litany of ancient titles denoting blue blood. Gerald Hamilton came last, the only commoner invited – an ecstatic moment of transcendental snobbery.

In real life, Isherwood tired of Gerald's persistent dishonesty, and wrote that although he did not look evil, there was an icy cynicism beneath the amiable surface. Brian was more indulgent: 'I knew Gerald was dishonest and could not be trusted with money. It was the way it was with him. And I dealt with him accordingly, but it did not stop me liking him. In life, if you expect a codfish to have the qualities of an eagle you are going to be disappointed.'

Gerald Hamiton spent his final years in London. 'He maintained the daily routine of a lifetime,' Brian said. 'He rose precisely at 5.45 AM – he was able to get so much more wickedness into the day like that. After the usual lengthy toilet, he made his way to the Hilton in Park Lane for a breakfast of freshly squeezed carrot juice. One morning, as he sipped his juice, he suffered a massive seizure. He was taken to the house of a woman friend and I went to see him later the same day. He was rambling for most of the time I was there, but suddenly the mist cleared. He sat upright in bed and looked at me: "I must now say goodbye to everybody." He fell into a coma and died in hospital that night.'

My pile of manuscript had been growing at the rate of three or four pages a day, until the screenplay began to take on respectable heft. Herod was pleasingly fiendish – torn apart by love and hate because of his beautiful wife, and mercilessly goaded and manipulated by his vicious mother-in-law. It was a pleasure to work with the old monster. Normally, I would write all day, knock off in the late afternoon and go out to play at night.

One evening, Dave and I were told to put on blazers and ties, as Brian explained our host was on the formal side. This was a wildly misleading description of the extraordinary night that lay ahead. We drove in a taxi to a residential part of the city I had not visited before, and were deposited at the gates of a splendid Italian villa overlooking the sea. It was an old house covered in a shock of purple bougainvillaea that climbed up the walls and on to the roof. The garden was tropical, with waving palms and lush vegetation, and a fountain of butter-coloured stone played before the front door. A black chauffeur in a grey uniform and thigh-high leather boots looked vaguely sinister as he leaned against a white, vintage Rolls-Royce parked in the gravel driveway.

'Stand by to repel boredom,' Brian groaned. 'He's invited that terrible old bore, Howie – the Pineapple Queen.'

'Pineapple Queen?' I said.

'Howie owns all the pineapples in Hawaii,' Brian explained.

'All of them?' Dave said doubtfully.

'Every last one. Which makes him very rich. Look at that

awful bloody car – have you ever seen anything so vulgar? And the chauffeur – how camp can you get? Remember, if he asks either of you to go to anything, make some excuse and say you're busy. He gives the dullest parties in town and is stingy with the drinks. And what he expects in return for a weak gin and tonic is a scandal – even in Tangier.'

We entered the house and were greeted by our host, suitably named Edward, an Englishman who had stepped from the Edwardian era. A tall man, who must have been in his mid-fifties, he was dressed in a blazer and cravat, with immaculate white linen trousers. Everything about him was narrow and thin – his frame, his lips and nose, and his strange, hatchet-like head. When he spoke his accent was so upper-class it was as if he were slowly being strangled with piano wire. 'I say Brian, how *frightfully* good of you to come. How *simply marvellous* to see you!'

The villa was not so much furnished with antiques as packed with them, like a shop: life-size, painted blackamoors holding torches flanked giant Chinese vases, while beautiful walnut cabinets were jammed with delicate porcelain figurines and finely wrought silver. I later learned that Edward was some kind of senior partner at Sotheby's. Brian leaned towards me, and said in a low voice: 'So this is where they store all the stolen stuff.'

We were led on to an open veranda where several men were seated in bamboo chairs. There were no women. Howie, the Pineapple Queen, a tiny man in a neat white suit, grew very excited at Brian's entrance. He whirred from his seat like a surprised partridge beaten from a covert. 'You're here! And nobody told me. Why didn't somebody *tell* me?' He turned to our host. 'Why didn't *you* tell me?'

'I apologise if I have been remiss,' Edward replied stiffly.

After effusive greetings, the naked insincerity of which drew a rolling of eyes and a black look from Dave, we settled down. Our host told us we were to be served the cocktail *de la maison*, which he was confident we would enjoy. 'All right,' Brian said, 'just so long as it gets here quick!'

There were ten of us for dinner and we were certainly an odd collection. I remember a tall, elderly Italian count in exquisite clothes, and his pouting, pretty-boy companion who sulked all night, and a couple of dull Englishmen in pancake make-up. Edward engaged in small talk designed to bring everybody into the conversation, moving from the weather – 'Jolly hot!' – to where we were all staying – 'Interesting, the Kasbah!' – to what we had all done that day – 'Never go to the beach – don't like the sand!'

'I don't go to the beach for the sand,' Brian said.

I sensed a sly, sudden presence to my right, perhaps a cat or a dog, then heard a shrill, piping voice that might have come from a child made of metal. '*Crème de Menthe Frappé!*'

Standing beside me was a dwarf in a pink satin suit holding a silver tray upon which was the most exotic drink I had ever seen. A large crystal goblet was filled with green liquid and crushed ice, and from it rose a stand of perfectly arranged mint sprigs. I stared at this apparition of dwarf and drink, unable to speak. '*Pour monsieur*,' the voice piped, '*Crème de Menthe Frappé*.'

'I do hope that's acceptable,' Edward said. 'Makes a pleasant change from gin and tonic, don't you think?'

'You can say that again, boyo!' Dave called out.

I took the drink from the tray and sipped it. It was quite extraordinary, neither too sweet nor too dry, too weak nor too strong, and had something mixed with it to take away the normal cloying quality of *crème de menthe*. It looked fantastic, as if prepared for a coffee-table book on cocktails, but quite apart from aesthetics and taste, it delivered the kick of a young mule. I made genuine appreciative noises. Two other dwarfs in pink satin suits had appeared to serve similar drinks to the other guests. Howie clapped his hands together at the sight of them.

During the course of the evening, Howie applauded everything. When somebody made a witty remark, he clapped; when the dinner was placed before him, he clapped; and he clapped when the wine was poured. He applauded references to books, films and plays, and actually rose to his feet to clap a couple of weak jokes. But I had to concede that the dwarfs were worth a round of applause, even a standing ovation.

'I *love* your little men,' Howie cried. 'Where did you get them? I've gotta have one for Hawaii!'

'They have worked for me for many years,' Edward said in a voice of ruffled decorum. 'They happen to be very good friends of mine.'

A gong sounded, deep and oriental, and we moved through to the dining room. A circular table was laden with silver, candelabra and flowers, and place-cards in ivory holders correctly identified each guest. Seats were taken, napkins unfolded and drawn on to laps, while Dave loudly admired the flowers: 'Bloody lovely, them!'

'So gratifying that you appreciate them,' Edward said with a moist smile.

The moment we were settled, double doors were dramatically opened and what now revealed itself to be an entire family of dwarfs entered – the men dressed in their pink satin suits, the women got up as miniature French maids in uniforms of black and white. Two of the men carried an enormous tureen of soup between them, while others toted bottles of wine and jugs of water. It was like dining at Snow White's place. The food was served with the precision of a three-star restaurant, without a word or gesture from the host, who continued to direct the conversation along safe and dreary paths. Despite the fact that this was a high-camp occasion attended only by men there were no sexual references of even the mildest sort.

Edward disclosed the arrangements he made with Jack

Barclay, in Berkeley Square, to have his Rolls-Royce changed every three years. This prompted Howie to begin an account in numbing detail of the travails of importing a vintage Rolls into Morocco. A tiresome business, not to be recommended. The anecdote was as exhausting as the experience, and Dave rudely interrupted to launch into a highly inappropriate monologue about rugby, which Edward affected to find riveting. 'And do you play yourself?'

'Not much now, but I used to be scrum-half, back in Swansea.'

'How very exciting!' Edward said, and seemed to mean it. His eyes, normally distant and dull, came alive when he spoke to Dave. He licked his thin lips.

The most extraordinary thing of all about that very peculiar dinner was the way in which the dwarfs seemed to anticipate everyone's needs. The moment a wine glass was low, a dwarf appeared to fill it; when the last guest lay down his knife and fork, the dwarfs marched through the doors to clear the table. Edward maintained a low drone of small talk throughout, and although his eyes darted constantly from guest to guest, he never issued a single instruction.

Afterwards, as we drank Turkish coffee and brandy on yet another terrace, I said quietly to Dave: 'An unusual evening.'

'Couldn't get any bloody weirder, could it, boyo? Edward is a nice bloke, but I could clean that pineapple pansy's clock. What a tosser!'

On cue, Howie appeared behind us and took each of us by the elbow, an intimacy that was vaguely suggestive and altogether repellent. 'My dears,' he crooned, in a soft, oleaginous tone, 'I want you to come with me tomorrow on an oceanic adventure. We're going for a sail on a fabulous yacht belonging to my friend. It's the biggest in the whole Mediterranean and you're going to love it.'

'We're busy,' Dave said, brutally jerking his elbow from Howie's caress.

'Busy! In Tangier! Don't be ridiculous! How can anybody be busy in Tangier?'

'Look, I told you – I'm busy!' Dave said. 'If I say I'm *busy* I'm *busy* – no ifs, ands or buts about it!'

'Suit yourself,' Howie said, wagging a finger in admonishment as he moved away.

'Won't catch me putting out to sea with that berk,' Dave said. 'Don't care how many bloody pineapples he's got.'

In the corner I noticed Brian deep in conversation with our host, and they both looked over in Dave's direction. There was something furtive and urgent in the glance. Dave had drunk copiously during dinner, seemingly oblivious that the dwarfs kept his glass permanently replenished, and had since downed at least three enormous snifters of cognac. As we took our leave his gratitude and goodwill towards our host verged on the hysterical, and his thanks became song: 'Thank you *ever* so much for having me. Lovely dinner! *Lovely!* Wonderful evening! *Wonderful!* Bless you, boyo. Cheers!'

'I *am* pleased you enjoyed yourself,' Edward said, his tongue darting along his lips. 'The pleasure was mine.'

As we crossed the gravel to our taxi, Brian said: 'That's what you get when your host has midgets for servants – an evening of small talk.'

'No need to take the piss,' Dave said, drunkenly belligerent, 'just because they're small.'

'They're fantastic!' I said. 'You finish a glass of wine – they top it up! You think you'd like a glass of water – they turn up and pour it! You fancy another potato, and there they are with the potatoes. Magic!'

'It's always like that – a military operation,' Brian said. 'Puzzled me for years. Edward sits there gibbering trivia and his dwarfs run all over the place and never get a thing wrong. One night I sat beside him, watching closely, and discovered the secret. Underneath the table, hidden behind the cloth, are two rows of buttons for the left and right hands. There are two buttons for each guest – food and drink. If the third guest from his left is short of wine, he hits the corresponding button and hey presto! The dwarf assigned to him arrives with the wine. He must have certain pre-arranged signals to tell them when the first course is over and so on. You notice that all the time he carries on that endless drivel about where to find the best olive oil in the South of France, he watches everybody like a hawk.'

'Well, he has to concentrate to get it right,' Dave said. 'He *cares* about his guests. He's a gent.'

'He was very taken with you,' Brian said. 'God only knows why.'

'Thanks a lot, I'm sure.'

'Love is blind,' Brian said. 'He asked me if you might care to go for a drive with him tomorrow afternoon.'

'Fair enough. It'll make a change.'

'Not that much of a change.'

One of Brian's friends who happened to be in Tangier during this time was the Honourable George Sandbach Borwick, half-brother and heir to the 4th Baron Borwick, and wealthy member of the Borwick baking powder family. Inevitably, Brian dubbed him the Baking Powder Queen. George was a conservatively dressed, quietly spoken man content to allow more forceful and colourful personalities to dominate, but he enjoyed close and genuine friendships in the theatrical world as a result of his role as a West End angel.

He was a great friend of Kenneth Williams and had financed his revue, *Pieces of Eight*. Famous for his manic, original and highly camp humour, and integral part of the national institution of *Carry On* films, Williams was in fact a depressive with a deeply serious nature. He was often a guest at George's Tangier apartment where he spent his time reading, doing crossword puzzles and pursuing an obsession with the precise meaning of difficult words and their etymology.

'Apparently, he's practically *asexual*,' Brian said with a disapproving shake of the head. 'Imagine being as queer as that and asexual with it.'

Kenneth Williams kept up a close and frequent correspondence with George, and had recently written recounting his experience on disc-jockey Pete Murray's BBC radio show. Even on the page, the words convey the swooping, nasal gymnastics of Williams' unique delivery and particular brand of anarchic humour: 'They have the listeners phone in, and you have to answer their questions. One woman said, "Can you give me any housekeeping hints?" and I said, "Oh yes dearie! Don't fart about between the slats of your Venetian blinds. Take them down and shove them straight into a bathful of soapy water, and avoid all the loo cleaners that don't have a screw top. You must have a good screw and then it doesn't give off that pungent stink that goes right up your hooter and half suffocates you, and let's face it, nothing is worse than a brown loo! When your friends go away saying to each other DID YOU SEE THE BROWN? then it is socially catastrophic, and keep the room simply ordered. Shove all the furniture up one end and do all your low dusting. Keep a wary eye on your rear. Then shove all the furniture back, and do the other bit. Does that answer your enquiry?" and there was a pause and a rather weak "Er, yes. Thank you" and the line went dead.'

As we made our daily excursions up and down the steep, narrow stairway from the house in the Kasbah to the square, we passed a white mansion with magnificent views overlooking the sea. It had been the home of Barbara Hutton, the Woolworth heiress, who had been a friend of Brian's for many years and shared his taste for sexual adventure with military men. Famous for her lavish parties, outrageous behaviour and reckless promiscuity, she enjoyed swapping stories of sexual exploits with her friend.

One evening Barbara Hutton told Brian that she had recently met an American Marine who had introduced her to the most exciting erotic experience of her life. 'Good gracious, Barbara,' Brian said, 'this verges on the historic. What happened? Tell me everything.'

'The Marine was six feet six, with a beautiful bronzed body in perfect shape. A magnificent specimen. He had this long, thick, tireless tongue that he used, dear Brian, with extraordinary force and agility – *to lick my belly button.*'

Brian waited, but there was nothing more to the story. 'Lick your belly button?' he said, disappointed. 'It doesn't *sound* very exciting.'

'Lick my belly button,' Barbara said, adopting an expression of the utmost seriousness, '*From the inside!*'

It was not long before the house in the Kasbah took on the same frantic, railway-station atmosphere of 83 Kinnerton Street, with numerous people dropping in. It became increasingly difficult to write. Jeremy, the young man who had lived in the place for several months and had decorated it so pleasingly, had returned and now busied himself painting the bedroom that opened on to the roof in preparation for the imminent arrival of a lover from California.

'Nice fresh clean white walls,' Brian said to me approvingly, as he inspected the completed work. 'Give this fellow from California something to look at while he's being fucked senseless.'

Brian was uncharacteristically respectful of Jeremy, who painted and wrote poetry, and had aristocratic connections. He meditated, with incense and candles burning, and Irish folk music playing in the background – not forgetting the score from Brian's movie *Playboy of the Western World*. 'Never travel without it,' he said ingratiatingly. He also smoked hash openly and regularly – as a spiritual aid, he said – using a stubby clay pipe known as a chillum, which involved draping a wet cloth around the mouthpiece to cool the draughts of harsh smoke it delivered.

'Using drugs for spiritual enlightenment is rather like drinking brandy for medicinal purposes,' Brian said. 'A cover for sensual pleasure. I'm sorry to say that if you need a drug to make you feel close to God, you have sadly missed the point. I'm sure that the most mystical of your gurus and yogis would agree with me.'

'It helps point you in the right direction,' Jeremy said. 'Gurus and yogis are already on a much higher spiritual plain than ordinary people and would naturally shun all drugs. For the rest of us it helps, that's all. You should try.'

And so it came about that at the age of eighty Brian smoked his first pipe of hashish. The chillum was packed, not with chips of the stale, desiccated substance encountered in London, but a hefty plug of pungent, fresh black hash that filled the house with its aroma. Inculcated into the advanced and elaborate art of smoking pure hash through a chillum, Brian puffed away manfully and was soon enveloped in a cloud of blue smoke.

'This a good idea?' Dave asked me quietly. 'This shit'll knock his block off.'

The pipe was duly passed around, and Jeremy put a symphony of Mahler on the gramophone.

'Nothing happening,' Brian said. 'Not a sausage.'

Unlike Brian, I began to feel the effects almost immediately, and looked across to see how Dave was doing. 'Bloody 'ell!' he said.

After a couple of minutes Brian said, 'Let's go down to the square and get a taxi to La Belle Hélène for supper.' Nobody moved. The Mahler had begun to sound like the Niagara Falls, the smell of incense was overpowering, and I held up my hand to shield my eyes from the blinding glare of the single candle. 'Look at the pattern the leaves of the potted palm throws against the ceiling,' Brian said. After a moment, he added, 'Extraordinary to think that the sound we are hearing – this great ocean of music – was created by a human being. *What a work of art is man.*'

Later, at La Belle Hélène's, we sat studying cumbersome menus, scarcely touching the chilled white wine in our glasses. The waiter arrived to take our order. 'I'll have a slice of lemon pie,' Brian said.

'Just dessert, then, is it?' the waiter said, eyeing us knowingly.

'No, no,' Brian said absently. 'We're here for supper.'

Jeremy ordered a plate of fresh fruit, Dave asked for a slab of chocolate cake with 'loads' of whipped cream, while I too settled for lemon pie – although I had a strong hankering for a Mars bar. Usually, at La Belle Hélène's, Brian questioned the waiters closely on the freshness of the fish, the age of the lamb, and would have studied the wine list with care. Not tonight. The lemon pie served as starter, followed by a further two slices as main course, and yet another slice, reasonably enough, for pudding.

Despite the radical departure from the dinner rituals of a lifetime, Brian seemed blithely unaware of the unorthodox nature of our supper. After consuming our multiple desserts, Dave and Jeremy drifted off separately, while Brian and I climbed into a taxi. 'All this hash smoking is really nothing but an affectation adopted by foreign tourists, like squirting cheap red wine in your face from one of those leather satchels in Spain,' he said. 'It had absolutely no effect on me *whatsoever*.'

It was inevitable, given the combination of Brian's personality with my own, that the strict work routine which governed the early days of our stay in Tangier became corrupted and lax over the weeks. No system on earth could resist the double dose of hedonism and idleness we brought to bear against it. Although a rough screenplay now existed in the form of a baggy and overlong first draft, I was to be found wielding the fountain pen or jabbing at the typewriter less and less. Increasingly, I accompanied Brian to lunch, and began skipping work. There seemed scarcely enough hours in the day to keep up with our strange social life, particularly as I was called upon to organise a couple of cocktail parties. Eventually, I ceased writing altogether.

One blazing day I came out of the house carrying a towel and a bottle of homemade suntan lotion, and ran into Brian on my way down through the Kasbah. 'On your way to the beach?'

'Thought I might go for a swim. It's so hot.'

'You're looking very brown. I had not noticed before. Positively bronzed – like a Hollywood film star.'

'Old trick I learned when I lived in Spain,' I said, shaking my bottle of suntan lotion. 'Olive oil and vinegar – none of your Coppertone for me! Rub this stuff on and you go black – fries you like a chop.'

'You have failed to pick up the nuance of my remark – the hint of irony. But I should know by now, subtlety is entirely wasted upon you. My point, Christopher, is that a writer should be pasty white and horribly pale, like a baker, not tanned like some playboy off a yacht. I brought you here to write, not swim and lie on the beach.'

'It's become a madhouse in there!' I said, nodding in the direction of the house. 'People coming and going all day long, music playing . . . how do you expect me to write? Jeremy meditating and chanting. Irish fiddle music playing all the time . . . it's just impossible. And the parties! Not to mention all the how's-your-father. Anyway, the first draft is pretty much complete. A few scenes here and there, a bit of this and that, and away you go!'

'Away we go indeed! If you could concentrate on the "this and that" over the next few days, we'll strike camp and go back to London at the weekend.' My face fell. 'What's the matter? London's not that bad, is it?'

'Reality,' I said. 'London's reality.'

PART III

London

London was reality, I told Brian. I was wrong. London was a nightmare. I returned to a world anxious to have a reckoning with me. As I waded through the post piled in my flat, I groaned out loud at the number of bills in red – final demands for gas, electricity and telephone. There were also threatening letters from the authorities written in the deadly, cold prose of institutional indifference. A stack from the Metropolitan Police concerned unpaid parking fines (although I had long since been unable to afford a car and had been happy to have it repossessed), and sinister missives from the ruthless crew at Camden Council demanded payment of rates. The communications regarding rates were written in escalating tones of severity, suggesting Big Trouble if I did not pay very, *very* soon. The last of these, delivered a week earlier, announced a move to obtain a warrant for my arrest.

The few cheques in my postbag in payment for articles did not begin to redress the problem. And my bank was being obtuse in regard to increasing my already considerable overdraft. 'A lot of people have been looking for you,' a friend who had stayed in my flat said. 'Unpleasant people.'

It was a period of considerable stress. Although I lived with money trouble as an Eskimo lives with ice and blubber, the entries in my journal for this period chronicle increasing desperation – an unpaid screenwriter and freelance journo on the edge of a nervous breakdown. Faced with financial meltdown, and the bouts of depression and despair this brought with it, I took down from the bookshelf a boxed Penguin paperback set of *War and Peace*, a Christmas gift, and began to read. There are people who cannot differentiate between literature and life, and fortunately, in my twenties, I was one of them. As Joseph Conrad wrote, 'I don't know what would have become of me if I had not been a reading boy.' While the unpleasant people drummed on my door, punched the bell and pushed nasty communications through the letterbox, I was far away in Mother Russia. Curled up on the sofa drinking cups of tea and nibbling Jaffa cakes, I anxiously anticipated a cavalry charge, as horses stamped and snorted on an icy winter's morning; I was fearful as Bonaparte's army moved upon Moscow; I suffered through Pierre's spiritual anguish, and was moved by his enlightenment.

Occasionally, I took time away from the upheavals of Russian life to make furtive expeditions to Fleet Street in search of commissions. Whatever my personal circumstances, I always found the Street of Shame a place of endless romance. In those days almost all of the major national newspapers were located on Fleet Street or close by. An army of journalists rubbed shoulders in the area's pubs and restaurants: Marxist–Leninist and High Tory leader writers drank together, reporters from the tabloids swapped gossip with distinguished foreign correspondents from the broadsheets, and a young journalist might stand on the edge of many circles and absorb Fleet Street's strange theories of how the world turned.

The excitement of breaking news and the tension of constant deadlines were palpable. I liked the Street best late at night, after the papers had been put to bed and were in the process of being printed. Lorries roared out of the various newspapers' loading bays on their way to London's railway stations with their cargoes of news. My walk home from Blackfriars to Bloomsbury took me along the length of Fleet Street – past the Cheshire Cheese, El Vino's and the Wig and Pen, past the Inns of Court and the Law Courts, around the Aldwych, and into Covent Garden – still functioning then as London's central fruit and vegetable market. I thought it a magical journey. As the lorries left Fleet Street, so others descended on Covent Garden and the market came to life. I often stopped at midnight at the all-night tea stall underneath the arch of Inigo Jones' St Paul's, the actors' church, and stood beside beefy porters drinking a mug of tea strong enough to stand a spoon in, enjoying a late supper of delicious, greasy bacon between slices of white bread. Despite the threats of electricity and gas boards, Camden Council and the Metropolitan Police, I felt I was at the centre of the world and it was an adventure to be alive.

And somehow, in between writing articles and extended sessions with *War and Peace* – happily, a long, long book – I managed to knock the script into some sort of shape. The verdict on the first draft was that the structure was essentially sound, but the story needed filling out. Herod was too much of a one-dimensional villain, Brian said, and suggested he should be more sympathetic, like the character of Othello. 'Give it a dollop of Shakespeare.' He also wanted more made of Herod's relationship with Mariamne, hinting that I was no great shakes at the lovey-dovey stuff. He was merciless in his mockery over a line I had put into the mouth of one of the wise men at his first sight of Jerusalem after a long, hard journey: 'We made it!'

'Good God,' Brian said. '"We made it!"'

'What's wrong with that?'

'Nothing – if one of the three kings is from Brooklyn. Reminds me of that old Cleopatra movie where she instructs a huge Negro standing with a roll of papyrus and quill, "Take a letter – take a *threatening* letter! Mark Antony, Rome . . ."'

'All right, all right.'

We were sitting in the upstairs room of the French House, in Soho, where we had met to talk about the script, or at least to spend twenty minutes talking about it during lunch. There was only one serious area of disagreement. Angels. There weren't any in my script, and Brian insisted they should be put in. I had written one scene in which the Angel of the Lord, although not actually *appearing* on screen, terrified shepherds sitting with their flocks by night as a disembodied voice. 'Are these shepherds supposed to be madmen?' Brian demanded. 'Hallucinating and running around the desert like they're off their rockers? Somebody put something in their gourd of sheep's milk cocoa?'

'I was attempting to create a scene that might be accepted by a modern audience,' I said with dignity. 'Trying to avoid the Christmas panto effect.'

'*I want proper bloody angels!*'

'It carries the risk of ridicule.'

'Listen, Thoroughly Modern Millie – put in the angels! I'll arrange a screening for you of Pasolini's magnificent film *The Gospel According to Saint Matthew.* He modern enough for you? See how a *genius* handles angels.'

'Pasolini made a film based on the gospel of Saint Matthew?' I said sceptically.

'Yes. And he had angels. So go and look at it.'

After lunch we came out of the pub and crossed the road on our way down to Shaftesbury Avenue. Sitting on the pavement outside St Anne's church was a man Brian would have called a tramp, now redesignated a homeless person. He was in bad shape, filthy and wrapped in an old blanket. 'Got change for a cup of tea, guv?'

Brian stopped and dug into his trouser pockets for a coin but couldn't find one. He pulled out a five-pound note instead and waved the money in the direction of the tramp, who viewed it with hostility and disappointment. 'I can't change *that*!'

'No, no!' Brian said. 'Take it!'

The man's eyes grew wide, and he took the note gingerly,

sensing a trick. He looked up and down the street with suspicion, as if involved in an illegal act, before whipping the note beneath his blanket in case his benefactor might undergo a sudden change of heart. 'Thanks, mate,' he said in an amazed murmur. 'Thanks a lot!'

'Remember, as you look up at the stars tonight,' Brian said, 'that the soft starlight you see has taken millions of years to reach us. I am told when you analyse starlight in the spectrum it contains the same chemicals that make up our bodies – bitumen, ozone, oxygen and so on. So if anyone ever tries to diminish you, just say, "Listen, you're addressing a walking piece of starlight."'

'Right, guv,' the man said.

As hard science, I suspect this data may be flawed, but as poetic inspiration it proved effective. Some outside force entered the tramp on the pavement, an injection of energy and spiritual rejuvenation brought on by the powerful combo of fiver and philosophy. But while Brian enjoyed bringing occasional succour and comfort to the needy, he also took pleasure in deflating the mighty. He could bless, but he also had a gift for hitting people hard beneath the fifth rib. 'Doesn't being a member of humanity ever get you down?' I once heard him ask an insufferably self-satisfied woman who considered herself very grand. 'I mean here we all are – *chained to the lavatory*!' And when his fellow beings made him despair, like the yob we came across one day vomiting over his own boots, he said: 'Take a look, Christopher, and be not proud – *that* is the species to which we belong!'

As we reached Shaftesbury Avenue, Brian seemed restless and reluctant to go home. 'I think I'm going to toddle over to the Festival Club in Brydges Place. It's a key club, and while I do not have a key, they'll let me in. I'll buy you a drink if you like, but I must warn you the clientele is *of a certain kind*.'

'Thanks, but I must go home and get some work done. I haven't been to the Festival Club in years . . .'

'You know it?'

'I used to go there with my mother in the school holidays.'

'Your *mother* took you as a schoolboy to an afternoon drinking club for *queers*?'

'She is a great friend of the owner.'

'Sometimes, Christopher, your complicated character leaves me speechless.' Brian shook his head and sighed. 'Well, I might just wander over there and see what's cooking. Don't forget my angels.'

Back in my flat I read through the screenplay without enthusiasm, confounded by Herod's lovemaking to Mariamne, while the unsolved problem of the angels gnawed. I sat without an idea in my head, doodling in pencil upon a large sheet of blotting paper. The next time I saw Brian I had to admit that I had accomplished nothing. 'I've been having a Big Think, but don't *actually* have anything down on paper.'

'Is this what you tell newspaper editors?'

'No. They'd just get nasty.'

'Writing for hire is a sordid business. While I do not wish to assume the mantle of the hard men of Fleet Street, I'm afraid even as a free spirit I have a duty to keep my writer on the rails. Inspiration, Christopher, is often generated by a moving pen. Do you think by chance that some time soon you might sit down and write a love scene between Herod and Mariamne? And the odd scene with an angel or two? Actually down on paper?'

'I'll try.'

'You can do no more. Let's go to the pub.'

As we walked down Kinnerton Street towards the Turk's Head, Brian turned to me and said, 'Look who it is, the richest girl who ever sailed the seven seas.' Approaching us from the other end of the street was a tall man, ramrod straight and immaculately dressed. The toecaps of his shoes glinted from a hundred yards. It was Lord Mountbatten, as illustrious and natty a toff as empire ever wrought.

Born His Serene Highness Prince Louis of Battenberg, great-grandson of Queen Victoria, nephew of the Tsar and Tsarina of Russia, and cousin of the King of England, he became Earl Mountbatten of Burma, GCVO, GCB, OM, First Sea Lord and Admiral of the Fleet, one of the three Supreme Allied Commanders in the Second World War, last Viceroy of India, best friend of the Duke of Windsor, uncle of Prince Philip, and architect of his marriage to Elizabeth, Queen of England, and beloved confidant of Prince Charles. Brian had met Mountbatten during the making of *Malta Story*, when he was Admiral of the Fleet, and they had been on friendly terms ever since. Despite Brian's irreverent aside, I had seen him nod silently when someone once described Mountbatten as 'the most distinguished Englishman alive'.

Mountbatten kept an ugly, modern mews house of brown tile and glass beside the Turk's Head – in what Brian asserted was the 'wrong end of the street'. Mountbatten broke into a smile the moment he caught sight of us, and stopped to talk. I was duly introduced as 'My writer', and Mountbatten politely enquired what it was we were working on. Brian ignored the question. 'How many lavatories do you have in your house?'

'Lavatories?' Mountbatten asked. Brian nodded. 'Let me see. I have two, now that you ask.'

Brian held up three fingers in front of Mountbatten's face: 'I have three!'

He turned on his heel and walked off down the street. I mumbled an awkward farewell and followed. I looked back to see Mountbatten, hands plunged in his trouser pockets, rock back on his heels. He let out an upper-class bark of laughter: 'Ha, ha, ha!'

As we took our seats in the Turk's Head, Brian said, 'When

I was making *Malta Story*, Mountbatten was a bit bored on the island with nothing much to do as Admiral of the Fleet, and used to come on the set nearly every day. He gave a cocktail party for us at Admiralty House and halfway through asked me if I was enjoying myself. "The party's marvellous, only I don't think there's much wallop to your navy drinks." He called over an enormous Marine. "This chap here doesn't think much of our navy drinks. Says they haven't got any body to them. Do something." The Marine came back in a few minutes holding a bottle of gin, a bottle of vodka, a bottle of brandy and a bottle of Scotch. He held them by the necks and emptied them into the punchbowl and Lord Mountbatten handed me a ladle full of the mixture. I took a good big gulp and the stuff nearly blew the back of my head off.'

I began to tell Brian about my money troubles. 'I came back from Tangier to considerable financial nastiness.'

'*Financial nastiness!*' Brian shuddered. 'Horrible – *horrible!*'

Despite my chronic finances, I now accepted that I would not receive any money from Brian, whom I understood was as hard up in his way as I was. It just happened that we lived beyond our means at different levels. (The small amounts he did hand over were delivered with increasing ill grace. 'There you are,' he once said, after giving me a tenner. 'You only want it to spend on *women*!') Indeed, Brian's own finances were so stretched that he had begun selling things from the house – an Edward Burra, *The Weeping Ship*, that he had bought in the war, had recently gone to a dealer for £4,000. He told me there were certain things in the house he would never sell: the portrait of St Bridget over the mantelpiece – painted by himself in the 1920s – a small Monet oil painting of a country house, and a bust of Nefertiti. The Monet had a highly dubious provenance and was almost certainly stolen. The Nefertiti, he said, was as old as the Nile and loaded with magic, and had been given to him by the Egyptian Minister of Culture. (I later learned that he had actually bought the bust in the gift shop of the Cairo Hilton.)

Brian listened to the details of the financial nastiness with compassion. 'Funny stuff, money. Comes and goes. Extraordinary how the debts mount up. These stupid electric and gas bills. In Russia it's all free.'

'At least when you were young you earned loads of money. I'm *always* broke.'

'No, no – I was often broke, the way film directors are. Feast or famine.'

'What did you do?'

'I sponged off my sister, Patricia. She lived in a house beside the Dorchester and had amassed a great deal of cash. She started with a tea shop in Chancery Lane, but was very shrewd and just went from strength to strength. A natural moneybags. She had this cat called Jezebel, a horrid thing that always jumped up to scratch me when I kissed my sister, but I used to take choice pieces of haddock and chicken around for the cat to keep on Patricia's good side. Once when I arrived with luxuries for Jezebel my sister was sitting with a friend who said, "Isn't he a nice brother?" I said, "I'm only keeping my name in the will." Patricia turned to her friend and said, "The bugger means it!"'

But Brian adored his sister, anchor to his bobbing life, and when she died at eighty-two he suffered. Years after her death, when members of the family showed him old film footage of her, he broke down and could not watch. 'Patricia had asked me some time before her death to scatter her ashes on Howth Head, overlooking the Irish Sea. And I was to throw roses on them and pour two bottles of champagne over them.' The ashes were sent across to Dublin, and Brian was driven out to Howth Head. 'I bought the champagne and stopped at a little flower shop on the way for the roses. "We never stock roses, sir," the lady told me apologetically. "We have no call for them out here." At that precise moment a man came into the shop with roses and I took two dozen off him.'

Patricia, Brian's beloved elder sister

Brian climbed over the cliffs of Howth Head, and found a suitable hollow covered with wild roses and flowering blackberry bushes. 'There was a slight breeze as I scattered the ashes and I got some up my nose. I then threw down the roses, opened the champagne and began to pour it out. I had been driven out by my old friend Harry Clifton's valet, Dodge. He caught my eye. "Bit of a waste, sir." So we both took a good slug from the second bottle.' Brian became momentarily lost in thought. 'So that's where Patricia rests – Howth Head, outside of Dublin. Perhaps we'll go there together one day and visit her.'

His tone changed, as if remembering our conversation was about pounds, shillings and pence. 'When Patricia died she left me £40,000 and another £40,000 in jewellery. She was a large woman, always dieting, and always with a bottle of brandy and a box of chocolates under the bed, and a case of champagne in the "catch-all", a little room next to the bedroom. For some reason she must have feared poverty because I found hundreds of banknotes pinned to the curtains in the bedroom after she died, and when I knocked over a little chair there was a large emerald ring pinned underneath. And emptying out the catch-all I found two Fabergé cigarette cases hidden among a pile of old newspapers, one emerald green enamel with an emerald catch, and the other white enamel with a diamond catch.'

I told Brian about all the letters from the council and the police, and the final notices. 'Those electric bills,' Brian said, 'they're a scandal. Once I went round to Patricia's to get her to pay my electric bill, but there was no fishing in my sister's waters that day. So I began to talk about a small Degas bronze I had seen in the Lefèvre Gallery of a female ballet dancer sunk down in a chair with her skirts spread all about her. I went on and on about its beauty until Patricia said it sounded lovely and asked how much it was. "Quite cheap, really. It's only £750." She wrote me out a cheque. I hurried round to the gallery and bought the bronze, and took it back to the house. "It's as beautiful as you said – and you're going to have such fun looking at it on your mantelpiece." "But Patricia, how will I see it – I have no electric light?" So she wrote out a cheque for the electric bill.'

The story cheered me up, but I returned to the draconian measures taken by Camden Council. I said that I feared imprisonment. 'How *ridiculous*!' Brian said. 'Locking up writers. It's like Russia! But I'm sure it's only a very light sentence for the rates. I'll come and visit you.'

'Thanks, Bri.'

'I'll bring lovely things from Fortnum's. Some of the lads are very good at shoplifting there. And it's only a matter of time before the millions pour in and we'll be awash with cash. I'm talking to all sorts of people. And the first thing I want you to do is go out and buy a nice big Rolls-Royce – I do hate to think of you having to take the bus.'

As might be expected, Brian's strategy for raising money for the film was highly idiosyncratic. He really did have meetings with money men, or long lunches at the Connaught at least, but no cash was forthcoming. I doubt if he ever stooped to discuss business, something I'm sure he suggested would be handled by his *people*. Except there were no people. Mostly, he told the businessmen endless funny stories. This enchanted and amused them but did not further the project. I failed to discover what really happened at any particular meeting, as I was never invited. It was *déclassé* to have the writer in tow, Brian suggested – they either bored everyone stupid by talking claptrap about existentialism, or droned on and on about royalty statements and subsidiary rights. Besides, it made the producer look desperate. *It just wasn't done*.

So I stayed out of things and let Brian handle it all. He lunched on several occasions with senior people from the Grosvenor Estates, meetings set up by his friend Stephen Vernon, who was married to the sister of the current duke. ('I don't understand it,' Stephen told me later. 'Brian never mentioned the film but talked about how the roof of his house leaks, making a nasty stain in one of his bedrooms, and why didn't they send somebody round to fix it.') There were also meetings with dodgy Arabs, a number of American producers, and Count Billy dropped by from time to time with the most unbelievable people.

One oddity who showed up on Brian's doorstep was an Italian with a pencil moustache and a thick accent. He had a mouthful of uneven teeth, haphazardly capped in gold, and a head of sparse, greasy hair dyed jet black. I remember he wore a narrow, stained tie, with a tiny, tight knot, and a nylon shirt gone grey with use and age, the collar of which flapped around his neck like a lifebelt. I reported the presence of this unattractive individual to Brian. 'There's some incredible spiv at the door, says you're expecting him. *Horrible* specimen.'

'The gentleman to whom you refer,' Brian said in a harsh tone of reprimand, 'is the London representative of the Banco Spirito Santo, the Vatican bank of Rome.'

I did not truly understand how perversely counter-productive Brian's behaviour could be until I introduced a merchant banker I had met at a dinner party. The banker expressed interest in the project, explaining that his bank had recently become involved with a number of European film distributors, and that there were deals to be done with Germany, France and Spain. He was a serious professional, so I worked to arrange a meeting. At first Brian tried to put it off. 'I so dislike the City . . . Such a long way . . . Banks are too depressing' and so on. The banker graciously agreed to go to Brian's house in Kinnerton Street one morning for an eleven o'clock meeting. I received a call at eleven-thirty.

'Who *exactly* is this bloody man Desmond Hurst?' the banker demanded.

At first I thought Brian had forgotten about the meeting, and not been at home . . . but it was worse than that. 'I can assure you he's made a great many films—'

'I don't care how many bloody films he's made!'

'Is there some sort of snag?'

'You could say that, you could say that . . .' Rage temporarily reduced the banker to incoherence. He collected himself and said in a cold, deadly voice, 'He told me to take my clothes off.'

I groaned inwardly, imagining the circumstances only too well. 'Oh dear – what happened?'

'What *happened*? I walked out the bloody door and bloody slammed it bloody hard – that's what bloody happened!'

'Oh dear.'

'*Oh dear!* Is that all you have to say?' The banker's voice began once again to rise in anger, beginning as a roar and ending in a comical squeal. 'I am a family man . . . A *normal* man . . . A senior partner at an old and distinguished City bank. You suggested I meet with a producer with a view to funding a film . . . I hardly have time to sit down when he suggests . . . *I take my clothes off!*'

'You're angry, naturally—'

'Bloody right I'm bloody angry. I don't care what you buggers get up to in your own time, but I do care about being sexually propositioned when I go about the bank's business. And as to that, let me inform you *officially* – we wouldn't touch your project with a bargepole. The bank is not in the habit of funding the enterprises of roaring perverts!'

The phone was slammed down. My first instinct was to call Brian and ask him what the hell he was playing at, but as I was to see him the following morning I decided to talk to him in person. Things were out of control and I wanted a showdown. Perhaps I could use the absurd situation to force him to be serious about the business side of the project. I might even have the exquisite pleasure of seeing Brian squirm a little.

We met at his house. As I waited in the hallway for Brian to put on his overcoat, I asked casually, 'How did it go with the banker?'

'Banker?'

'The man I sent along yesterday.' A sarcastic edge entered my voice. 'Merchant banker. Well-cut pinstripe suit, white shirt, highly polished shoes. Old School Tie. Rather posh. A little on the formal side. Strictly business. Quite important in the City, actually.'

'Oh, him. He has yet to phone me back.'

'Actually, he called me directly after your meeting.'

'Oh?'

'Yes. With the most categorical rejection imaginable.'

'*Rejection!*' Brian sounded scandalised. 'He hasn't even read the script!'

'I don't think he'll be bothering. In fact, he turned the project down on more personal grounds. He was really rather cross when he spoke to me. No, not cross – *incandescent* with rage. Said you told him to take his clothes off.'

Brian did not squirm. In fact, he hardly reacted at all. After a moment's reflection he said, 'Good-looking chap, but self-important. Pompous – but bankers usually are. The money goes to their heads. They act as if it's theirs, rather than they've grubbed it up from everyone else. Gives them a false sense of power.'

'This man was a potential backer! He can raise millions for movies – he has access to money in Europe! He was introduced through a personal friend and took the time to come down here to meet you at home. He expressed genuine interest. *And you propositioned him!*'

'He was queer, that one – I'm telling you. I remember the first time Big Freddy came to see me. He got up to go to the loo. As he went out the door I said, "And take your clothes off while you're out there!" I saw a shudder run through his entire body.'

'Big Freddy is a *male prostitute*. This man is a *merchant banker*!'

'There is no need to raise your voice, Christopher.' Brian adopted a grand manner meant to convey that my outrage over his behaviour was middle-class, and the talk of money common and unartistic. 'You seem *peculiarly* impressed by merchant bankers.'

'They have money – we need money. This was serious. And now he's screaming down the phone that we're perverts and he'll never lend us a penny.'

'Ah, I see. You're upset because your society friends will now think you're queer.'

'I'm upset because you have completely destroyed any chance of raising money from an important source. I'm upset because you show total contempt for my efforts and no respect for my contacts. I'm upset because all the unpaid work I put into this always seems to come to nothing.'

My speech sounded shrill and pompous and I knew it. This made me even more angry. Not only was Brian not squirming, he was not in the least bit embarrassed. (Actually, I never saw him embarrassed by anything – the closest was when he told a dirty joke to a monk who failed to laugh. Brian just looked at the ground for twenty seconds.) Most galling of all, he didn't give a hoot about the lost opportunity.

We walked out into Kinnerton Street in silence. Brian set a dignified course in the direction of the grocer to buy an orange for his champagne breakfast, while I stomped off to the Wilton Arms and sat at the bar sulking. He arrived in his own time and joined me, while I remained surly and uncommunicative. We sat side by side, saying nothing.

'Shepherd's pie or Cornish pastie?' Brian asked.

'Haven't decided.'

There was another silence as we concentrated on our drinks. Brian said quietly, 'You should have seen his face!'

The scene appeared before me. I imagined the arrival of the banker at the front door – the manly handshake and stilted small talk about weather and traffic. The tightly folded umbrella, and tailored overcoat with astrakhan collar, are put away in the hall cupboard. The guest is led into the drawing room, and invited to sit. He lowers himself into the quicksand of the ancient sofa with as much dignity as such a manoeuvre allows, professionally balancing his slim, black leather briefcase on his knees. Brian takes up position in his wing-chair throne, drops a few names, and trots out a theatrical anecdote or two. And then, after ten minutes, as the banker politely prepares to steer the conversation towards the business at hand – he is asked to remove his clothes.

'*You should have seen his face!*' Brian chuckled and caught my eye. Reluctantly, I started to laugh. Brian put his hand to his mouth, screwed up his eyes and began the wheezing giggle that often accompanied the memory of a particularly wicked or outrageous act. I laughed and laughed. Tears came to my eyes.

'What's the point of being in the film business if you can't have a bit of fun?' Brian said, giving me a nudge.

I laughed until it hurt. Laughed and laughed and laughed.

I arrived at Kinnerton Street one morning to find an extremely tall man standing on his own in the front room warming himself in front of the fire. He did not introduce himself but launched into an incomprehensible monologue. 'I had dinner with her again last night. At the Ritz. We had the most delicious lamb cutlets. Served pink. She loves them pink like that. And a bottle of Léoville-Poyferré 1961 – do you approve? A whole bottle – not a half.'

Mercifully, Brian came into the room at this moment and I was temporarily spared further bewilderment. The man was introduced as Harry Clifton. 'Take Harry to the Nag's Head, will you, Christopher? I'll join you directly.'

We made our way to the pub where Len Cole, the publican, greeted us. 'Dear boy, how are you? What's it to be?'

I offered to buy Harry a drink. 'That's *extremely* kind. *Extremely* kind. And in due course I would *love* to join you in a drink. I would *love* it. But first, I must have a few words with mine host.'

'At your service, dear boy,' Len said.

'Do you have hard-boiled eggs?'

'Many. *Very* hard-boiled indeed.'

'And do you have ham?'

'Certainly. Lovely ham.'

'Good. Please shell two very hard-boiled eggs and prepare a small dish of salt and pepper mixed together, and provide me with two slices of lovely ham with the fat cut off.'

'Right-ho.' Len turned to me. 'And a Guinness for you, dear boy?'

'Please.'

Harry hummed to himself tunelessly while Len drew the Guinness, and set about shelling the eggs and preparing the ham. As I made to say something, Harry gazed down at me from his great height and smiled kindly: 'I would rather not speak just now, if you don't mind.'

Len returned with the shelled eggs and slices of ham on a plate, a small dish of salt and pepper, and my Guinness. The landlord and I watched with fascination as Harry dipped both ends of the first egg into the salt and pepper, and carefully rolled it up in a slice of ham. He devoured it in two bites and set about preparing the second. In less than a minute both eggs had disappeared.

'Delicious!' Harry looked down on me benignly. 'I have not forgotten your generous offer of a drink but hope you will forgive me if I *insist* that you allow me. Landlord, do you have champagne on ice?'

'Certainly.'

'Then a bottle of iced champagne, if you would be so kind.'

On cue, Brian came through the door carrying an orange. Len poured Harry a glass of champagne, then picked up the orange from the bar without being asked and began to squeeze its juice into a glass. Harry took the bottle of champagne and topped up my Guinness. We moved to a table where the conversation made it clear that Harry was in line – behind the Duke of Westminster – to finance our movie. Brian spoke of our recent trip to Tangier, and my work on the script, concluding proudly: 'Christopher writes with a fountain pen.'

'Oh, I like to hear that,' Harry said with unnerving enthusiasm. 'Yes, I like that *very* much. And *she'll* like that. Do you have the pen in question on your person?'

'Yes, I do.'

'May I hold it?'

'If you like.' I took the pen from my jacket pocket and handed it to Harry, who held it tightly in his right hand and stared hard at me. Unsure whether I should meet his gaze or look away, I glanced at Brian for some insight into the ritual under way, but his manner suggested that nothing unusual was happening. Harry began to roll my pen against his forehead.

'He's the real thing,' Harry said to Brian, handing back my pen. 'I will let *her* know. How clever of you to find the right writer for your story.'

'And we have St Thérèse working hard for us,' Brian said.

'Good, good,' Harry said, nodding seriously. 'And Tomaster provides guidance, no doubt?'

'Of course. And St Bridget in the wings.'

Later, I was sent for sausage, mash and fried-onion gravy. These were kept at one end of the bar in three separate metal warming containers with glass covers. The sausages, for some reason, were twice the length of an ordinary sausage and cooked until they had a burnt, black crust around them. Brian and I thought them very delicious. The pub cat, an enormously fat Persian Blue named Mr Moggs, liked to sleep stretched across the top of the containers, attracted by the warmth. He did not seem to mind being lifted up and down with the lids as Len served food, but it meant that various quantities of cat fur worked themselves into the mix. Sometimes it would only be the odd hair, but there were times when whole tufts from Mr Moggs attached themselves to the mashed potato. I had previously remarked that this was somewhat off-putting. 'Helps take your mind off worse things,' Brian said.

'Like what?'

'Len cooking them! The coughing, the wheezing, the fag ash – *the dirty fingernails*.'

(The other publicans on Kinnerton Street conducted themselves in a businesslike and professional way, but Len Cole marched to the beat of a different drum. Despite his grand manner and affected accent, he lived upstairs in conditions rumoured to be authentically eighteenth-century –

the last time the place was cleaned, according to the pub wags. Len's appearance was in keeping with the squalor of his surroundings: a cigarette was forever wedged between nicotine-stained teeth, an inch of ash perpetually juddering on its end; his trousers were greasy and stained, and his shapeless pullover of indeterminate colour had long since lost its elbows. There were regulars who drank after hours who swore they saw Len pee in the washing-up water. Members of his family who lived in America grew so concerned for his welfare that they rashly imported him to live with them. But there must have been some antibiotic culture contained in the slime and filth of Len's Nag's Head, for the cleanliness and antiseptic nature of the New World did for him. He was dead within six months.)

As we tucked into our sausages and mash, a woman passed our table and acknowledged Brian with a cheery, 'Hello, Bri.' Harry immediately rose to his feet. 'Oh, don't get up for me, please,' the woman said.

'Tallulah Bankhead *always* got to her feet when *men* entered a room,' Harry said. 'Isn't that so, Brian? A man would come in and Tallulah would stand.'

'That's nice,' the woman said nervously, and scuttled away.

After lunch Harry said goodbye to us in the street, once again subjecting me to a disconcerting stare. 'He's the real thing,' Harry repeated, 'but he doesn't *understand*. I'll talk to her.'

Back at the house I said, 'I'm glad I'm the real thing, but what is it I don't understand? And who on earth is the woman he goes on about – the one he takes to the Ritz?'

'Ah, yes, the woman he dines at the Ritz. That would be God.'

'*God?*'

'Harry dines with God once a fortnight – to keep in touch with the other side. Harry has always gone to the top and never messed about with minions. He might have a sherry

The wealthy eccentric, Harry Clifton, at home at Lytham Hall

with a bishop or a cardinal, but for dinner it has to be God. He believes God to be a woman he calls the White Goddess.'

'But who is she?'

'Doesn't exist. Harry sits at a table for two by the window and the head waiter duly takes his order for two. Food is served for two throughout the evening. The wine waiter pours wine for two. Except nobody is there, of course. At least, God does not deign to make Herself visible to mere waiters and diners. Harry sits there for hours, talking happily to himself.'

'Don't the staff find it . . . *odd*?'

'Not really. They're used to it. Harry used to use the Ritz as a café in the old days, and kept a suite there throughout the year, and had his own wine cellar. He once invited me to dinner and asked how I liked the soup. I complained mildly that it was a bit thin and not very hot. This was a mistake. Harry called the manager and demanded that he send over the major-domo of the Berkeley, which was situated across the road in those days. Harry then ordered my entire dinner to be brought from the Berkeley, saying that he presumed *their* chef could provide decent, hot soup. It was duly pushed across Piccadilly in a great silver trolley. I was so embarrassed that when I left the Ritz I tried to hide my face in my overcoat.'

'Harry's quite *eccentric*, wouldn't you say?'

'That is the word that attaches itself to Harry. If he were poor and of modest origins he would be put in a straitjacket, locked away in a padded cell and fed from a safe distance with a long spoon. But he's very rich and aristocratic, so he's found to be eccentric and charming. Big tipper, Harry – and *lovely* manners.'

Henry Talbot de Vere Clifton, I came to understand, was a wealthy aristocratic scion from a long line of half-mad giants. He was enormously rich and owned great swathes of Lancashire, and his forebears were equally as unconventional and untrammelled. The men had originally met in Hollywood when Brian was working as an assistant to John Ford, and Harry was in the throes of one of his many voyages around the world.

'Tell me more about Harry,' I said, sinking into the sofa and deciding not to work that afternoon.

'I had a close friend in California called Misho Ito, a famous Japanese dancer,' Brian said. 'Misho was on tour in Japan and I got a letter from him, asking me to meet a young Englishman off a ship whom he had met at the British Embassy in Tokyo. I drove my shabby but elegant Peerless convertible to San Pedro, the port for Los Angeles. Down the gangway of a rusting tramp steamer came this extremely tall, distinguished young Englishman, with no shoelaces in his shoes, and wearing the dirtiest white shirt I have ever seen. I could see at once he was *quite* an eccentric. As we drove through San Pedro we stopped in the middle of the town at a red light, and a big crowd surged across the road. Harry stood up to his full height in the convertible and pointed at them. "Look! Look, Brian – *Americans!*"

'We got into Los Angeles, and under the impression that Harry was a poverty-stricken young Englishman doing the world on the cheap, I put him in a very small, inexpensive hotel in Hollywood. I introduced him to Jack Ford, who took a liking to him because he was *so* eccentric and gave him a job as an extra in one of his pictures, for seven and a half dollars a day. Harry turned up on time every day and at the end of the week collected his pay. Then on the Friday, he turned to me and said, "Would you and your friend, Mr Ford, like to have dinner with me tonight?" Jack said, "Yeah, let's go." We were directed to the main hotel in Los Angeles, the Ambassador, and arrived to find that Mr Henry Talbot de Vere Clifton had installed himself on one whole floor. It was only then that I discovered he was one of the wealthiest landowners in England.'

Harry owned Lytham Hall, in Lancashire; a large part of the town of Lytham St Anne's – including the funfairs; vast landholdings in the county; a further 27,000 acres and Kildalton Castle on the Isle of Islay; lochs, rivers and land on the island of Lewis; Kylemore House, beneath the Nine Pins of Connemara, Ireland; a hotel in Dublin and numerous properties in London. ('There was no railway station for Lytham Hall so Harry used to pull the communication cord, stop the train, jump down and throw the driver a fiver. Then he would climb up the bank and over the fence into the grounds.')

Lytham Hall had originally been bought in 1606 for £4,300 by Cuthbert Clifton – later knighted by King James I. In due course it was demolished and replaced by the Georgian building that stands today. With the establishment of the Clifton Estates, the family set about improving the lot of the community. (Harry's mother was known to quote the strange aphorism, 'Kill socialism with love.') The land was drained, and a lifeboat station, cottage hospital and parish church were built – the church was peculiar in that it was adorned with two spires, a result of a pair of Clifton sisters at the time being unable to agree on the design.

'When I came back to England from Hollywood I decided to look Harry up at Kildalton Castle. I went up to Glasgow by train, then took about three different boat journeys before I eventually arrived on Islay. There was a man to meet me with a handcart for my luggage. I was shown into the castle, an enormous pile of imitation Gothic, and sat in the Great Hall. One bare electric light shone on about two hundred deer's heads coming out of the wall, all with eyes that seemed to be glaring at me. Harry came down the stairs in a great African robe and golden turned-up slippers. "Oh, there you are, dear, dear Brian. Come at once into the African room."'

The family had collected precious objects for hundreds of years, and every night at dinner some treasure was placed beside the dinner table. One night, it might be a gold candelabra seven feet high; the next, a jug and ewer given to Josephine by Napoleon. (In the days when Harry's father, Talbot, was still alive there had been stranger post-prandial rituals. When an effort to adopt a pygmy family – 'with child preferred' – failed, Talbot bought his wife a pygmy pony from Iceland, and the animal was led by the butler into the dining room each night after dinner and fed from the table.) If members of the family were quarrelling, they would eat in the dining room at separate tables.

'The castle was haunted by various ghosts,' Brian said, 'positively enjoyed and possibly imported by the family. According to a Chinese lady of high rank, who was staying there, one of the lavatories was haunted. She came rushing into the drawing room and told us she had been interfered with by a tall ghost with a long black beard wearing only a kilt, and that she would never go into that lavatory again.'

Brian soon learned that his friend Harry was merely an eccentric chip from a monumental family block of eccentricity. The castle had originally been acquired by Harry's father, Talbot, and his mother, Violet, was still alive when Brian first visited it. One day as he sat beside her on the lawn eating chocolates, she spoke of her past life. 'When my father was ambassador to one of those small countries below Mexico, the old boy was in love with me in quite the wrong way. Along came Talbot, who was much taller than myself. I took to him at once because I wasn't going to marry a shrimp. When I told my father, he said, "Marry him, Violet, and breed a race of half-mad giants."' At that moment, her younger son, Michael, who was six foot seven at seventeen, leaped across the lawn with nothing on but an old kilt, shooting at a rabbit with a bow and arrow. 'And as you can see, dear Brian, I've done it.'

Harry's father Talbot was described by all who knew him as a man born out of his time, better suited to the life of an Elizabethan pirate or explorer. He had come into his full inheritance at the age of sixteen, and the money gave him the freedom to travel and do as he wished. He set about creating a dangerous and challenging world of adventure for himself, exploring Mexico, California, Alaska, the Arctic and the Far East. He planned treasure hunts to the Cocos Islands, weathered revolutions in South America, and was struck down with yellow fever and malaria. He died in the arms of his wife on an expedition to West Africa.

Violet Beauclerk – Harry's mother – came from similarly ancient and individual stock. She was the great-granddaughter of the eighth Duke of St Albans – himself the descendant of Charles II and Nell Gwyn. Talbot remarked of his wife, 'It took a king and an orange girl to forge her.' The daughter of a British diplomat, she was born in Rome where because of fever she was suckled first on goats' milk, then on wine. The father was a profound melancholic who sat for hours in

Harry Clifton's parents, Talbot and Violet

his library behind a locked door, drawing his fingernails up and down the writing table moaning, '*Taedium vitae, taedium vitae!*'

In Talbot, Violet found the man of her secret dreams and romantic fantasies. The couple met in the Peruvian Andes, where Talbot came across his future bride lying on a rock, reciting poetry to a plunging waterfall. They became engaged and sailed back to England to be married, and on the journey home Violet received advice that she was to follow all her life. 'Never let your husband see you in bedroom slippers,' the captain of the ship told her. 'It galls a man's finer feelings – sends a lot of marriages to the bottom.'

After marriage, Talbot showered his wife with the jewels of his family: diamond wings to wear in her hair, an ancient chain of golden birds from the East, and a priceless necklace of gold-brown diamonds to match her eyes. She wore the jewels at every opportunity, even when dining alone with her husband. One friend was surprised to find her so adorned eating supper in the tiny cabin of their racing yacht.

Away from the enforced austerity of hard travel, and the discomfort and privation that went with that life, the domesticated Talbot was wildly extravagant. Although he busied himself collecting orchids and playing the organ – turning a wing of the castle into one enormous instrument – he occasionally attempted to re-create the excitement of his youth in sprees of reckless gambling. Once when he ran up enormous debts in Paris, he sent a telegram reading 'SELL BLACKPOOL'.

Violet attempted to draw moral strength from these cash haemorrhages, explaining to Brian: 'Because we always spend more, not less, than we can afford, we are saved from ever feeling complacent or rich.'

'There was a story Violet told that moved me to tears,' Brian said. 'It has stayed with me all these years and still moves me.' While walking along the seashore near his home in Ireland, Talbot found a corked bottle given up by the sea. Inside was a sheet of paper covered in writing on both sides. At the top of the first page the handwriting was tiny and precise, but grew increasingly loose and uncontrolled as it charted the fate of three survivors whose ship had been torpedoed. At first the note expressed hope, but soon thirst became the obsession. One man died, and then another. And then hope died in the lone survivor. On the edge of sanity, he wrote a bitter attack on his wife, cursing her as the cause for having gone to sea. The writing was now wild and sprawling, matching the desperation of its author. But then a profound peace settled on the parched, doomed man. The last entry, written in a bold hand, defied thirst, starvation and death itself – 'God is Love'.

After Talbot's death, Violet never wore her jewels again; partly out of penance, she said, and partly out of love. 'Violet had Talbot buried on the hill opposite Kildalton Castle and at midnight would go up on to the roof to commune with him,' Brian said. 'She had named a part of her body after every place she had visited with Talbot where they had made romantic love together. One night, we all hid behind the chimneys to watch her. She undressed and stood there naked, beautiful and very tall. She pointed to one of her breasts: "This, Talbot, is your Isfahan." And so she continued, pointing to various parts of her body and naming each place they had visited and made love.'

This strange, ancient Catholic family, both rich and unconventional, appealed to everything in Brian's nature. Back in London he saw a great deal of Harry socially, although as no film had presented itself in England he decided to return to Hollywood. 'That seems a pity with all your knowledge,' Harry had said. 'Have you got an idea for a small film that wouldn't cost very much – without these terrible American accents?'

Brian said he had a film he wanted to make that would cost £3,000. The next morning the bank manager called. 'A tall young gentleman has been in here and has placed three thousand pounds to your credit. The cheque is perfectly legal and stamped . . . however, it is rather strange.'

'How strange?'

'It's written on an opened-out Gold Flake cigarette packet. Signed by somebody called Harry Clifton. Is it any good?'

The money funded Brian's first film, *The Tell-Tale Heart*, based on the Edgar Allan Poe story of a murderer who betrays himself because he is convinced he can hear the beating heart of his victim. 'I selected the story because it was sensational film material, and was also in the public domain – that is, I didn't have to pay for the rights. I hired a cameraman but there were no professional actors in the film. The detectives were played by two electricians, the old man by a painter, and the lead by a lover. We used recordings of Tchaikovsky and Debussy for the soundtrack as we could not afford to compose special music.'

Fox bought the film for quota, a system set in place by the government of the day intended to help the British film industry – 'Staggering to ruin, as usual.' For every hundred feet of American film shown on the screen, UK distributors were obliged to buy seventeen feet of film made in Britain. 'This gave rise to a series of the most ghastly films with budgets up to £10,000. These were generally shown once at ten o'clock in the morning and never again.' *The Tell-Tale Heart* was sold for £4,000 at a pound a foot – a profit for Harry of £800, as the film had gone £200 over budget.

The making of the film meant that Brian grew closer still to the Clifton family, and he became a frequent visitor to both Lytham Hall and Kildalton Castle. 'Harry met my sister, Patricia, and they became great friends. Whether it was a mother/son relationship or not, I don't know, but she became his financial adviser. She made and saved him a lot of money. When he was selling a piece of land near Lytham for £300,000 Patricia went up there and discovered that there had been bribery among the local officials and ended up bringing Harry back £900,000 – three times what he expected. She also advised him to invest in Sardinia years before the Aga Khan thought of it. When my sister did a good deal for Harry, he would give her a beautiful emerald or a sapphire necklace, or jewels of great price.'

Brian began an affair with Harry's beautiful sister, Avia – so named to celebrate the adventure of flying. What started as an amusing and exciting episode took on a tempestuous life of its own and he found himself engaged. 'You haven't got any money, have you, darling?' Violet Clifton said, when she heard of the engagement. 'As Avia is rather extravagant, we are going to settle £8,000 a year on you.' This was an enormous sum at the time. In addition, Avia lavished expensive gifts on her fiancé, including an engagement present of diamond and sapphire shirt studs. Brian complained that they were so large they made him look flashy and vulgar. 'Never mind, dear,' Avia said, 'they'll do for film dinners.'

One night after the engagement, as Brian dined at Lytham Hall, he looked down the table at the long, Norman–Byzantine faces of the family and knew that the marriage would be a disaster. 'Violet rang me up in London and said, "We have put the wedding banns in the Catholic church at Lytham. Will you go to the nearest Catholic church to you and do the same?"'

Lacking the courage to tell the truth, he fled to Paris. Avia followed. Brian awkwardly explained his misgivings and his nature, and his jilted fiancée seems to have been remarkably understanding. Avia even stayed on to live with him briefly before an amiable parting. She later married the doctor of King Ibn Saud, of Saudi Arabia, and sent Brian a photograph of herself sitting by a fountain in the royal palace, surrounded by attendants. 'Come and visit me in Arabia, my darling. I have eighty slaves. You'll *love* it.'

Harry and Brian shared an interest in the spiritual world, which they both accepted and experienced as a separate reality that often bled naturally into everyday life. 'The coffee servers at Claridge's in the thirties dressed like Turks,' Brian said. 'One, a Mr St George, had told Harry's fortune and impressed him. Convinced he was a great healer, Harry set St George up in a clinic in Sudbury Town. I visited him and he made my arms lift up without any will to do so on my part. St George said he couldn't tell me the name of my spirit guide then but would do so on my next visit. That weekend, I was dozing in a chair after a good lunch when I suddenly felt my arm being lifted up and drawn towards my desk. I had heard about automatic writing and thought the spirits wanted me to write something down, so I went to the desk where there was a pad and a pen. I wrote, *This is your spirit guide, Tomaster*. I later discovered that he was a musician and harpist to a German king at Dollinger, in Germany. Then my hand wrote, *Omnia vincit labor* [Work conquers all]. Not a motto I would have chosen for my coat of arms, but particularly relevant to me at the time as I was going through an idle period. This was my first experience of automatic writing. I still do it when I have a puzzling question, and I ask Tomaster for the answer – this will prove invaluable for the film. The writing is always very round and childish but in English. Once he wrote, *If you will come to Dollinger, there is a ruin on the top of the mountain. I will appear to you.* Years later I passed through Dollinger but never dared go up to the ruin.'

A second spiritual encounter involving Harry left Brian thoroughly unnerved. He was staying at his friend's house in Pickering Place, off St James's Street, and had taken Harry and his valet, Dodge, to the station to catch a train for Lytham, and did not return to the house until late that night. 'A voice came down the stairs. "Is that you, Mr Hurst?" "Yes, Dodge," I said without thinking, and went to bed. Lying in the big four-poster, I remembered that Dodge had left that morning for Lytham. I went upstairs – I don't know where I got the courage from – but there was nobody there.' He dressed quickly and left the house, never to return. Harry merely nodded when told of the incident: 'The house used to belong to Nell Gwyn. Ghosts go up and down the stairs but never come into my room.'

During the war, Harry Clifton asked Brian to store a quantity of beautiful sixteenth-century Dutch stained glass, including an exquisite central panel of the Madonna in blue. He objected, saying he lived in the most unsafe room in London, with a very large north window and a very large east window, and when the anti-aircraft guns went off in Hyde Park the whole building shook. But Harry insisted, saying he knew the Madonna would be safe in Brian's care, and the glass was shipped to the studio.

'Some time later I was working at Denham and got a terrible feeling the blue Madonna was in danger.' Brian managed to get a phone message through to the film director John Ford, who was staying with him, to move the Madonna and place the glass in the corner of the studio behind a large screen. 'Half an hour later a bomb dropped nearby and both studio windows were completely shattered. A large, heavy ormolu French clock, which was on top of a bookcase, was blown clear across the studio, which was about thirty feet wide, and through a strong wooden door. The windows were boarded up and remained so for the duration of the war, but the blue Madonna survived untouched.'

Through Brian, Harry became a close friend of William Butler Yeats, who shared their interest in the occult (Harry also became one of the few early collectors of paintings by the poet's brother Jack). On receiving a gift of a superb Chinese carving in lapis lazuli, Yeats wrote a poem of that name and dedicated it to Harry – one of the very few of his works dedicated to a specific individual. 'I dare say, Christopher,' Brian said, dismissing my naïve murmurs of awe, 'that you'd write a poem and dedicate it to me if I gave you a piece of lapis lazuli the size of your head.'*

The affair with Harry's sister, Avia, was one of a number of heterosexual relationships in Brian's youth. Sometimes, to listen to him, he gave the impression that he had been a straightforward, lusty lad. One story of an encounter with a girl on a train, when he was returning from the war as a young soldier, had a cigar-smoke-and-locker-room quality: 'We began to talk and eventually ended up together in the lavatory. I sat her up on the sink and we set to it. I was bruised all over because every time the train took a twist or turn of any kind, I was hurled against the wall. It took for ever, but I was extremely randy as I had been without women for a very long time. We came out for lunch and then we went back and set to it again. Eventually we reached London. As we parted, she said to me, "Soldier, that was a long, hard ride – and I'm going to have *Hot* and *Cold* from the taps

*Harry was the last of the Cliftons of Lytham, and died in November 1979. Ownership of Lytham Hall passed to the National Trust.

embedded in my bottom for the rest of my life."'

I once joked that if Brian undertook Freudian analysis he would discover he was a latent heterosexual. 'It's quite true,' he said. 'If I had ever met a Guardsman with tits on his back, I would have married him.' It was the crudest sexual reference I heard him make, but contained a psychological truth: he was emotionally frightened by women, not physically repelled. And although deep down he suspected his true nature as a teenager, he was confused to find himself unexcited by girls, but mysteriously attracted physically to boys. At the time he thought that this was merely a lack of confidence with the opposite sex, a phase he would grow out of, and assumed he would naturally develop heterosexual appetites in due course. The reality of his sexuality was held in abeyance. In Northern Ireland, in the first quarter of the twentieth century, homosexuality was such a taboo subject that individuals scarcely admitted their secret natures to themselves, let alone spoke of it. It was impossible to know how many others shared the same urges and feelings – and it would have been so much less complicated to be heterosexual. (Belfast is not the easiest place to be openly homosexual today.)

As a young man, Brian claimed to have greatly enjoyed sex with a number of women, although there was usually an opportunistic aspect to these relationships. The women he had affairs with tended to be rich, older, or married. A wealthy widow named Hilda, whom he had met in London when he was an art student, was so smitten she moved to Paris to be close to him. 'She didn't exactly give me money, but bought my paintings which were still only student works. I needed the money, not least because I liked to use expensive colours like cerulean blue and chrome yellow.' Hilda was a kind but silly woman of forty-five, with two grown sons, while Brian was in his early twenties. 'She was in the habit of dressing young, with inappropriate frocks and fluffy curls. I took her to the best hairdressers and the chic dress shops to persuade her to look simple and elegant, but when I came to take her out at night the curls and frilly dresses were back.'

Hilda wanted to get married, and Brian thought it would be a comfortable arrangement. His sister, Patricia, was violently opposed to the idea. 'If you marry that woman, I'll never speak to you again.'

'But Patricia, Hilda has over £12,000 a year.' This was a vast sum in 1924, large enough even for Brian to overcome his unexpressed but deep reservations. 'After the marriage had been decided, we went to a hotel where we were to sleep together for the first time. My art-student friends hung around outside in the street, and if I was successful I had arranged to go to the window and light a cigarette.' Theatrical, even *in extremis*, Brian lurched half-drunk to the window of his hotel after love-making, and lit *two* cigarettes.

Hilda gave him a large sum of money to buy a house for them to live together on the rue Joseph Bara in Montparnasse. The sons – sixteen and eighteen years old – were brought over from London to meet their future stepfather. Brian showed the boys life in the Latin Quarter, and they were instantly won over. 'You must marry mother,' the eldest said. 'You know how silly she is. She'll fall into the hands of some bounder who will spend all her money.'

'But that's *exactly* what I will do.'

'Yes, but you'll see she has a good time.'

The disaster of marriage was averted by Lady Duff Twysden, the impoverished admiral's daughter who had run off to Paris with her lover, and celebrated her thirty-sixth birthday with Brian, his art-student friends, Liam O'Flaherty, James Joyce, and thirty-six bottles of champagne. 'You can't go through with this marriage,' she told Brian emphatically. 'You'll destroy your life.' He dreaded the inevitable scene with Hilda, and begged Lady Duff to go along with him for the encounter. 'I went and explained myself to Hilda.

There were tears and remonstrations, but she came to realise the marriage would not be a success.'

The threat of matrimony always seemed to bring out the honest homosexual in Brian, and had actually propelled him into his first love affair with a man. While at art college in Toronto, before he moved to Paris, he met Ruth, a married woman who was a classical pianist. 'We used to go to a hotel and make love. She had all these diaphanous clothes and I enjoyed sex with her very much. But then she told me she wanted to give up her millionaire husband and get married, which was the last thing I wanted.' The prospect of marriage alarmed and depressed him, and there was a row.

'I was very distressed as I returned through the brown slushy snow to the house where some of the art students lived. The only other person at home that night was this friend of mine, Norman. He asked me what the matter was and I explained. Somebody had given Norman a bottle of Burgundy on the quiet – Toronto was "dry" then. We poured the contents into two water glasses and drank it down. Although we weren't drunk or anything, we had "drink taken", as the Irish say.

'We were alone in the house, and Norman was sitting on the arm of my chair. I began to kiss him and we both got excited. I said: "Let's take our clothes off." We began to make love. Norman then astounded me by saying, "Will you bugger me, Brian?" I did it but I could see that he wasn't enjoying it.

'The next day at school, he wouldn't look at me or come anywhere near me. As he was very beautiful and always surrounded by the best-looking people in the art college, I found myself jealous. He avoided me for days and finally I confronted him in the cloakroom. "You haven't spoken to me for four days!" He answered, "Look what you did to me!" I asked him why he had made the request, and why he didn't tell me to stop. "I didn't know what buggery was – I didn't want

Norman, described by Brian as the 'love of his life'

you to think I was such a bloody fool, having asked you to do it and not know what it was."'

Both men were sexually naïve, and alarmed at the passion they aroused in one another, but Norman became the love of Brian's life in a relationship that lasted, on and off, for many years. Although he often spoke of Norman, the love affair was already fifty years in the past, and even then it was never exclusive. Love and sex seem to have been separated very early on in Brian's life, and almost all his relationships were transactional in one way or another, and carried few illusions.

The lack of sexual self-knowledge in a man like Brian seems scarcely credible today, but he even went through his time at war in the all-male world of the army as an innocent. 'When a sergeant left Gallipoli for the hospital ship, he said, "Move up into my bivouac, sergeant. It's much safer than yours. Young Willie has his bivouac beside mine. He's my bum-boy." I hadn't understood what he meant. And later, while I was in Cairo, there was this rich man who was very kind to me. He used to take me to Groppis, an expensive restaurant famous for ice-cream and pastries. Then he would take me on to his *dahabiya* [sail boat] on the Nile. We would recline on cushions while musicians played Arabian music. On the boat's two masts were two soundboxes and the wind blowing through them made a beautiful sound. One night, after we had been on the Nile, he brought me home to the hospital in a buggy. As I was getting out, he pulled me back on to the seat and said, "I would like to take a kiss from you." I said, "Don't be silly, men don't kiss each other." I was still very innocent.'

The equanimity with which I accepted and mixed in Brian's homosexual world strikes me as strange today. Should I not have been shocked or threatened, or at least *bothered* in some way by its alien and excessive nature? But I wasn't, and treated it as the parallel universe that it was, stepping in and out of it at will.

Odder still, I never questioned the voracious and relentless sexual appetite that Brian displayed as a man already in his eighties. True, these were the days before Aids, but even so, his promiscuity was frenzied, and the imagination fails to conjure up the sexual energy he must have possessed in his priapic prime. He was, however, the soul of discretion as far as I was concerned, and shielded me from any direct experience of his sexual world. I neither heard nor saw anything overt, even when we shared a house in Tangier.

Brian lived life as an adventure, both when he was young and old. He told me: 'The French say, *Croquez le pomme!* Bite the apple! Not *Grignottez le pomme*, or *Pas de pomme pour moi, merci*. Adam was not the first sinner, but the first man to take up the challenge of life. The first hero. And it was what God wanted. Adam took Great Big Smacking Bites from the apple of the tree of life, and it tasted so good he ate the core as well.'

The window that opened on to Brian's world was certainly an education for me, and full of surprises. Sexually, all sorts of people proved to be not what they seemed. I had met a

Dominican dancer through friends, an intense character who was ferociously heterosexual, and pawed all our women. He had turned his ample Dutch girlfriend into an exquisite dancer, and they put on displays of the merengue, rumba and tango in their small apartment in Earls Court. He also had a very pale and very shy ginger-haired Scottish boy called Ian as a friend, who was training in classical ballet. I sent them both round to Brian – suitably forewarned – to see if he could introduce them to anybody influential in the dance world.

'Did Eduardo drop by?' I asked later.

'He came with a Scottish lad. I had a few friends round at the time for a drink and I must say we were all very impressed. Put on quite a show.'

'They danced – here in the front room?'

'Yes. Modern athletic stuff. Not usually my sort of thing, and there's not a lot of room. But this was precise, clever pirouettes and twirls around the coffee table without a single collision or ricochet, or any damage whatsoever. A talented duo. Very avant-garde – and they know how to grab an audience's interest. The performance was enacted entirely *desnudo*.'

'You're not serious?'

'Most certainly. They were rather unsuitably dressed for a proper display of their balletic skills, so I asked them to remove their clothes. Dancers are natural exhibitionists. They leap at the chance to perform before an audience whether they're scantily clad, dressed in heavy winter overcoats, or buck naked. Those boys are in fine shape. It was quite something. That Scottish lad has the whitest body I have ever seen. You could spend a lifetime counting his freckles.'

'*Ian!* He took his clothes off as well?'

'He was a little reluctant at first but I told him – *It takes two to tango, Jock*.' Brian shook with mirth at his little joke. 'Do you have any other friends like that?'

'I don't know.'

The correct answer should have been, *God only knows*. Time spent with Brian had taught me not to draw conclusions about anyone's sexual orientation from appearances or mannerisms. The endless stream of super-masculine Guardsmen and the conservatively dressed family men with children and long, if not happy, marriages, displayed no external trace of their homosexuality. On the other hand, fussy, effeminate little men dressed in strange clothes, often from the BBC, exhibited treacherous heterosexual traits, secretly asking for girlfriends' telephone numbers behind my back, squeezing their knees beneath restaurant tables and whispering hot, left-wing love in their ears when I was out of the room. The last vestige of surprise at these revelations was torn away one Saturday morning when I found a pub-loving, rugger-playing hearty wrapped in a towel, cleaning his teeth in Brian's downstairs bathroom. I had known him quite well over a number of years and dined with him and his wife at their house in Clapham Common, while toddlers screamed in an upstairs bedroom. We were both stunned to see one another. He rallied first, and begged through a mouth full of toothpaste, 'You won't tell Cleo?'

A steady stream of closet queens came for lunch, some of whom seemed scared even to be in Brian's presence. (One man complained that he found it impossible to find a lover. 'Not just in the closet,' Brian later said wickedly, '*On the shelf* in the closet.') Although he had never disguised his own sexuality, he was sympathetic to those who did, remembering the days of social ostracism and criminal prosecution. I doubt he would have approved of 'outing', which he would have seen as too blunt and brutal a weapon to use against members of his own tribe, however cowardly.

But he did enjoy disconcerting and undermining the staid and the pompous. He told me of an incident when Sir Harold Nicolson, diplomat, writer and closet queen *par excellence*, visited him for lunch. Brian had arranged for a tall Polish boy to be sitting naked in an armchair behind the door, unseen by the distinguished personage as he entered. 'I'd like to introduce Stefan,' Brian said. 'Stefan – Sir Harold Nicolson.' As Sir Harold turned, he was confronted by the naked Pole, with outstretched hand and member. Sir Harold fled.

One lunchtime I arrived to find that an effeminate, sweet-natured man from Nottingham, the same age as myself, had taken up residence. Paul's loneliness was palpable and when I offered to make him a cup of coffee he almost burst into tears. 'Oooh, Christopher,' he said, 'you're a *real* pal!'

Later I confided to Brian, 'I wouldn't have thought the new lodger was your type.'

'Hardly. He's down here for a sex-change operation.'

Some time later I dropped into Kinnerton Street one evening for a pre-arranged drink. Paul opened the door. He was very friendly and gave me an awkward hug, then blushed furiously. He sat in a chair in the drawing room gazing at me with a smile that made him look simple-minded. When he left the room for a few moments, I asked Brian, 'Is he all right? Looks like he's on some mind-bending drug. Is it the hormones?'

'He's been like this for several days. Since your last visit in fact.'

I was a little slow off the mark. 'What's the matter with him?'

Brian lowered his voice: 'He's in love!'

'Oh, Christ!'

'He asked me if he could dress up in his Sunday best for your arrival tonight. Twin-set of tweed in earth tones and a string of imitation pearls, wouldn't you know? Between you and me, he looks a bit like one of those county-crowd matrons with Labradors. I told him I thought it best not. Suggested he should take things slowly as you were rather old-fashioned and easily shocked. More Jane Austen than

Lady Chatterley, I told him.'

'Thank you.'

Paul returned to the room. He was dressed as a man, but was done up as if on a date, neatly dressed and carefully coiffed, reeking not of aftershave but of Chanel. The three of us made small talk over a glass of wine. Brian watched me closely, a look of wicked amusement on his face. Paul fidgeted and never took his eyes off me, and when I made some weak attempt at humour he threw back his head and roared with inappropriate laughter. He followed me to the front door when I made to leave. 'I always have a good laugh when you're here,' he said ambiguously. 'You don't half cheer me up, honestly you do.'

'That's good to hear.'

'Is it?' he said, becoming coy. 'Perhaps, if you're in the area some evening, we could go out for a snack. Have a few beers and a few laughs.'

'I don't come over here much in the evenings.'

'I just meant if you were in the area – you know, footloose and fancy free. Feeling a bit bored.'

I avoided Kinnerton Street for a week or so, not wishing to lead a girl on. When I finally turned up for a pre-lunch work session, there was no sign of Paul. Nothing was said, so finally I asked after him. 'Not pining, are you?' Brian said.

'Not exactly. I just wondered where he was. He seemed a nice sort.'

'He has fled. He had the temerity to object to certain of my friends, can you believe. Said they frightened him.'

'That would mean the rough trade that pitches up drunk after midnight, would it?'

'It would not. I am an elderly gentleman who is tucked up in bed and fast asleep by eleven. I take my occasional pleasures in the late afternoon – if I'm lucky. Or any other time, if the opportunity arises. But never after midnight, and never with drunks. Don't be so bloody impertinent.'

'I stand corrected.'

'As the rent boy said to the Marquis de Sade. No, what happened was that a couple of the lads were a little cruel to him in their jokes. I told Paul he needed to be more robust if he was going to try and live life as a transsexual. People take the Michael. That's the way it is.'

'Poor Paul.'

'*Poor Paul!*' Brian mimicked. 'Damn hypocrite! I didn't notice his true love around here these past couple of weeks to hold a distressed maiden's hand.'

'You didn't really expect me to babysit your drag queen tenant did you?'

'He's not a bloody drag queen, you heartless ignoramus. A drag queen is a queer who likes to wear women's clothes. Paul's a poor boy who believes he's a woman trapped in a male body. He's frightened and lonely, without any friends, and came down to the big city to have his cock cut off. Miserable in the present – terrified of the future. No one to talk to. Do you understand? He liked you. You could have bought the poor sod a drink!'

Brian was right. I could have bought Paul a drink. Listened to what he had to say. Said a few encouraging words. Been a little kinder. Gone out for a beer and a laugh. I thought of sad, lonely, gentle Paul and felt ashamed of the miserliness of my humanity, and it must have showed. Brian sighed, and made the plucking gesture with his right hand that he used when he wanted to take his words back.

'There was nothing you could have done. I'm a bit upset about it, that's all. On Saturday night a couple of Guardsmen made fun of him. Told him he was an ugly runt as a man, and would make an even uglier woman. Laughed at him. Paul ran to his room and cried all night. Then he got depressed. He had been shaken and hurt. He packed his suitcase and took the train back to Nottingham.'

'It can't be easy being a transsexual.'

'You have a way with understatement, Christopher – almost a masterly touch.'

And then there were the full-blown tragedies.

A regular visitor at Kinnerton Street was an elegant, good-looking Indian in his late thirties called Khurshid, a steward on Air India who worked the London–Bombay run. Whenever I saw him he was smartly turned out in his airline uniform, although Brian told me confidentially that he was the son of a rajah. This was several notches above your common or garden maharajah, Brian made clear – information that is precisely contrary to the facts. But whatever his ranking in the social hierarchy of the sub-continent, Khurshid displayed exquisite, aristocratic manners, and was something of a favourite because he brought Brian large tins of caviar described as 'excess to requirement' from First Class.

The love of Khurshid's life was a youth who became known as the Boy from Bridgwater. I never met him, but Brian was not impressed. He suggested the boy was unattractive and uninteresting, and of such low intelligence that a drop of five IQ points would produce leaves and branches. He lived at home in a council house with his family, where he was abused and mocked for being gay. 'Can you imagine the scene when he introduced Khurshid to this clan of smock-frocked Somerset yokels?' Brian said. 'They did not see the elegant and educated man we like and enjoy – whose home as a child was a palace, and who had a hundred servants and a score of painted and bejewelled elephants at his call. No. They saw a queer nigger. It's not been easy for Khurshid with the Boy from Bridgwater. The path of true love does not run straight down there in the West Country, especially the love that dare not speak its name.'

And then one day I entered the drawing room to see Khurshid sitting on the sofa, looking terrible. I had never seen such a change in a person. His eyes were sunk deep into his skull, his hair was wild, and his face covered in stubble. His hands were held together over his knees, endlessly working a handkerchief. The Boy from Bridgwater had committed suicide. Overwhelmed by the pressure of his life, and lacking the courage to cope with a hostile family and exotic lover, he had locked the lavatory door in the council house, and hanged himself.

'So sorry . . .' I murmured. Khurshid's natural graciousness forced his eyes to smile kindly, acknowledging my clumsy attempt at commiseration. It was a moment of normality when for an instant the world was as before, then suddenly the eyes went dead, and he sank back into the oblivion of his loss. It was a terrible moment, and it scared me.

Later, I asked Brian, 'How long will it take Khurshid to get over it?' It was a question from someone who had yet to suffer the death of parents, family and friends. At the time I accepted the half-truths and clichés of the emotionally unscarred – that time heals all wounds and soothes all hurts, and night's attendant terrors vanish with the dawn. I did not understand the inevitable and universal sadness at the core of human life.

'He'll never get over it,' Brian said.

Characters of exquisite eccentricity stepped through the front door of Kinnerton Street and into the drawing room, like actors making an entrance on to a stage. Although, had they been professionals, many would have been accused of over-acting. One or two had also rather overdone it on the greasepaint and powder, and Major Donald Neville-Willing was a case in point.

I have a precise memory of the major *flying* into the room. I mean that I retain an image of him actually entering in flight. I accept that this cannot truly be the case, but there was so much flutter and fuss as he flapped through the doorway that his feet did not seem to touch the ground. A small, neat figure immaculately dressed, he arrived in a cloud of talc, exuding lemon cologne and snobbery. Not a hair of his elaborate, snowy white, sculpted coiffure was out of place. The lines of his face had been filled with a delicate film of make-up, while a subtle application of mascara and liner around his eyes softened the effect of harsh morning light. Around his neck hung a square, silver monocle as a prop for constantly fidgeting fingers.

'Now listen, listen, listen,' the major said, his tongue darting in and out of his mouth, as words rattled from him in nervous, staccato bursts like Morse code, and his shoulders moved up and down as if he were running on the spot. 'I have to tell you first before you hear the story from some other vicious neighbourly tongue.' There had been an altercation in the street early in the morning, when two men arguing over a parking place entered into a shouting match. It became so bad that the police were called and a constable duly arrived to restore order. The argument raged on, waking the major from his much-needed beauty sleep – 'To be this beautiful a body needs at least ten hours.' Infuriated, he had pulled on a silk dressing gown – 'You know, Brian, the gorgeous one with the large and daring Chinese motif' – and thrown open the window. Thus attired, with flowing, white hair unbrushed and wild, the major called down imperiously into the street: 'Would you men mind taking your argument elsewhere!'

The constable turned and looked up towards the window: 'Why don't you mind your own business, *madame*!'

The major's eyes closed in appreciation of the exquisite humour of the situation, his shoulders gyrated, and he began to bend forward in balletic collapse, waving his monocle from side to side in helpless mirth. 'Well,' he said eventually, drawing breath and straightening himself, 'I'm off to tell the story up and down the street. Before unnecessary slander and obloquy are added to ginger things up.' As he turned to go he became overwhelmed by the hilarity of it all once more. The shoulders folded inwards, the monocle shook in his hand and he doubled up: '*Why don't you mind your own business – MADAME!*'

After the major's departure Brian was silent for a moment. 'Christ,' he said, as we heard the front door close. 'I'd hate to be as queer as that.'

The major was a neighbour of Brian's who lived a couple of doors down in a tiny, bijou house with an even tinier bijou garden. After I came to know him, he would hail me from the window of his front room: 'Young man, pop in and have a dish of Darjeeling,' or, 'The sun is over the yardarm in some benighted foreign part, come and partake of a glass of nutty Amontillado.' The interior of his house was as elegant and exquisite as its owner, with similar flourishes of over-decoration. The major at rest was a different kind of bird from the major in flight: instead of constant flap and flutter, he became very still and rigid and upright. Tea-cup or sherry glass would be held at a precise angle, just so, as he took tiny, delicate sips and spoke non-stop. 'I do so love talking about myself.'

Not many people listened to the major's stories, and he well knew he was regarded as something of a freak and figure of fun, but he was a kind, gentle man and I genuinely liked him. As he prepared to impart a scandalous nugget of gossip about some famous person, his voice fell, the eyes became like saucers, and he raised his eyebrows: 'Are you *sure* you're twenty-one?'

He described himself as a hard person, 'with every attitude one hundred per cent effeminate'. This was noted early on as a report from the major's preparatory school confirms: *Excels at sewing.* His ambition as a young man was to be an entertainer, and he found a job in revue. 'But when people ask you to sing and then they start laughing for no apparent reason . . .' In the 1920s he was notorious for playing 'effeminate' roles – so notorious and so effeminate that he found it wise to leave both the stage and the country. He went to New York but it was the Depression and times were hard. He worked the High Society scene at night and a machine in a metal cap factory by day, but money was so tight that he was unable to pay his hotel bill. The manager asked what he could do in lieu of payment: 'I can arrange flowers.' He was given fifty dollars to do the flowers for a banquet and excelled with a glorious extravaganza of bronze and yellow chrysanthemums, and also returned twenty-nine dollars in change. Within a year he was made assistant manager of the hotel.

Donald Neville-Willing seemed unpromising material for the soldier's life, and I was curious how the major received his commission. It was the central prop around which his butterfly personality fluttered, and featured prominently on his visiting cards and stationery, and he was known everywhere as 'The Major'. I asked Brian if the rank was genuine. 'Yes. But don't ever ask what regiment the major served in.'

'What regiment *did* the major serve in?'

Brian lowered his voice and whispered: '*The Catering Corps*.'

This was unfair, as the major was living in America at the outbreak of war and could have avoided military service altogether. He had persuaded rich friends in the States to pay for two ambulances, and joined the American Field Service, a voluntary medical outfit, and took ship with them to Egypt where he wangled a transfer into the British Army. He was told he wouldn't have to do any fighting but would go on the General List as a 'Gadarene swine', and became the oldest second lieutenant in the war.

He later served in India, where he found the British women insufferable and blamed them for 'losing' the country. The major liked to tell a story of a typical confrontation with one of these harridans. 'What do you think Stickey's gone and done?' the woman said of her husband. 'He's gone and dropped dead on me. *On dance night!*' At the end of the war the major was transferred to the Canadian Army in Holland and was put in charge of the restoration of civilian amenities like electricity and roads. Prince Bernhard was on his staff – 'Biggest son of a bitch I ever met.'

The high point of the major's career was when he became the manager of the Café de Paris, a nightclub off Piccadilly Circus. A beautiful room drearily lit, it was unfashionable at the time and moribund. The major changed all that during his seven-year reign, and brought over world-famous performers including Liberace and Marlene Dietrich. Exhibiting an innate knack for publicity, the major instructed Liberace to turn on the interior lights of his Cadillac the moment the car hit Piccadilly so people could see who was inside. At the Café de Paris his considerable organisational skills and adoration of show business bonded naturally, and he became a minor celebrity himself. Noël Coward – whom he disliked – called him 'Major, baby'; W. H. Auden wrote a poem about him; his photograph appeared in the papers standing beside the famous and titled.

Private happiness, alas, did not march in step with public acclaim. The major proved to be unlucky in love, but late in life enjoyed a relationship that lasted five years before disintegrating. This love had long gone by the time I arrived on the scene, but he still mourned its loss. 'You can imagine the sort of household the major and his lover inhabited,' Brian said. '*Fussy* would be one way to describe it. The love object was one of the *silliest* people on earth. Drove us all mad. They drove *each other* mad. But Donald was shattered when the twerp went off. He became very depressed.'

To cheer the major up on his birthday, after he had been on his own for a while, Brian took his friend Big Freddy round to the house. Brian told the major to close his eyes, saying he had a *big* surprise. The major opened his eyes – to find that Big Freddy had exposed himself. The major ran shrieking into the upper reaches of the house and refused to come down until the birthday treat was taken away. He was forever wary of Brian from that day on.

Some time after I first met the major, he proudly showed me around his house and garden. At the end of the tour, which did not take long, he said, 'There's a darling room downstairs I want to show you. Are you poetic? And soulful? Otherwise you might make fun.' Uncertain how to reply, I followed the major down narrow stairs to a tiny basement bedroom. 'This room is decorated like the bedroom in the little cottage we had in Sussex. We had to give it up – just couldn't afford it. We were heartbroken. So my friend and I created this fantasy room where we could escape, and used to come down here and lie on the beds and pretend we were in the country. Before he left me and went away.'

The major sat on one of the beds and gestured to the other. 'Go on, lie down! See how peaceful it is.' I did as I was told, and lay absurdly in the narrow bed beside the major, hoping rumours of this experiment in astral travel to rural parts would not get back to Brian. 'Can you hear the birds? The wind in the trees, the babbling brook?' The major became quiet and lay totally still, like a waxwork, small feet akimbo, manicured hands clasped together across his chest, and eyes closed as if he were dead. Perhaps he was. Drugged insensible with nostalgia, paralysed by loss and sadness. Poor old major. He was one of the loneliest men I have ever met.

Although we never worked at the weekends, occasionally on a Saturday I would go to the house or the pub to join Brian for lunch. This was always a social occasion attended by an unpredictable mixture of men and women, made up of the great and the good, and assorted lesser mortals including one or two drawn from the criminal classes. There was always a sprinkling of the more amusing villains to be found around the Belgravia hostelries, presumably following the same irrefutable logic as the American armed robber Willie Sutton who said, when asked by a psychologist why he robbed banks, 'Because that's where the money is.'

It was on Saturday afternoons, after these lengthy lunches, that Brian was often visited by Big Freddy, who had been consort and friend for twenty years when I first met him. Freddy was a married man with children, but had made a profession out of servicing the wealthier and more demanding elements of the London homosexual scene.

Big Freddy had been introduced to Brian by a strange creature known as the Lion Man. 'I called him the Lion Man because he was a South African with tawny blond hair and golden eyes who liked to pretend he was a lion. It got him very excited and aroused. I had to put up with him crawling round the floor and making lion noises. He had a very good growl and quite an impressive roar. He wanted me to tell him off and beat him when he didn't perform his tricks properly, but I'm too indolent to be a sadist. One day he brought Freddy to the house – six feet six inches tall, and quite extraordinarily handsome. He was like a Minoan prince with small waist, broad shoulders, beautiful dark curls and *everything* in proportion.'

Freddy was neither a soldier nor a policeman, but had learned his trade on the door of one of London's smart hotels. He seems to have been very unstable as a young man, when Brian first knew him. 'A friend was visiting and had parked his new motorbike outside the house. While we were talking Freddy quietly left the room and took the bike for a ride round Belgrave Square. It was a powerful machine and he didn't have a clue how to ride the thing. The bike also had L-plates on it, which meant it was illegal to carry a passenger, but Freddy picked up a friend and gave him a ride. This attracted the attention of the constabulary.

'Freddy roared around Hyde Park Corner without killing anybody, which was a miracle, and then took off up Park

Lane pursued by the police. He abandoned the bike close to the Dorchester and made a run for it, hiding behind a hoarding surrounding the Hilton, which was being built at the time. The police caught the passenger who proved to be sadly lacking in character and yelled, "It wasn't me, it wasn't me – it was him behind that hoarding."'

Flushed from his hiding place, Freddy began to climb the scaffolding around the partly-finished building. Up and up he went, while a large crowd gathered below to watch the drama. He reached the top and, unable to climb higher, began to crawl along the arm of a giant construction crane. There was a collective intake of breath from the onlookers below as he took off his shirt and stood on his hands.

'By now all traffic had stopped and a huge crowd had gathered in Park Lane. There was a groan, and a woman screamed as the shirt floated down and people thought it was Freddy plunging to his death. The police eventually coaxed him down. He fell the last seven or eight feet, breaking his ankle and hurting his knee badly, so he was taken to St George's Hospital and put at the very end of a big ward where he couldn't very well escape. I went to see him there and asked him why he had taken his shirt off: "I was hot."'

Brian arranged for a brilliant lawyer friend, David Jacobs, to take the case. 'David appeared in court wearing his usual full morning make-up (he had other make-up for afternoon and evening). Nevertheless, he was a great and most impressive barrister who argued eloquently that Freddy was nothing but a confused lad who needed help – one of the more extravagant examples of English understatement.'

Freddy was remanded in Brixton Prison for a psychiatric report, and finally sent for four weeks to a psychiatric hospital just outside London. 'I visited him there and felt distinctly uncomfortable. The patients would look at me strangely as I passed through the billiard room, and I kept a careful eye on their cues. One poor boy was filled with such excessive grief for the death of his mother that he couldn't stop weeping. There was also a charming girl who was distraught because her lover had stopped making love to her.'

The resident psychiatrist had enrolled Freddy into an unorthodox treatment to allay the girl's psychological anguish, suggesting he take her for a walk in the woods. 'You mean, doctor, I can go the whole way with her?'

'Yes. That's what she needs.'

After about a month, when Brian drove down on one of his visits, he was summoned to the doctor's office. 'I realised that he was trying to find out my connection with Freddy. One or two of us were concerned what he might have said to the authorities and the possible legal consequences. I thought it best to put the quacks firmly in their place.' As soon as he was shown into the office he went directly to the doctor's desk and sat down behind it, forcing the man to stand somewhat foolishly in front of him. Before the psychiatrist had a chance to speak, Brian said, 'Tell me, doctor, how do I get into this hospital – where fucking is prescribed for certain of your patients?'

No more questions were asked. It became clear that the authorities were eager to discharge a difficult patient whom they did not consider a danger to society. Brian drove down in the Bentley on the day of Freddy's release to take him back to London. 'I'll do my best for him,' Brian said to the doctor who came out to say goodbye.

'Rather you than us.'

From my first encounter with Big Freddy I found him a sinister and unfriendly character. Whenever I saw him I kept my distance, and our relationship settled into one of mutual distrust and dislike. This became set following a conversation after a typical Saturday lunch held in the house. Big Freddy arrived as we were all drinking coffee. I was talking about an interview I had conducted with the art forger, Elmyr de Hory. He was a slick talent, but a tainted one, and had recently put on a successful exhibition of paintings and drawings in the style of Dufy, Matisse and Picasso. A stateless Hungarian, de Hory's life was bedevilled with legal complications and international litigation, and a ceaseless quest for nationality – any nationality – that would give him a passport.

De Hory's arrogance was monumental – he maintained that *his* Matisse drawings were superior to those of the artist himself. 'If you look closely at a Matisse drawing under a magnifying glass you see a break in the line where he looks up at the model,' he told me. 'In mine there is no such hesitation. It is more fluid. I can make a drawing in the style of Modigliani right now and ten minutes later I can make you a drawing in the style of Matisse. I have been able to put myself in these artists' souls, hearts and heads. And that is a special talent because most artists walk on one road. I can walk on different roads.'

Brian, who knew de Hory, added a few of his own comments – mainly that while he could imitate the work of great artists, his own work was vulgar and derivative. And then Freddy spoke: 'I visited the silly sod when he was over here staying at Claridge's – you can bet somebody else was paying. Afterwards he gave me a tenner. A tenner! I didn't say nothing, but waited till we were back down in the lobby with lots of people around. Then I turned on him, tore up the tenner and threw it in his face. I grabbed him by the throat and he was so scared he looked like he was going to shit himself. I shouted at him so everybody could hear, "You tight-fisted little faggot, I've a mind to smack you so hard you'll look like one of your Picassos."' Freddy let out a nasty laugh.

After an awkward silence somebody said, 'You don't get much for a tenner these days.' The conversation moved on, but I had seen the pleasure with which Big Freddy had recounted his bully's tale. De Hory was a small, nervous man in his early seventies at the time, no match for the Minoan prince, in whom violence lay forever close to the surface. Big

Freddy was trouble, and his story strengthened my determination to keep my distance.

Apart from that Saturday lunch, I had not seen Brian for a couple of weeks, and although I had returned to a routine of cranking out articles I was still broke. Papers and magazines did not pay upon submission, but weeks after publication, so my front door remained a no-go area. I was stalked by a particularly unpleasant bailiff who sat for hours outside my flat, while I lay low inside, silent and still as the dead, happily reading the Russian. One day the bailiff pounced upon me and caught me by surprise when I unwisely stepped outside thinking the coast was clear. He threatened to take all my furniture away and took sadistic pleasure in watching me make frantic phone calls to arrange a loan. We sat together for an anxious half-hour while I waited for cash to be sent over. He was a tiny, talky little runt of a man, and pointed to a scar that ran across the top of his bald head. 'See that? Some bastard waited for me behind a door in his house and hit me with a metal curtain rod. He went to prison, of course – I am supported by the full weight of the law in my profession. But some people take things personal.'

I said nothing, secretly admiring the scalper, and weighed the coffee mug in my hand against the full weight of the law, calculating the consequences of smashing it into the bailiff's joyless face. The front doorbell sounded as a friend arrived with funds. 'Saved by the bell,' the bailiff said, jolly as Santa.

Less than a week later, having avoided the clutches of the bailiff, I was finally arrested for non-payment of rates to Camden Council, and taken to Clerkenwell Police Station. 'They don't consider this a very serious crime, do they?' I asked the pleasant but bored constable who had made the collar, as we trudged past the junkies and hookers of King's Cross on our way to the nick. 'Put it this way,' he said. 'I'm not going to be promoted for this morning's work.'

Granted bail on my own recognizance, I later appeared before Hampstead Magistrates' Court where I begged for mercy, and was given time to pay with an ominous warning of the consequences for failure to do so. I could tell by the way the magistrates looked at me that they did not like my type. The editor of the *Observer* magazine took pity on my plight and offered me a month's employment at two hundred quid a week. This involved working in the office on a dreadful series the magazine was preparing called 'The Making of the British'. At an earlier editorial conference someone came up with the idea of commissioning obscure professors from minor universities to write various historical articles on the island story. Suitably illustrated with woad-smothered natives and ancient, hirsute kings, the series was supposed to provide a cheap, educational filler for the summer months. As a concept it was hardly inspired journalism, but the actuality was a disaster. The historians delivered late, and they delivered long. The work submitted was atrocious. Almost every article was uniformly badly-written, often in dense jargon that was scarcely comprehensible, and some of the pieces were book-length. As one sub-editor waded through a pile of turgid manuscripts he murmured in disbelief, 'These people are *professors*! At *universities*!'

The mass of copy was placed in the hands of deft sub-editors who hacked and hewed at the dread prose to turn it into intelligible English, a labour of Herculean proportions. My job was to do as I was bidden by these increasingly gruff and bad-tempered men, including placing small paragraphs in local papers throughout the country alerting readers in advance when their town or village was to be mentioned. Excited natives were then supposed to run out and buy the *Observer*.

Occasionally, I did some ruthless cutting myself – 'Here, fillet a thousand words out of this,' a sub might say, handing me a stack of copy the size of my *War and Peace*. I was also used to deliver bad news to academics over the phone. As a freelance journalist hardened by rejection, and inured to the brute treatment of commissioning editors, I was surprised to discover how sensitive the Ivory Tower brigade could be. One scholar had submitted a five-thousand-word article on the cost of bathing in the fourteenth-century, and a sub found it mildly interesting that one had to be well-off in the Middle Ages to afford a hot bath. I called the author who was pleased to hear the paper wanted to use the piece, surprised that it would have to be cut, and stupefied to learn we only wanted one hundred and fifty words.

It was a deadly time, but I was paid at the end of every week – a novel experience I found seductive. The daily routine was therapeutic, and I came to admire the skilful subs as they worked their way methodically through reams of dire copy, like ancient gods giving shape and meaning to chaos. But it was a dull life and I felt caged. 'I'm so bloody bored I could kill myself,' I said.

'*You're* bored,' a sub growled. 'This series is going to make our dear British readers wish they were Mongolian.'

One summer's morning, as I toiled unhappily in the stifling office, Brian called. 'You have an *office*! And you're *in* it! How *very* peculiar.'

'Working on a big historical series,' I said importantly. 'Buried in work. Deadlines. Pressure. You know how it is in Fleet Street.'

'I can imagine. But this lunchtime forego your usual three-hour session at El Vino's and get over here.'

'I'm afraid that's out of the question,' I said, laughing indulgently. 'I'm lucky these days to get away for a half-pint and a sandwich in the Blackfriars.'

'Bugger the Blackfriars! Get over here! It's important. Sir Michael's coming to lunch.'

Herod the Great – *himself! Finally*. Brian was right, this *was* important. I took the bus to Knightsbridge, a journey that seemed endless, but I was excited to be meeting the man who was to play Herod, and it gave me time to think. I was relieved that I had cleaned up Herod's description, and cut references to his 'dropsical' and 'syphilitic' features – not a great way to reel in a star, as Brian explained. I had tightened the dialogue and finally added some Big Emotional Scenes between Herod and Mariamne – actors enjoyed a chance to rant and wail, Brian said. I had also taken out parenthetical stage directions that apparently irritated the gifted and derailed the untalented: (Aghast), (Amazed), (Surprised), (Ecstatic), (Depressed), and so on. 'You don't want to see an actor doing "Aghast". You really don't.'

On arrival at the house I was briefly introduced before Brian excused himself and went upstairs for some reason. We were left alone and it was evident that Sir Michael Redgrave was painfully shy. He was dressed in an old tweed jacket and corduroys, and had on the floor beside him a white plastic bag that I thought might contain the script and the great man's notes. Although I was anxious to talk about the film I understood that it would not be appropriate for either of us to mention it until Brian returned. Besides, I had never spoken to an actor in my life about a script, let alone one who was unarguably one of England's finest. I wondered if Sir Michael would be intellectual and analytical, or emotional and intuitive – would he be critical and difficult, or manipulative and charming?

'Sorry if I'm late,' I said. 'The bus took for ever.'

There was silence. After a while, Sir Michael said, 'Prefer the bus, do you? To the tube?'

'There's no tube that really connects Knightsbridge and Fleet Street, that's the trouble.'

Sir Michael nodded. Silence fell again. A minute passed. Maybe two. It felt like an hour. Sir Michael rifled inside his plastic bag and pulled out a bottle of brandy. 'Drink?'

'No thanks.'

Sir Michael Redgrave

Sir Michael replaced the bottle inside the plastic bag. Another silence; more time crawled by. Sir Michael pulled out another bottle. 'I have whisky.'

'That's very kind, but no thank you. I have to work this afternoon. Spirits at lunchtime make me sleepy.'

We sat in excruciating silence once again until Brian entered. Sir Michael immediately rose from his chair, pulled an envelope from the plastic bag and placed it on the desk. The men embraced and Sir Michael made for the door. He turned to face me: 'Goodbye.'

'Goodbye.'

Brian accompanied Sir Michael to the front door and I heard them muttering conspiratorially in the hallway. The words were indistinct but there was something urgent in Sir Michael's tone, almost panic. The front door opened and closed, and Brian returned and took up his seat in the winged chair. 'You made a very good impression on Sir Michael.'

'I *am* pleased.' The sarcasm failed to find its mark. 'Brian – I came all the way from Fleet Street for this meeting. I thought we were going to talk about the script. Sir Michael asks me if

I prefer the bus to the tube, offers me a belt of booze from a plastic bag, and says goodbye.' A suspicion entered my mind. 'He does know, I suppose, that I'm the man who wrote the script?' The suspicion grew. 'He has *read* the script?'

'Set all that aside,' Brian said, dismissing my questions with a wave of the hand. 'This is much more important. A very delicate matter. I am asking you to perform a service for Sir Michael in the utmost confidence. This is strictly between the three of us. I know I can trust you.'

'What is it?'

'Sir Michael has had a spot of bother with Big Freddy.'

'Oh, Christ!'

'Hear me out! Big Freddy is on a cruise in the Caribbean with his wife and children. I don't know what happened, maybe he's been gambling on board or something, but he has been sending daily telegrams to Sir Michael demanding money. Naturally, these have been ignored. But Big Freddy has a spiteful streak – he has threatened to go to the papers.'

'What? And tell them Sir Michael's queer? As if they don't already know.'

Brian looked at me searchingly, and seemed to be considering whether to continue. 'There are a few "in" jokes about Sir Michael in our circle. "Sir Michael Redgrave, I'll be bound," and, "Sir Michael is unable to come to the phone just now, he's all tied up!" Do you understand?'

'Bondage?' I said, attempting to appear knowing and nonchalant.

'And the rest. Our friend likes to walk around naked in a suit of armour so that it cuts him . . .'

'Good grief!'

'And Big Freddy provides a special service. He takes a needle and thread and pierces the left nipple, carries it across the right nipple and pierces that, and then takes the needle down to pierce the tip of the foreskin—'

'I don't think I want to hear any more,' I said, repelled.

'So you can see why Sir Michael doesn't want this to get into the *News of the World*.'

'It's blackmail, pure and simple.'

'Nothing pure and simple about it. It's rather sordid and complicated. Sir Michael has given me five hundred pounds in cash to wire to the ship. Naturally he doesn't want his name involved, and neither do I for a variety of reasons. I am asking you to go to the P & O office in the City and wire the money to Big Freddy. You might need identification, I don't know. They will give you a receipt. Will you do this for me?'

'I suppose so.'

Brian handed me the envelope and I counted the money and put it in my pocket. I tried to cover the fact that I had been shaken with a display of righteous indignation. 'It's a bit rich – I mean, you owe the milkman God knows how much, and I've been arrested for non-payment of rates, and here's Big Freddy getting away with blackmail . . .'

'Crime pays. Life's not fair. The rich get richer and the poor get poorer – it's all a bleedin' shame.' Brian stood up. 'I have shocked you, I can see. Perhaps I should have spared you the grisly details but you have always previously taken a prurient interest in revelations of a sexual nature. But I thought you should know what it was all about. When Sir Michael called me he was in something of a state. He is greatly concerned, really quite frightened. I hope you understand there is nobody else I would trust to do this.'

At the P & O office in the City I paid over the money, gave my name and address and was handed a receipt. The wire was sent. I telephoned Brian to say that the mission was accomplished, and returned to the *Observer*. There was a vague air of resentment in the office when I entered, although no one on that civilised team would have been so crass as to suggest that by taking a couple of hours off I was not pulling my weight. 'Sorry to be so long – I'll make up the time tonight. I had to pop out on behalf of the Empress of

Ireland and pay off a male prostitute blackmailing a famous theatrical acquaintance.'

'Very funny,' a sub said. '*I've* had a *particularly* frustrating time with King John.'

It would have made sense for me at this stage to focus on finances, seek other sources of income and concentrate on my journalism. Instead, I suggested Brian write his memoirs.

He was, of course, much too lazy and temperamentally unsuited for such an undertaking, so the burden inevitably fell upon me. And naturally, this new and self-inflicted task was unpaid – although I was offered an unspecified but generous cut of the enormous, sure-fire, future profits. But as we had spent so much time together, and I had heard so many of Brian's stories, I thought it worthwhile to record them. Tall stories, war stories, funny stories, sad stories, Irish stories, gay stories . . . stories accumulated over a long and original lifetime. I knew even then that together they pictured a vanished and more elegant world, but saw them at the time as little more than well-spun yarns.

Now I realise their true worth. Brian told stories as a way to process life, to parcel up the pain, order the chaos and confusion, and endow meaning to the pointless. Experience was held on to and made valuable by transmutation into anecdote, preferably amusing. Brian put at least as much effort into the story of his life as he did his life's work of film.

Immediately, the memoirs became known as the Big Bestseller. 'When the Big Bestseller and the Box Office Blockbuster hit the market, Christopher, you'll be so very rich. I wonder what you'll do with all the money?' That was easy. Try and extricate myself from the sucking swamp of debt that the Box Office Blockbuster had helped land me in.

The process of getting his memoirs into book form, I explained to Brian, would involve interviewing him on tape. This would then be transcribed by our mutual friend,

Valerie – who lived in a flat in Ann's Close, the courtyard behind the Nag's Head. I would then shape and edit the text. And so, I now began to spend even more time at Kinnerton Street, armed with a tape recorder.

'*Hans Moore Hawthorne!*' I exclaimed when first told of Brian's baptismal names, as I sat chronicling childhood memories for the Big Bestseller. 'What happened to Brian Desmond?'

'That comes later,' Brian said impatiently, and went on to paint a picture of childhood bliss. He told stories of happy, carefree days dominated by a good and gentle father, set against an idyllic, albeit shabby-genteel background of an Ireland of low, white-washed cottages, green fields and blue remembered hills, caressed by soft, God-sent rain. The kindly and indulgent *da* was the beloved local doctor upon whom the grateful poor (whom he never charged) pressed small presents. Wittily, his humane father would often say of a patient, 'That Mrs Murphy has *magnificent* symptoms.' The doctor administered to the sick at all hours of the day and night, journeying to them through all weathers in one of his three modes of transport: an old Crossley motorcar, a pony and trap, and a horse for mountain paths.

This remembered world was rich in detail: the trap, for instance, had the varnish peeling from it and a plank missing from the floor. Brian told of accompanying his father on emergencies, when his task on arriving at a cottage was to boil water. One night father and son arrived at a woman's cabin to find her husband lying dead on a pallet of rags in the corner. 'I lay beside that fellow every night for forty years and I never liked him.' Wealthy and titled landowners adored the splendid doctor, whom they never treated as less than a social equal despite the mildly mocking and superior manner he adopted towards them. His popularity meant that he was given permission to shoot over everybody's land and fish in their rivers. A rota was devised for the nine children (six surviving from Brian's first mother, and three from his step-mother): 'You three go sea fishing, you three on the rivers and you others go shooting.'

Then one day Brian happened to mention that his father had worked on the metalwork for the *Titanic*. 'Unusual, that,' I said. 'A doctor working on the metalwork of an ocean liner.'

Brian was silent for a moment. His pale blue eyes scanned me closely, an indication that he was about to break new ground. 'How about this for the very first line of my memoirs: *I am truly in a predicament – an Irishman chained to the truth*.'

'Very good. But none of your friends will believe it.'

'I have the impression that you find the portrait of my childhood too rosy?'

The extent to which Hans Moore Hawthorne, a.k.a. Brian Desmond, had invented himself would be revealed to me gradually over time, but somehow the country doctor *da* with his collection of impoverished patients and their magnificent symptoms, together with his indulgent, aristocratic chums, never really rang true. 'A bit *too* charming,' I said.

'Not a word of truth in it.'

'Your *da* wasn't a doctor?'

Brian shook his head. 'And there was no pony and trap, no Crossley motorcar. That's the way I would have liked it to be, not the way it was.'

The portrait of carefree days drawn in a score of well-turned anecdotes was replaced by a reality infinitely more bleak and cruel. Brian grew up poor in South Belfast. He was born in 1895 in the family's small terrace house in Finvoy Street, the seventh child of the seventh child, a circumstance the Irish believe casts a destiny of profound good fortune. He emerged from the womb partially covered in a caul, also considered to be a source of great good luck. Irish sailors used to give large sums of money for a caul in the belief that to possess one meant its owner would never drown. Less romantically, anyone could pin a name on a lucky infant born with a caul by paying the local minister five shillings. 'My father had a close friend called Tom Moore with a son called Hans who gave the priest ten bob. And my mother's grandfather's name was Hawthorne, so I came to be christened Hans Moore Hawthorne.'

Robert Hurst, his father, was a blacksmith in the Belfast shipyards and worked on the delicate ironwork for the interior of ships – including the *Titanic*. When he was employed he was decently paid, and the large family lived well enough on a diet of porridge, potatoes and stew, but when there was no work life became desperate. Brian remembered being so hungry he picked up stale crusts in the street.

His father drank. In an attempt to prevent him going to the pub, Brian's mother would hide her husband's clothes, but his compulsion was so great he would take one of his wife's black dresses and go out. 'The neighbours would say to me, "We saw your father in the road and he wasn't very well." That meant he was clinging to the wall, drunk.'

Brian's mother, Esther, died giving birth to her eighth child, a little girl who also died. During the confinement the midwife had been given strict instructions to keep the pregnant woman sitting up because she had dropsy, but in the excitement of the birth she was laid down briefly and water flooded her heart. Brian was three and a half years old, but remembered his father's tearful, angry shouts at the midwife, 'You have lost me my Acey!' Esther was buried with the baby girl resting on her arm. Brian was told that his mother was so beautiful that she was needed as an angel in heaven and could not stay on earth.

Childhood memories of his mother were few. Prematurely aged by childbirth, and suffering from consumption, she was dead at thirty-four. 'I remember running into the house one day and asking her for a biscuit. I was still dressed then as a little girl, because in Ulster we believed that the fairies only

The Hurst family in Belfast, 1897.
Brian is sitting on his mother's knee

stole little boys and didn't want little girls. My mother was lying on the sofa heavily pregnant with her last child. I didn't know that then, of course, but I remember her struggling to get up, and taking an age to pull herself right round the room to get to the glass barrel on the mantelpiece to give me a biscuit.' A second memory was of being taken to the circus and given a ride on an elephant. 'The only other thing I remember is being put into a carriage for my mother's funeral.'

Robert Hurst was left with six surviving children (a second child had also died at birth). The eldest, Patricia – thirteen years older than Brian, but the sibling he loved most throughout his life – took over the house, a job she did indifferently. His father soon remarried, to his wife's first cousin, Margaret Shilliday. Both women were descended from Brian's great-grandfather, David Hawthorne, who was born in 1750 and lived to be 108. Four days before he died he returned from a day's fishing singing happily and swinging a fish he had caught.

Despite drink and intermittent unemployment, Robert Hurst tried to be generous to his large family. 'One pay-day he took me to a shop near the Short Strand and bought me a beautiful little green overcoat with an imitation astrakhan collar. I loved that coat but I didn't get much chance to wear it because it was always put into pawn on Monday and taken out again when pay-day came round.'

An old woman called Nancy used to come to the back door of the house carrying a heavy basket full of bits and pieces for sale that people had given her: pins and needles, scraps of ribbon, odd china plates and cups. Occasionally she would go over to the 'town', as North Belfast was known, to buy things for the family. 'She came back one day when a troubler – *agent provocateur* – had been active in the shipyards. There had been an incident of some sort and as a result a Catholic was pushed into the river. As he swam to one side they pushed him away with long poles, and when he swam to the other side the same thing happened. Exhausted, he swam to the middle and drowned. As Nancy told the story she said, "Ah, it was quar'n hard to see him die, even if he was a Papish."'

The old woman's great talent was for making pancakes. 'She would hang up the griddle over the fireplace in the kitchen, dust it off with a goose wing and rub it with bacon fat. Then she would pour her pancake mixture on to the griddle with great precision. They were always exactly the same size. We would sit around watching and waiting, and were handed pancakes with a big lump of butter in the middle. I have never eaten such delicious food as we had at home in the good times. Nancy had to sleep out and we were all very sorry for her. Finally, we got together with the neighbours and found her an old hut, but before Nancy could move into it she was found dead from exposure.'

The family was brought up Protestant. There was much Bible reading in the front parlour, and on Sundays the children were sent in batches to Bible class. 'We were given two sixpences, one for the collection and the other to buy ice-creams as a reward for going. As we came to the door of the church one Sunday, my brother Bobby began to search frantically through his pockets. He looked at me with a tragic face of absolute despair: "I have lost God's sixpence." Happily, he had not lost the one for ice-cream.'

The stepmother made no secret of favouring her own offspring, and Patricia was forced from home by the woman's jealousy. 'Every time your father looks at your long, golden hair he sees your mother,' an aunt told her. She was sent to Scotland, and later moved to London. Brian had no good memories of his stepmother, and the stories he told of her suggest persistent psychological cruelty.

At the age of seven he was urged to hang up a stocking from the mantelpiece on Christmas Eve. 'Be sure to do it, now, so Santa Claus can fill it with good things,' his stepmother told him. He hung up a long black stocking and lay awake most of the night in anticipation. 'Everybody, except my father, was waiting for me when I came down in the morning. The stocking was full of knobbly objects and on the top was a great big golden orange, shining like the sun against the black fireplace. I rushed over, pulled the stocking down and took out the orange. But when I looked inside I saw it had been filled with ashes and cinders. The family laughed at me. Even my own brothers and sisters. I laughed weakly with them, and then ran out of the house. I hid and cried.'

At the age of eight Brian began to take the breakfast of his father and two older brothers, Robert and Jimmy, to the vast smithy inside the shipyard. Two hundred blacksmiths worked in the enormous building, and the noise from the great steam hammers and the heat from the furnaces made it into an inferno. 'Anything my father and brothers did not eat, I would get. Then I would join a group of boys standing outside the shipyard workers' canteen and the men there would bring us out what they hadn't eaten. I would return home with the breakfast basket full of wood for the fire which I'd picked up in the shipyard.'

One day Brian sat patiently watching his father eat breakfast, waiting for him to finish. 'I must have been looking sad for my father suddenly looked up and said kindly, "I haven't given you much of a mother, Hans, have I?"'

Consumption, the scourge and terror of the age, which had already claimed Brian's mother and his stepmother's first husband, hung over the family as a perpetual threat. When Brian was barely nine, his stepmother escalated her cruelty from casual spite to deadly malevolence. Speaking quietly with great deliberation, she looked into the small boy's eyes and said, 'Your mother died of consumption. This is a hereditary disease and when you are nineteen, you too will die of consumption.'

The child took the stepmother's statement as fact: he was a consumptive under sentence of death, with ten years to live. He became obsessed by the fate awaiting him, and began to visit the local library to read medical books relating to tuberculosis. And when a friendly aunt came to visit from Scotland, she found her nephew kneeling in the lane beside the house examining his spit for blood.

Aunt Sarah – his father's sister – was a tall, stately woman who Brian remembered as wearing beautiful, striped Edwardian dresses. She considered herself a cut above her brother's impoverished and struggling family, having married a businessman with a string of steam laundries in Govan. Throughout his childhood, Brian was clad from head to foot in the cast-off clothing of his aunt's eldest son. Aunt Sarah was generous and kind-hearted and seemed to understand the mean streak in her brother's wife. On finding her nephew crouched over his own spit, she asked him what he was doing.

'I have consumption, you know.'

'Who told you that?'

'My stepmother.'

Nothing more was said, but a day or two later Aunt Sarah took Brian to see a chest specialist who gave him a thorough examination. The doctor handled the situation skilfully. Instead of dismissing the condition, which the child would have suspected to be mere consolation, he delivered the verdict from the next room, leaving the door open so Brian could overhear. 'That fellow – *consumption*! He has the finest pair of lungs in County Down!'

The next time his stepmother morbidly reminded him of his consumptive fate, Brian was able to contradict her. 'Oh no, I haven't got consumption. I have the best pair of lungs in County Down. I have been to Dr Smiley and he said so.' (His stepmother's prophecy was later fulfilled to the letter, but striking her closest and most loved child – the eldest, Robert James, died of consumption aged nineteen.)

It was a time when all Ulster schoolchildren took any work they could to earn money, and one of Brian's first jobs was peculiar to the deep-rooted tensions of the neighbourhood. 'It concerned Catholic neighbours of ours. I was given a penny to open the door of their kitchen – front doors were usually left open in our part of Belfast – and shout, "Paddy beats his ma!"'

Brother Bobby, who was always kind and generous to his younger brother, sold the *Belfast Newsletter* on a street corner in North Belfast. Brian often went with him and in order not to be forgotten attached his night-shirt to his brother's with a big safety pin. When all the papers were sold his brother would take him to a grocery shop and buy a bag of broken biscuits.

At twelve, Brian got a job driving a grocer's pony and cart delivering groceries, and was paid four and sixpence a week. 'The grocer's pony became very ill and could only move at a walk. Somebody told me that the pony should be given turpentine and I asked the grocer for fourpence to pay for it. He wouldn't give it to me so I bought the turpentine out of my wages and gave it to the pony. But the next morning when I went in to harness him, the pony was dead.'

The death made him miserable, a mood that deepened when his half-brother Thomas fell ill. 'He was my favourite, a lovely little chap with a pale face and deep blue eyes. I used to hurry home from work so I could nurse him. I would put his potty under him, clean him up and feed him. People said about Thomas, "They're watching him." That meant that the angels were watching him and that he would die young. Thomas died when he was three. *He was taken up lest evil change his understanding or guile deceive his soul.*'

At thirteen and a half, Brian's father took him to the schoolmaster and received permission for him to leave school, on the grounds that his family needed every penny it could earn to survive. He went to work in the Bloomfield Linen Factory, starting at six in the morning and earning a basic wage of five shillings a week. 'I learned to weave the fine Bessborough tablecloths, enormous things about twelve feet wide and very long.

'Sometimes, in the evenings, I went with friends to the music halls in North Belfast. Coming back, we used to hurry past the Short Strand, where a community of Catholics lived by the side of the River Lagan. If the local boys saw us, and they outnumbered us, they would surround us and make us curse the king. If we refused, we got a beating. South Belfast wasn't always peaceable either. On Saturday nights there were terrible fights in all the streets off the Newtonards Road, Ballymacarrett. People used to come from North Belfast to see the fighting.'

Shortly after he began work, at fourteen, Brian fell in love with his stepsister, Annie. 'I took her into a field and tried to do things to her. She ran home and told my stepmother. I got a beating first from my stepbrother, Robert James, and then from my stepmother. Finally, my father told me to go upstairs and take off my clothes. He came up to give me a hiding with the taws, a long piece of leather cut into strips at the end, a kind of domestic cat o' nine tails. I crouched cowering in the corner, a miserable object. He didn't have the heart to hit me.'

At sixteen, Brian first became aware of the sexual confusion within him. 'I was friends with two girls at this time. One was called Clara, a beautiful girl with snowy white skin and the marvellous complexion that often goes with brilliant red hair. I took her into the wasteland around where we lived and used to wonder why I didn't get excited like the other boys, who were always talking about girls. I felt easier with the other girl, Maggie, a very warm, good-hearted girl, and I was able to kiss and fondle her. But then I went into an alley with a boy. It was so nice and exciting that I made him do it again the very next night. We often went for walks in the wasteland after that. The constant beatings from my eldest stepsister, Martha, and my stepmother, had implanted a fear of women in me and made me wary of them.'

The monumental presence of the *Titanic* during the years of its construction dominated the shipyards of Belfast and the surrounding area as a familiar landmark. Brian's father proudly took him to see the great ship launched. 'When the news came back of the ship's sinking, a tidal wave of grief struck Belfast. There was not a street in either North or South Belfast that didn't have a house in it with the blinds down, because there were some four hundred technicians from the town on that maiden voyage.'

Days later, his father fell ill. It was as if the sinking of such a magnificent vessel, the apogee of the shipwright's craft, had broken the man's spirit. He took to his room, confined to bed. Brian's stepmother and a family friend, Euphemia Johnson – known always as Famey – nursed the dying man. The nine children did what they could, and sat in the front room after they returned from work each day waiting with dread for the inevitable. One evening Famey came down the stairs, and paused in the doorway: 'You have lost a friend.'

At first Brian felt numb, as the large family around him prepared for the funeral and went into mourning. He seemed strangely distant from his emotions, almost unmoved. Two nights after the funeral he was delegated to take Robert Hurst's black boxes, containing the hammers of his trade, to give to his father's closest workmate from the shipyard. 'It was only when I left the mate's house, and had handed over the hammers, that I truly realised my father was gone. My grief was terrible. Overwhelming.'

Our taping sessions were usually haphazard and did not follow any chronology – a story from the First World War might come after an anecdote about a film made thirty or forty years later – but on the day that Brian decided to chain himself to the truth, and first spoke of his true childhood, he talked of nothing else and the tape ran for a couple of hours. I had offered to stop a couple of times when he was overcome by the painful return to the past: particularly the deaths of the pony, his baby brother and his father. 'No, the memories are coming back – let's press on.'

At the end of his account of a loveless childhood scarred by want and loss, he seemed to have shrunk and somehow become simultaneously very old and very young. It was a sad little boy from the backstreets of Belfast who said, 'So there you are – now you know why I made up a happier childhood.' And yet it was an old man who complained he was tired and wanted to sleep, and seemed troubled. It was not just recalling unhappy memories, buried so deeply for so long, that had upset him, but the length of time he had spread the lie. 'I should never have denied my true father. Robert did his best for us. Nine children to feed and clothe, married to a sour wife, work uncertain – who wouldn't drink?' It was difficult to know if the old man spoke for the child, or the child spoke for the old man: 'I loved him.'

PART IV

Ireland

'Never been to Ireland!' The voice merged pity with outrage, as Brian reeled beneath the dreadful intelligence that I had not set foot upon the Emerald Isle. 'That explains *a lot*.'

A plan was being made to go to Ireland for a week to meet the man whose play, *Born to be King*, had originally inspired Brian with the idea for the film. This was Major Stephen Vernon, an unknown quantity to me, who was married to Lady Ursula, sister of the then Duke of Westminster. The play had originally been written to be performed in Kinsale, County Cork, in the open air, moving from one location to another. It had been staged only once, with Brian playing Augustus. He assured me that he had been a triumph – the very essence of imperial Rome; assuming the purple came naturally to him, he explained.

I had finally been given the play to read, which I found stilted and wordy. It was understandably unsuitable as a screenplay for film but I thought that a couple of the speeches could be pruned and incorporated. 'I've told Stephen that you're bowled over by it,' Brian said. 'Wildly inspired. But that you had to go back to the drawing board for the film. He's thrilled to be involved. And don't forget the duke's good for a few million.'

Brian then broke the news to me that I would have to share credit on the picture. 'Nothing that will detract from you as a screenwriter. Just a line in tiny type – *Story by Stephen Vernon*. Something like that.'

'Won't it suggest that Stephen Vernon wrote the Bible?'

'Are you saying that it should read, *Story by Major Stephen Vernon, Matthew, Mark, Luke and John*?' Brian smiled at his joke. 'But I take the point. How about, *Inspired by a play by Stephen Vernon*?'

'I suppose I can live with that.'

'Good. Then that's settled.'

'How will you word the Executive Producer credit? His Grace the Duke of Westminster, the Duke of Westminster, or just Westminster?'

'Whatever he bloody well wants.'

It was decided that as I had never visited Ireland before, we should make the journey by ship. 'So much more romantic to approach Cork by sea,' Brian said. 'After all, this is a great occasion – Christopher inculcated into one of the great mysteries and wonders of the world. Magical Ireland.' He telephoned a few days before we left to say that he had spoken to his travel agent who had informed him that there was an overnight boat to Cork from Swansea. 'The most comfortable cabin is a double on deck. The singles are in the bowels of the ship, and dark and airless I fear. So what's it to be – privacy and discomfort, or shared luxury?'

This was a loaded and delicate question, as it meant that we would have to sleep in the same room, an intimacy so far avoided. I was touched by Brian's tact, and felt no qualms at all as I replied without hesitation, 'Shared luxury, please.'

'Thank God for that.'

We took the train to Swansea, a long, slow journey. Over cups of tea and currant cake, Brian told me about his early film-making in Ireland. His second film, after *The Tell-Tale Heart*, was an adaptation of J. M. Synge's bleak play, *Riders to the Sea*, a story about a widow who loses her husband and all of her sons to the sea. 'It is the best and most dramatic one-act play written this century and I used many of the actors from the Abbey Theatre, in Dublin, including Sara Allgood. I realised that to make one's mark as a director it was necessary to ride into the business on the back of a great writer. We shot the film in the west of Ireland and I was able to use local fishermen for the scene where the last son's body is washed ashore.

'Our art director was actually a fine sculptor, a wild man who used to put a long piece of seaweed into his bum like a tail and run up and down the beach yelling and screaming like a banshee. This caused consternation and scandalised the local population. We had built a set, three-sided with no roof, to shoot the sea through the windows, and I was accosted about it by the local priest, accompanied by a young girl and her grandmother. He complained that his parishioners were using the structure for immoral purposes. The priest turned on the girl and harangued her, saying he had heard she had visited it with her boyfriend. The grandmother spoke up: "Leave her alone, Father. Sure, all we have in Ireland is the drink and *that*."

'The film was released in Ireland and America, but not in Britain, and Gracie [Fields, the producer] never got her money back. So there I was with two artistic films to my name but no sign of any new film on the horizon. I was considered brilliant but not commercial.' Brian shuddered. 'Avoid this fate at all costs! It is the leper's bell that a producer's left ear is tuned to hear from a hundred miles away, as his right rejoices in the sweet ringing of the cash register.'

Brian had returned to London on completion of the film and worked occasionally in his friend Norman Duncan's bookshop in Lower Belgrave Street. 'I was sitting there alone one Christmas Eve. Nobody had been in all afternoon except a friend who only wanted to borrow a book. At six o'clock I decided there was no point in staying open any longer. I had just locked up when the bell rang. I opened the door and there stood a poor, shivering Indian in a turban, clutching a small bag.

'He asked me if I would buy a tie for two and sixpence. I

had in my possession at the time only three half-crowns but I bought a tie. He looked so frozen that I said, "Please come in and warm yourself at the fire." We sat chatting for a while and I made him some hot tea. Then he suddenly said to me, "I want to tell you three things. You are going to get a letter asking you to go and see someone. The result of that meeting will be that you'll be under contract for a long, long time. And you will be changing your car next year to a great big one."

'I bought another tie for two and sixpence and the Indian went away. He could hardly have turned the corner when a letter fell through the letterbox. It was an invitation from the Chief of Production of British International Pictures, at Elstree Studios, to visit him in the new year. The studio had begun work on an Irish picture called *Ourselves Alone* – a translation of Sinn Féin – and they wanted me to take a look at what had been done so far. I went along early in January and watched what they had shot. Thinking I was talking myself out of a job, I said, "Nobody talks like that in Ireland. The dialogue is impossible." They asked me to read the script, and I took it away and opposite each shot I made a little sketch, perhaps three hundred small drawings in all. When I brought it back they asked me if I thought I could direct it. "Blindfolded with my hands tied behind my back!" Then they wheeled in the usual accountant who said the usual thing: "All the money has been allotted and there's nothing left to pay you. Not very much, anyway." They insulted me with an offer of £150, but it was £150 more than I had so I took it.

'After I finished the film I was given a contract for £40 a week, which was a top salary for a director then – plus £500 every time I made a film. In one year I made *Ourselves Alone*, *The Tenth Man*, based on a story by Somerset Maugham, *Sensation*, based on a newspaper story, and *Glamorous Night* by Ivor Novello. We really had to go at it then – making films was rather like scrubbing and washing at the tub. And I bought my great big car – a drophead Rolls-Royce, that belonged to Betty Carstairs, the Standard Oil heiress, who had spent more than £20,000 on the bodywork alone. So Christopher, if you ever come across an Indian in a turban selling ties – buy two!'

In Swansea we boarded the ferry for the overnight journey to Cork. The cabin was oddly shaped, but spacious for a boat, and the single beds were in opposite corners. After unpacking we made for the bar, already filling up with enthusiastic drinkers. We found a table and I went off to buy tumblers of Irish whiskey while Brian scoured the room for victims.

'A very nice girl over there,' he said. 'I shall ask her to come over and sit with us.'

'Over where?' I looked around the bar which did not contain anyone who could possibly be described as 'a very nice girl'.

'There!' Brian said impatiently, nodding through the blue haze of cigarette smoke in the direction of the far corner, an area that took in everyone. 'You don't expect me to point, do you?'

I looked again. Isolated among the laddish throng were two unlikely contenders: a middle-aged woman a yard wide with long, stringy hair, sitting with her back to us, and the fantastic figure of a gypsy in layer after layer of colourful skirts and scarves, positioned with purpose at a table loaded with pint pots and shot glasses. 'Do you mean the fat old bag with the greasy hair or the gypsy woman about to tie one on?'

'The *beautiful* one,' Brian repeated, '*over there*!'

But I could see no such beauty, and shrugged. Some time later I left the bar for fifteen minutes to go back to the cabin and retrieve a packet of Gauloises. On my return I found two nasty-looking youths sitting with Brian at the table. 'This is Ted . . .'

'*Ned!*'

'This is Ned, and his friend . . . I'm sorry, I didn't catch your name?'

'What's it to you?'

'And his friend Wozzittoyu. Fetch us a round of drinks, Christopher, if you would be so kind. Wozzitobe, gentlemen?'

Depressed, I set off to fetch draught Guinness and glasses of whiskey. When I returned Brian whispered in my ear. 'Extraordinary thing. My eyes must be going. This Ned was right across the bar sitting down – I was *sure* it was a girl. I was thinking of you. Honestly.'

'You should have those peepers tested soon, Bri,' I said, looking at the toughs at the table, 'before they declare you legally blind.' Ned was a raw-boned, spotty, lank-haired individual who had no redeeming qualities whatsoever, except that he was not in the least effeminate and was far from being a very nice girl. He regarded us with animal, snarling contempt. His single possible attribute was that he was an improvement on his friend, who was already half drunk and seemed poised to erupt in verbal or even physical abuse. For the next couple of hours Brian bought drinks and told his unreceptive audience stories featuring Charlie Chaplin, John Ford, James Joyce, Laurence Olivier, John Wayne and the Duke of Edinburgh. Ned listened with open disbelief. The friend sat through everything, blank and silent, drinking steadily and slowly turning green, as his desire for violence was subdued by a growing need to vomit.

The anecdote concerning the Duke of Edinburgh, as told to Ned and his friend at our table in the bar of the night ferry to Cork, was surreal. 'Prince Philip was a young naval officer at the time and we were all together at a luncheon at the Ritz,' Brian said airily. 'There were some charming young women among the company. Beauties from the best families in the land. But I remember looking at this handsome fellow and thinking what a husband he would make for Princess Elizabeth, as she then was. Afterwards, he took me to White's – a club I had never set foot in before nor have since. We drank Buck's Fizz in silver goblets. I drove him back to his uncle Mountbatten's house, in Chester Street, because he didn't have a car.'

'Bollocks!' Ned said mildly. 'You don't expect me to believe the Duke of Edinburgh didn't have a motor?'

'Sad, but true. A prince of royal blood, destined to marry the Queen of England, but motorless.'

Brian rose to go to the lavatory, and while he was away Ned asked, 'Your friend a fucking nutter?'

'Yes. But the stories are true.'

'What – he made all them films and knows them film stars and toffs?'

'Yes.'

'Fuck me,' Ned said, turning to his companion. 'The weirdos you meet travelling.' His friend did not respond – he had passed out in his chair; drool hung from his open mouth and his nose ran.

Brian returned and stood by the table, evidently about to turn in. 'Gentlemen, it is time for bed.' Surely Brian would not invite either of these horrors back to the cabin? Would he? *Not a nightcap in the cabin! Please don't invite them for a nightcap in the cabin!*

'I'll bid you goodnight. Sweet dreams.' I felt light-headed with relief as we moved away from the gruesome duo. It had been a tense couple of hours. Brian said with feeling, 'What a *ghastly* pair! Probably escaped from prison.'

The modesty with which we undressed would have done credit to the most chaste and prissy Victorian spinsters. Brian turned on a single lamp to ensure maximum discretion as we each stood facing opposite walls in silence. Trousers were artfully taken down beneath dressing gowns and pyjama bottoms quickly pulled on. The same delicacy governed the removal of shirts and putting on of pyjama tops. Neither of us cast a glance in the other's direction before we slipped beneath the covers. It was a fastidious exercise, on both our parts, in rampant asexuality.

In the morning the ship ploughed through a fine mist of grey rain as it made its way into the Cork estuary, a scene more nondescript than magical. We tied up in the city's docks and took a hire car to Kinsale. 'I brought a Saudi Arabian sheikh down here some time ago to meet Stephen,' Brian said as we looked at the countryside. 'Thought I might be able to separate him from a million or so, but nothing came of it. The sheikh looked out the car window at this lush green pasture and said, "Tell me, is all this done through irrigation?"'

The car sped on and Brian settled back with a look of pure happiness on his face. 'Good to be back in Ireland,' he said. 'Sad, mad Ireland.'

After a while, he began to chuckle. 'What are you laughing at?' I asked.

'About five years ago I travelled to western Ireland to look for locations. I had persuaded an actor friend of mine, Dudley Sutton, who had married the American heiress Marjorie Huntington-Hartford, to buy an option on Liam O'Flaherty's novel *Famine* for £500. We set off in a great limousine and were driving through a little town called Spiddal, in western Galway, where there were two long lines of men on either side of the road breaking stones. We were held up for a long time until Dudley wound down the window and said angrily, "What the hell is going on?" One of the workmen leaned on his hammer and said with great charm, "I don't really know, sir, but I *believe* we're narrowing the road."'

On the journey, Brian told me of a trip to Ireland many years earlier with John Ford. 'Like you, Christopher, I took Jack Ford on his first visit to Ireland. I wanted everything to be marvellous for him as he had fantasised about the place for so long. We got off the boat at Dun Laoghaire and it was miserable – sleeting and freezing. We were to take a train to Galway, and I asked a porter to put us in a warm carriage. He led us to a train with steam rising up around the carriages, and it was really lovely and warm. As we waited, we read our newspapers, and half an hour went by. Then we read each other's papers. Through the steam, I caught sight of the porter. "This *is* the train for Galway?" "Oh sure, not at all, sir, not at all. The train for Galway left this twenty minutes and more. I thought all you wanted was a warm carriage, so I did!"

'When we eventually arrived on Galway Bay, where Jack's family originated, his cousins immediately went out and killed a chicken and made a wonderful stew. It snowed most of the time and on the train trip back to Dublin we lost our luggage, so we went to the station near Phoenix Park to see if we could find it. It was late at night and still snowing hard, and the station was deserted. We found a little door with "Lost Property" written on it, and knocked. It was opened by a fine-looking Irish boy, very drunk. We explained about our luggage. "Lost your bags, have you? Come on in and take any two you like. I have shelves *stuffed* with bags."

Brian had been instrumental in getting John Ford to buy Liam O'Flaherty's book, *The Informer*, which became one of Ford's most successful films. 'The three of us went to Paris together, where Jack embarked on an extended binge. He had promised me he would stick to beer and wine, but I went into his room and saw three empty bottles of cognac under the bed. Two or three times over the years he would get drunk in depth and I would have to send for the ambulance. But having been brought up by a classic drunk, I knew how to deal with him. On this occasion he was fairly far gone. He looked at me and said, "Brian, what island am I on?" There was a pause, and he said, "When's the ambulance coming?"'

At Kinsale, snuggled at the end of its beautiful estuary, Ireland began to creep up on me. We checked into a hotel overlooking the harbour and as no breakfast had been served on the boat, went into the dining room. 'A rather featureless, lacklustre establishment, I'm afraid, but we must make do,' Brian said. 'I find these paper napkins and pats of butter wrapped in silver paper *too* depressing. I'll talk to the management.'

The manager of the hotel was summoned and presented himself at the table – a rumpled, obliging character. 'We are here on film business and will be staying in your hotel for several days,' Brian announced. 'Mr Robbins is my writer – a scenarist of great talent. We will possibly be visiting with some frequency, but as creative artists you must understand we are easily downcast. Would you be good enough to replace these thin and rather unpleasant paper napkins – known in the trade, I believe, as *serviettes* – with a couple of nice big linen ones?'

The manager was a man who responded to importance, but was so overwhelmed by the magnificence of Brian's manner that he had difficulty concentrating on the detail of the demand. He stood gawping at the end of the speech, unsure what was required of him. Brian held up the paper napkin between two fingers as if lavatory paper had found its way on to the table. 'It would be appreciated if you could replace these squares of Kleenex with white linen napkins.'

'We don't have any linen napkins,' the manager said sadly.

Brian sighed, dug into his pocket and pulled out a fiver. 'Then be so good as to send one of your lads out to purchase a couple.'

'I'll not accept your money, sir,' the manager said, holding up his hand, determined to rise to the occasion. 'There'll be linen napkins on your table the next time you sit down to eat.'

'Thank you. And while you're here, could you arrange to have these fiddly bits of butter wrapped in silver paper replaced by a big dollop of golden Irish butter?'

'Forthwith,' the manager said, falling into the style of things. 'No trouble at all.' He called across a waiter. 'George, take the butter pats in the silver paper away and bring a slab of golden Irish butter, will you?'

'What?'

'The gentleman does not care for wrapped butter. He wants a proper piece cut from a slab.' The waiter stared at Brian with deep suspicion and walked off, shaking his head. 'May I welcome you to Kinsale, gentlemen,' the manager said. He turned to me. 'It is a particular privilege and pleasure to welcome a literary gentleman. And may your film business be a grand success.'

As he moved away, Brian said, 'Ireland's the last place in the world to take writers seriously. Except, of course, France, where they take them too seriously.'

Later in the morning I discovered a small sitting room on the first floor of the hotel with some shelves of books, and was idly looking through them in search of something to read when the manager entered. 'A shaming collection, I'm sad to say,' he apologised. He placed himself in front of the books and gazed at them with scorn. 'Agatha Christie and Ian Fleming – in *paperback* – and the complete works of Bulwer Lytton, as if anyone cared. Books by the yard. That's what it is, *books by the yard*. And not even leather-bound. I am disgraced – but it's an impossible thing in this day and age, when the world is ruled by men of business, to be given money for a few decent books. The guests are condemned to watch the television, terrible though it is.'

'Books do furnish a room,' I said. Out of context the phrase sounded arch and idiotic, which was pretty much what it was *in* context.

'Now, Mr Graham Greene – there's a fine writer – and of the Catholic persuasion. Do you by any chance know the gentleman?'

'I'm afraid not. I've read him, of course.'

'*Of course*,' the manager said, somewhat sharply. 'And Mr Saul Bellow. The American. Now there's a talent. A master. A colossus. There's some Irish in him somewhere, to be sure, even though he is of the Jewish persuasion. Would you have met Mr Bellow on your literary travels in the film business?'

'We've never met, no.'

The manager was beginning to lose faith – I could see the doubt and disappointment in his eyes. He had invested such high hopes in me, and here I was in the process of being defrocked as a small-time literary impostor, friend neither of Greene nor Bellow. 'Gore Vidal,' the manager said, throwing me a bone. 'I saw him talking eloquently on the television some time ago on the subject of the impending collapse of the American civilisation. Clever and funny he was, although I think he'd had a few . . .'

'I've been looking for you,' Brian said, entering the room.

'The manager is about to ask me if I know Mr Gore Vidal,' I said, giving Brian a cue and hoping to restore my tattered reputation.

'*Extraordinarily* good-looking as a young man,' Brian said, lowering himself into an armchair. '*Very* handsome. And knew it. Full of himself. He came down to a luncheon party I gave at a house I used to have in the country outside of Oxford. It was a sunny day and we were all standing on the lawn having drinks before lunch. As a change from champagne, I served Château-d'Yquem, the exquisite nectar of Sauternes, the only white wine on earth the *Bordelais* deign to be classed as a First Growth. I came upon Gore holding forth and dominating the conversation, holding his glass cupped in his hand as if it were brandy. I said, "Young man, you'll find this rare elixir is chilled to precisely the right temperature. It is a mistake to warm it." His hand moved like lightning from the bowl of the glass to the stem.'

Gore Vidal hit below the fifth rib, I thought – a difficult blow to land.

'A fine lesson in the grand etiquette,' the manager said with a laugh. 'If ever I'm at a garden party here in Kinsale with a glass of rare elixir chilled to perfection, I'll not have my big clumsy hand round the bowl.' It was uncanny how Brian could inspire the most sensible and down-to-earth people to ascend virgin peaks of pretension and snobbery.

'Mr Hurst has known all the great Irish writers,' I said. 'You name them – Liam O'Flaherty, Sean O'Casey, James Joyce, Yeats . . .'

'Joyce and Yeats,' the manager said with an intake of breath, instantly reverential. 'Is that God's truth?' Although he continued to stand, figuratively the man was on his knees as a supplicant, awaiting the benediction of personal anecdote from one who had communed with the saints of Irish literature.

'Yeats was hopelessly in love with Maud Gonne, the Irish patriot,' Brian said. 'She refused to marry him, making his youth miserable. Maud's adopted daughter, Iseult, had married my friend, the writer Francis Stuart. Yeats was in love with her too and had proposed before she married Francis. I used to stay with Francis at freezing Largh Castle, which was not a castle at all but a blockhouse built by the English to keep the Irish down. The back yard was haunted, and you could see the wall where rebels had been chained and shot in the eighteenth century.'

'Terrible, terrible,' the manager said, discreetly avoiding looking at me.

'Yeats used to come to the castle to visit Iseult. He couldn't keep away, although he had no real connection to her. He used to recite his poetry to us, explaining that no word should be over-emphasised and that simple music on a harp, flute or soft tin whistle should be played behind it. He read "Byzantium" and I asked him what he meant by the lines:

A mouth that has no moisture and no breath
Breathless mouths may summon;

I hail the superhuman;
I call it death-in-life and life-in-death.

"Oh, I was away," he replied – meaning he was dreaming in another dimension, for he was deeply involved with spiritualism and the occult. He once said, "The Eskimo worships the creator of the Universe through a piece of white whale bone, the North American Indians through their symbolic totem poles, the Maoris through a carved piece of wood." And here he paused, before pronouncing these wonderful words I consider a great truth: "What the world's million lips are thirsting for must be substantial somewhere."'

'Fascinating, fascinating,' the manager said. 'I could stand here all day listening, but you'll have to excuse me – I have a hotel to mismanage.'

At lunchtime we returned to the restaurant to find linen napkins at our place settings, and a full pound of butter upon a side plate in the centre of the table. Stephen Vernon was to join us to talk about the screenplay. 'Normally, of course, I'm invited to stay at the house,' Brian said, 'but I've checked in here to give Stephen and her ladyship a chance to look you over. See if you pass muster. It's not that they're snobs, you understand, but there was an unfortunate incident on a previous occasion when I was here with someone who turned out to be quite unsuitable. A bit of an alcoholic. And touched by kleptomania. There was noise at night and things went missing. Stephen and Ursie laughed it off, but the butler took a very old-fashioned view of things, not being used to cinema people. Put his foot down – no more riff-raff at Fairyfield.'

'I *quite* understand,' I said acidly.

'But don't worry. We pass as gentry – even though we are a couple of shits.'

It seemed that Stephen's life story was a mixture of high romance and tragedy. 'Best-looking man of his generation,' Brian said. 'Officer in the Irish Guards, decorated for bravery in the desert war in North Africa. He meets Ursula, who was a lovely creature as a young woman, and falls deeply in love with her. It was to be the society wedding of the year. A duke's daughter, beautiful and disgustingly rich, and a charming, handsome, young war hero. Yum-yum. Envy stalked the land.

'And then a spectre from Stephen's past appeared. An older man went to the duke and said that he had been Stephen's lover on and off for a number of years. That he had bought Stephen out of the army, set him up with accounts at Fortnum's and Harrods, and sent him to Savile Row tailors and bootmakers in St James's. The duke spoke to Ursula, whom he adored. There were tears and she told her father she knew that Stephen was not a hundred per cent in that department but didn't care. She loved him madly and would marry him even if she were cut off without a shilling. The Grosvenors may have their faults, but being middle-class isn't one of them. The duke called the bounder back, greeting him with the words, "My Ursie shall have whom she wants. How much for you to disappear for ever?" He was given a hundred thousand pounds to fuck off to Australia, keep his mouth shut and never set foot in England again.'

'Good for the duke!'

'Quite so. Ursula and Stephen were married in a magnificent ceremony. I had a seat very near the front, naturally. They lived a charmed life. Invited everywhere by everyone – masses of interesting friends in London, wonderful house parties, horse breeding in Ireland. One of their horses won the Irish 2,000 Guineas. They were very popular – interested in literature and the theatre. Had actors and writers around them. A genuinely glamorous couple. They behaved in a way that almost gave rich people a good name. And then – *disaster!*

'Stephen is struck down with polio. Crippled. He cannot walk and the whole of his right side is paralysed. Naturally, they withdrew from the social scene and escaped to the house here – Fairyfield. Nothing grand, just a big old rambling Victorian villa with a separate cottage for the live-in help. A butler who doubles as chauffeur, a cook, a gardener and a woman to clean. Stephen pursues a scholarly life and becomes religious. He suffers through a series of painful operations – forty-six in all, I believe. They help somewhat, but even today he can scarcely walk and has to be lifted in and out of the bath by the butler, and has callipers and needs a stick. But Ursula has stood by him, and suffered through it with him. They remain devoted to one another.'

'A love story, then.'

'Yes. A love story.'

Stephen appeared at the door of the restaurant. He was still a good-looking man, with thinning, jet black hair and a classical, fine-featured face. He made his way across to us, limping and hobbling slowly. It was obvious that he hated his infirmity not only because of the physical handicap it imposed upon him, but also for the added burden of self-consciousness. We stood and I was introduced.

As we sat down Brian made unintelligible signals to me across the table with his eyebrows, which moved up and down and from side to side. His behaviour was so peculiar it was impossible for Stephen not to notice. We both watched mystified as the eyebrows continued to jerk and twitch. Finally, Brian nodded at my plate and winked. None of this facial semaphore conveyed anything at all to me. 'Your napkin,' he said at last, through clenched teeth. 'Give Stephen your napkin.'

The management had only gone as far in its largesse to provide two linen napkins, and any third party was expected to make do with the standard issue of a paper square. 'I'm sorry,' I said, offering my napkin to Stephen. 'Of course.'

'Why on earth should I have his napkin, Brian?' Stephen said with a laugh. 'Don't be ridiculous.'

I explained the situation while Stephen listened with amusement. 'Oh Brian,' Stephen said. 'Dear, dear Brian.'

The lunch was a great success. At the appropriate time, when I was given my cue, I launched into my vision of the screenplay – the charging white horses of the opening, the nightmare of Herod, the journey of the wise men in winter, through high mountains and snow, the murder of Mariamne, the massacre of the innocents – and the birth that changed the history of the world for believer and non-believer alike. Stephen seemed carried along by my enthusiasm, and I was careful to make clear that the screenplay was a departure from the play while respecting the ideas behind it. I could tell I had given a good performance by Brian's expression of Mandarin satisfaction.

'You have passed muster,' Brian said later, after he had been telephoned by Stephen to invite us to move to Fairyfield. 'No more of this hotel food, which leaves a lot to be desired.'

The memory is hazy, but somehow on the final evening in the hotel I had the rare good luck to meet a raven-haired, green-eyed local beauty, whom for the purposes of this narrative shall be known as Miss Flynn. Things went fast with Miss Flynn, who made it clear that while her morals were rigid and severe with regard to local lads, enabling her to enjoy a spotless reputation in the town, she welcomed the opportunity to relax them with the occasional foreigner. After touring the hotspots of Kinsale – of which there were a surprising number – we returned to the hotel. Miss Flynn was not to be lured to my room, but agreed to a nightcap in the 'library'. I rang reception in a mood of Brian-like extravagance and ordered a bottle of champagne. On being told the price I whispered, 'Make that half a bottle.' After forty-five minutes I gave up all hope of the champagne arriving, but Miss Flynn proved very friendly on the library sofa without it. The room was cosy, deserted, and once I had found the light switch, encouragingly dark.

At an advanced stage in our lovemaking, during a particularly inappropriate moment, the door opened. Framed in the doorway as a dark outline against the light in the corridor was a waiter with a tray upon which stood a champagne bucket and glasses. I heard the man's muffled, 'My God!' Before quickly pulling the door shut, he said, 'I'll wager you'll no longer be wanting the drink.'

Miss Flynn became hysterical. 'It'll be the ruin of me,' she wailed, made distraught by the thought that the waiter might have recognised her. I calmed her, saying that it was quite dark, and while the waiter no doubt had seen too much, it was unlikely he would have recognised us. He would shortly find out my identity, as I had given both my name and room number to reception, but Miss Flynn's anonymity remained secure. She seemed somewhat reassured by this, but said she must go home before further calamities befell her. I pointed out that if she left now the receptionist and the night porter were bound to spot her, whereas if she hid in my room and slipped away at dawn her reputation would remain unsullied. Miss Flynn accepted the irrefutable logic of my argument. I opened the door of the library, and peered down the corridor to make sure that the coast was clear before we made a run for the lift.

Safely inside my room, Miss Flynn once again abandoned her small-town inhibitions. Before she prepared to leave at dawn I asked her when we could meet again. I was likely to be in Kinsale at least another week, I said, and had an image of love-filled evenings. 'Not here. Not in Kinsale.' There was desperation in her voice. She explained that the story would be around the town before the day was done, and to be seen about with me would be an admission of guilt. 'They'll put two and two together and make the usual forty-four. This is a town that talks and never has a good thing to say about anyone.'

'You mean the whole town will know what I was up to last night? What will they do – stone me?'

'Ah, they won't care about you at all. You're an Englishman. But it would be the ruin of me.'

I suggested an evening in Cork – surely a large enough city to get lost in? The idea made Miss Flynn nervous. She had friends and relations in Cork, she said. 'Dublin would be better. Or London.'

'You can't be serious! They are hundreds of miles away. We're both here – in Kinsale!'

'You're a cold sort of man, Christopher Robin,' Miss Flynn said, 'to make love to a girl one night and not want the bother of a journey to see her again.'

'It's not that. It just seems such a waste.' Genuinely, I wanted to weep, for I was taken with Miss Flynn.

'It would be the ruin of me. The absolute ruin!'

The last I saw of Miss Flynn was as she ran across the wet grass of the hotel garden at first light, and turned to wave and blow a kiss before she disappeared from my life. We spoke on the phone, but never did meet in Dublin or London. A serious local involvement intruded – a fine fellow with prospects, Miss Flynn informed me – and it was not to be.

At 10.30 the following morning I received a call from Brian. 'Where the hell are you? I want my breakfast.' We took off on a tour of the pubs of Kinsale in search of champagne but found it was not a drink much in demand by the locals. Brian carried an orange from one pub to another and grew increasingly frustrated. 'I'm *starving*!' I suggested coffee and toast at the hotel. 'No, no – not two days running. At my age you have to be careful. It would be too great a shock to the system. A small Guinness, perhaps.'

In one establishment an old, tramp-like man sat at the bar with a young scruff half his age, talking non-stop, and urgently imparting the wisdom of hard, personal experience. 'Listen to the advice of a man who took a terrible wrong turning in his life and learned from it – *never marry when you're on the dole.'* At another pub a bleak individual stood drinking on his own, before leaving without a word. A man close to us shook his head: 'What a *sad* man – not a story in him!'

I told of my experience the previous night. It was a pleasure to have an adventure of my own to recount for a change, and a comic sexual one at that. Brian was greatly amused. '"*I'll wager you'll no longer be wanting the drink!*" Very good. An Irish experience from start to finish. Embarrassment and clumsy charm on the part of the waiter, the fear of recognition and moral hypocrisy from the lascivious Miss Flynn. "*It'll be the ruin of me, the absolute ruin!*"And so it would – if anybody ever puts a name to the local colleen involved in such disgraceful conduct with a heartless English cad. We'll have to hope the waiter did not recognise Miss Flynn's lily-white thighs, otherwise you'll have to marry her.'

The butler came to the hotel to drive us to the Vernons' home, Fairyfield, which proved to be a comfortable house hidden behind high rhododendron bushes, with a spectacular view across the estuary, and a steep, secret garden down to the water. 'Presumably, the name of the house refers to the Little People?'

'Yes. I expect there was a sighting on the grounds at some time,' Brian said.

'I was sort of joking.'

'Joke about it at your peril. I had a friend with a castle that had a large lake clogged with leaves and water lilies. I asked him why he didn't clear it as it must have been full of fish. "For God's sake don't mention it!" he said. "I dare not have it cleared, for if you look closely you will see a fairy ring in the shape of the leaves and the fairies are said to dance on it at night. If I cleared it, every servant in the house would leave." I once asked my own father if he believed in fairies. "Not *exactly*," he told me. "But I wouldn't be surprised if I saw one coming down the lane."'

'*You* don't believe in fairies, do you?' I asked suspiciously.

'Not really.'

Lady Ursula was everything Brian had promised: soft, gentle, quietly spoken, gracious, unconcerned with clothes or make-up, and genuinely welcoming. The house was run by the butler, Gerrard, a stocky, quiet man with a thick Irish accent and easy manner. It was clear that he was indispensable, and was known in the town as the Napoleon of Fairyfield. Before lunch we gathered in front of the fire in the drawing room, where the butler poured everyone generous measures of Paddy whiskey. He then disappeared, to return after half an hour to announce in a sombre, dignified voice, 'Luncheon is served, my lady.'

Lady Ursula led us into the dining room. Having passed muster, with my bag unpacked in my cosy bedroom, it struck me as unfortunate and unnecessary that Brian should choose to pass on the story of Miss Flynn to my host and hostess at our first lunch together. There were embellishments: Miss Flynn not only had the creamiest thighs in Kinsale, but also tottered on the most extreme and provocative high heels ever seen in the town. When surprised *in flagrante delicto*, at the height of her pleasure, she was screaming the names of the saints. The waiter at the door was so overcome by the shock of it all that he remained under the doctor . . . and so on.

When we returned to the drawing room for coffee I had Brian to myself for a minute. 'Very funny,' I said. 'And very humiliating. Thanks a lot.'

'There's no pleasing you. You always seem upset when people assume you're queer – I establish your reputation as a red-blooded young stud rogering the local wenches and you're still upset.'

'True, I don't wish to be taken as your catamite—'

'That makes two of us.'

'—which doesn't mean I want you to broadcast compromising stories told to you in confidence.'

Brian looked genuinely contrite, but I should have known better. Lady Ursula and Stephen came into the room. 'I have been reprimanded, Ursie,' Brian said. 'For the shocking story I told at lunch. It was, apparently, highly confidential and top-secret. Christopher is concerned that he will be banished from the house as cinema riff-raff and sent back to the hotel.'

'It is very naughty of Brian to tell such outlandish tales,' Lady Ursula said. 'I so enjoy his stories, but don't believe a word of them.'

'Ursie!' Brian said, pretending to be shocked.

'Dear boy,' Stephen said to me, 'you must understand that we live a quiet life, cut off down here in the country. We *love* cinema riff-raff.' (Just how cut off became clear in a subsequent conversation. Stephen questioned me about a technical film term he had seen in a review by George Melly in the *Observer*, wondering whether it referred to a camera angle, editing technique or whatever. The dictionary had failed to come up with a definition. The term was *fellatio*.)

The routine at Fairyfield was an easy one. I was woken at nine by Gerrard, who deposited a strong cup of tea beside my bed, pulled the curtains and announced without variety, 'A nice soft day, sir.' This could mean that it was drizzling lightly, raining steadily or raining hard. I would dress, and go down to the drawing room to have breakfast by the blazing fire and read the *Cork Examiner*, a paper that made light work of the world. Through the window I could see Lady Ursula in the garden, dressed in an ancient and threadbare overcoat, feeding the birds on stale bread. It was a tranquil, easy-going, comfortable and old-fashioned existence compared to the frenzy and worry of my London life, and I settled into it happily.

After breakfast, I would join Stephen in his study and we would go through the script, enriching it with historical detail. He told me that polio had forced him to change from a man of action into a scholar overnight, and the metamorphosis was not easy. He never complained about his plight, but joked about it in a leaden way. 'The terrible thing about being a cripple is that it makes you a sitting target for bores. You can never get away fast enough when you see them coming. Holidays are the worst, when you are left stranded by the hotel pool or on the beach. The bores circle like sharks. They can smell the helpless and just fall on one. It's dreadful, and there's nothing to be done.'

Stephen had developed a love and knowledge of history in general, and biblical historicity in particular. He had made a close reading of Josephus and knew his work intimately, and was well versed in the history of Herod and his offspring. Brian could never quite see the point of our interest and emphasis on historical truth. He was interested in Jesus as God, not as a historical figure, and the Bible as sacred text, not fact. Stephen, who struggled endlessly with doubt and anger, admired Brian's absolute, childlike faith. Although embroidered from a rag-bag of ancient, pagan trappings, his Christian vision was unshakeable. 'I find it more reaffirming than a thousand sermons from a thousand priests,' Stephen said. 'Does it affect you?'

'Yes. He makes me wish I believed. He is genuinely spiritual, although how he keeps his faith so pure and uncontaminated by his wicked, wayward life is a genuine religious mystery.'

'Perhaps he's a saint – a male version of St Agnes, the beautiful thirteen-year-old Christian martyr who was thrown into a Roman brothel and emerged a virgin. Dear Brian,' Stephen said, smiling, 'and his picnic ways.'

Brian's presence in the study where we worked was occasional, bordering on the rare. 'I wonder where he goes and what he gets up to?' I said.

'I dare not ask and do not wish to imagine.'

Late one morning I came across him in the corridor outside the study carrying a bulging plastic bag. Brian gestured to me to approach quietly, indicating that the contents of the bag were some sort of secret. He opened it to reveal a muddy collection of small tubers. 'Know what these are?' I shook my head. '*Topinambours*,' he said with a flourish. 'Jerusalem artichokes.' He beckoned and whispered conspiratorially, 'Follow me.'

We went down the stairs into the kitchen to be greeted by a scene to warm the heart of any fan of BBC period costume drama. The cook was by the stove stirring a pot, the cleaning lady was peeling potatoes, the gardener was drinking his eleven o'clock mug of tea, and Gerrard, the butler, was buried in the sports page of the *Cork Examiner*. Our entry was scarcely remarked, indicating that the group was used to Brian coming and going. So this was where he spent his mornings – downstairs with the cook and butler!

Brian gave the bag of Jerusalem artichokes to the cook and explained they would make a fine soup for the following day, when there were to be guests for lunch. '*Topinambour* soup.' Giggling, the cook repeated the word, mangling the pronunciation. 'No, no, no,' Brian said. '*Toe-pee-nam-bore!*'

Brian carefully coached everyone in the kitchen in the correct pronunciation, working particularly hard with the butler, to whom French did not come naturally. 'While you,' Brian said to the gardener, 'could pass for a Frenchman. One more time, all together . . .'

'*TOE-PEE-NAM-BORE!*' We sang the word in unison, like children in a nursery, and burst out laughing.

'Now, here's the plan for tomorrow,' Brian said. He addressed the cook: 'You, Mary, enter the dining room with the tureen as usual, and when Gerrard lifts the lid and you offer the soup to the assembled guests, you announce in ringing tones, "*Topinambour* soup, my lady!"'

'Oh, I *couldn't*,' Mary said. 'I'd kill meself laughing.'

'There will be *no* laughing,' Brian said. 'That's the joke. The whole point of the exercise. Now, after we've all had a good slurp of the stuff, Gerrard here picks up the tureen to offer seconds, and goes up to Lady Ursula, "A drop more *topinambour* soup, my lady?" Straight-faced. Natural and normal. Well, butler-like anyway. It'll stupefy them.'

'It will that,' Mary said, shrieking with laughter. 'It'll *stupefy* them. I'll *kill* meself laughing.'

'Anybody who laughs will not be considered for a part in my movie. I've had my eye on Gerrard here for the captain of Herod's guard. A natural. I can see him massacring innocents right and left.'

'Oh, I wouldn't like to do *that*, Mr Hurst,' the butler said.

The gardener had been very puffed up by the remark that his pronunciation was so good he could pass as a Frenchman, and was eager to demonstrate his cultural refinement with regard to the cinema. 'Is it true, Mr Hurst,' he asked, 'that you made that *magnificent* film *Playboy of the Western World*. It was shown up in Cork in the big cinema there, so it was.'

'One of the greatest satiric comedies ever written,' Brian said, nodding. 'We mostly used actors from the Abbey Theatre in Dublin, and most of the budget came from Ireland. I only had five weeks to make the film but considered it worth the risk to get *Playboy* on the screen. The National Film Finance Board, in London, provided fifteen per cent of the budget for some reason I never fathomed. They sent a spy to watch over this piddling amount, because they didn't believe I could make it in the stated time and would then snatch their money back. You know the English!'

'Not at all,' Mary said, looking at me kindly. 'What a thing to say!'

'Synge originally set the play in Mayo but it's built up now, so I went all over Ireland looking for locations. I eventually found a long, lonely beach at the village of Inch, on Dingle Bay – later used by David Lean for *Ryan's Daughter*.'

'One of the most beautiful places in the wide world,' the

gardener said. 'Although I've never had the pleasure of visiting it *personally*.'

'My great friend Gerald Hamilton visited when I was filming,' Brian continued. 'The weather was very bad, and Gerald was very bored. So bored he became quite ill. The lady who owned the cottage where he was staying found he had a high temperature. "Now would you be a Catholic or a Protestant?" she asked. Gerald explained he was a Catholic. The woman gave a sigh of relief. "Glory be – you understand, it would be awkward to have a dead Protestant lying about in the village!"' The kitchen broke out in understanding and sympathetic merriment.

'A tinker came to me while we were filming and said, "If I bring my caravan, my wife and seven children, my dog and my donkey, will you give me a pound a day and dinner?" It seemed reasonable. They were a colourful lot and provided excellent background and atmosphere. I lived in a caravan on location and the boy who cleaned it said, "Oooh, this film, sir, it's bound to be an enormous success because *everybody* in Inch will come and see it."

'The finished film was shown in New York where it ran for twenty-eight weeks at the 55th Street Playhouse and was highly acclaimed. It also played here, of course, and received good reviews – and you know how difficult it is to please the critical Irish about their classic authors. On Irish television they asked me why I had used an Englishman, Gary Raymond, for that most Irish part of the playboy. "Gary is not an Englishman," I told them. "His grandmother was born in Galway, he's a gypsy and his real name is Lee. He's therefore far more Celtic than the people of this town of Dublin, who are nothing but the descendants of Danes, Normans, Vikings, Elizabethans and Cromwellians."'

'Ah, you were hard on those Dubliners,' the gardener said with satisfaction.

'*Playboy* opened the Boston Film Festival and was invited

Brian at work as a young director

to the Edinburgh Festival, but never released in England. But what can you expect of those English?'

'Don't be carrying on teasing the lad,' Mary said, winking at me.

'I went to Dublin to see Irish Film Finance, who had put up the money, and asked why they didn't make British Lion put the film out. The answer was, "If those good folk living beyond the long ride of the Irish Sea don't want to look at our film because it is *marred* by literary merit, they needn't!"'

The talk about *Playboy* made me ask Brian if it had been possible for him to make films in Ireland at the peak of his career. 'More than that,' he said. 'I had plans to help create an Irish film industry.' Together with his friend, the Irish peer, Lord Killanin (who, alongside Terence Young, appeared on our letterhead, Four Provinces Films, the only thing of the company that existed), he was prepared to work to attract film-makers to the country.

Brian offered to forego his Rank contract, at a great loss of income, and move to Ireland to help build the fledgling industry. It had been estimated that the Irish government would need to invest £100,000 to prime the pump. Brian flew to Dublin to talk to Sean Lemass, the Minister for External Affairs.

'Which part of Ireland do you come from, Mr Desmond Hurst?' the minister asked.

'Northern Ireland.'

The minister looked at the aide sitting beside him. 'Mr Desmond Hurst means, of course, the Six Counties.'

'No, Mr Lemass, I do not mean the Six Counties. I mean what is now and always has been the dominating province in Irish affairs – Ulster.'

And on that note, the government decided not to advance the £100,000, Brian renewed his contract with Rank, and early plans for an Irish film industry were shelved.

There were ten of us for the *topinambour* lunch, a genial group except for a plump, horsey man who established narrow, philistine credentials even before we sat down. He managed to vilify Americans, queers, modern art, rock music and the unemployed within half an hour. '*Minor* aristocracy,' Brian whispered in my ear. 'And broke. This is how it takes them.'

My encounter with the man was brief and savage, and of breathtaking rudeness. On being told I was a screenwriter and a journalist he informed me bluntly that the rotten gentlemen of the press were worse than prostitutes, and that films were not worth watching. He proposed horsewhipping for hacks, tight censorship for the press, and looked forward to the day when *all* cinemas became bingo halls. Before I could respond he had moved on. 'I do hope I don't have to sit next to the Broke Titled Gentleman,' I said to Brian, as we went into the dining room. 'I might bust him on his bulbous conk.'

'No, no – sit as near to him as you can. Enjoy the fun. Leave the Broke Titled Gentleman to me.'

Brian bruised him gently early on; gored him badly later. The butler and the cook trooped in with the soup, and it was worth the morning spent rehearsing in the kitchen to see Stephen and Lady Ursula lock eyes in a look of utter stupefaction as Mary solemnly intoned, '*Topinambour* soup, my lady.'

'What the devil soup is it?' asked the Broke Titled Gentleman (also known as Jack), taking the bait. '*Terpenumbra*?'

'*Topinambour*,' Gerrard said. 'Jerusalem artichoke, my lord.'

'The butler is naturally using the French word,' Brian said with condescension.

'Tastes good, whatever it is,' Jack said, irritated.

During the soup course Brian took pains to suggest that his career in the cinema had made him rich beyond his own calculation, although in reality, of course, he was even more hard-up than the Broke Titled Gentleman. He then proceeded to patronise Jack further with stories of impecunious aristocrats, the gist of which expressed profound pity for their plight, and altruistic pleasure in occasionally being able to relieve their distress.

'When I made *Hungry Hill*, I had impoverished Irish aristocrats *begging* me to use their crumbling piles, poor things,' Brian said. 'On the first day of shooting, my fellow directors Carol Reed and Michael Powell came to wish me luck. Normally one chooses a simple scene to start, with one or two actors, but I had about fifty women breaking up rocks as well as Margaret Lockwood and Dennis Price arriving in a pony and trap. Scenes with horses are notoriously difficult because, like children, monkeys and other animals, they always steal the scene. Michael Powell said to me, "God, if this were the first day on a picture of mine I'd shoot myself." Carol Reed said, "If you're like me, the first day on a set marks the beginning of sixteen weeks of anguish." One's fellow directors are encouraging blighters!'

'*Hungry Hill*?' Jack said. 'Never heard of it!'

'Based on the famous novel by Daphne du Maurier,' I said.

'Don't read books by women.'

'While I was going round Ireland looking for a castle for the film,' Brian continued, 'I visited Bantry House, owned by Mrs Shellswell-Whyte, the great-granddaughter of the Earl of Bantry, Ambassador to France at the time of the French Revolution. He had brought back countless treasures from an auction at Versailles, where nobody had dared bid for royal possessions. These included a set of tapestries in mint condition made for the wedding of Marie Antoinette which now hung in the gloom of Bantry House. Mrs Shellswell-Whyte had shut up most of the place and lived only in the great hall with its huge granite pillars – she ate in one corner, cooked in another, wrote in another and slept in the fourth. She asked me to stay for lunch and called a boy, giving him a shilling. "Get on your bicycle, Patrick, and go into the village and buy four herrings." The boy returned with the herrings and that was our lunch, consumed in this faded splendour.

'And there was the Earl of Fingall, the premier Earl of Ireland. "Please use my castle, Brian, because I have no money and my roof is leaking." He could not afford to run his castle either, poor man. In the enormous dining room he had built a small modern house, but the windows in the little house did not coincide with the big windows so one looked out on to a piece of faded tapestry or a badly painted ancestor. On the landing were more than a dozen receptacles of all sorts, strategically placed to catch the rain drops, which made a charming musical sound. So we fixed his roof for him.'

'How much does a film company pay to use a castle?' Jack asked, unable to suppress his curiosity.

'No idea, really,' Brian said, grandly vague. 'I leave that to my people. But *thousands* and *thousands*.'

It was clear most of the guests knew Jack was strapped for cash, and they seemed to enjoy his discomfort over the stories of leaking roofs and needy landowners. He went quiet for most of the lunch, but was revived enough as the pudding was brought in to launch a renewed assault on the queers who had infiltrated the Irish government and were destroying the country. I waited for Brian to strike, but he said nothing.

At the very end of lunch Brian innocently mentioned the name of a wealthy landowner known to everyone as the Captain, who unlike most of his peers actually had some money. 'Good friend of mine,' Jack said, no doubt relieved to have someone of financial substance introduced into the conversation. 'Capital fellow.'

'I don't pretend to know him as well as *you*, of course,' Brian said. 'Not *intimately*, that is. But I have stayed in his magnificent house. Beautiful and extensive grounds, as I'm sure you know. I was there once with a good-looking blond actor who said he had heard stories about the Captain. That he was *like that*. The actor had been put up in a huge bed in the Empire Room and locked the door in case the stories were true. Just as he was falling asleep, the doors of the great wardrobe in the room slowly opened to reveal a secret staircase. Up it came the Captain, who approached the actor's bed. "I say, it's absolutely freezing. I'm perishing with cold." The actor, whose austerity was not oppressive, threw back the bedclothes and said, "Get in." In the morning, when he told me the story I asked him how it had been. "Rather like being made love to by a plank."'

'That is an *outrageous* story to tell,' Jack said, breathing heavily. 'A completely unsubstantiated and malicious slander.'

'I agree that you shouldn't take the word of an actor,' Brian said. 'Not this one, anyway. But the Captain's predilection was later confirmed by a nun – a Mother Superior, no less.'

'*Preposterous!*' Jack had turned tomato-red.

'The Captain had loaned the dower house just inside the gates of the castle to some nuns, whose convent in Armagh was being decorated,' Brian continued blithely. 'I was going for a stroll through the grounds and came across the Mother Superior. She asked me to try to persuade the Captain to go to Mass on Sunday and I said I would. At that moment a handsome young Irishman came through the castle gates, tall and strong with clusters of dark curls. "Who's *that*?" I exclaimed, in spite of myself. "Oh sir," she said simply, without condemnation, "*That's* the Captain's little weakness."'

The Broke Titled Gentleman left the house in a rage, after offering brief thanks to his host and hostess, foregoing an offer of coffee, brandy and cigars. 'You were very hard on Jack,' Lady Ursula said. 'He's harmless, really – just silly and stupid.'

'He asked for it,' I said.

'And got a filleting with a very sharp knife,' Stephen said. 'Well done, Brian.'

Whenever we went into Kinsale, Brian always visited the parish church, St Multose – one of the oldest in Ireland – to light candles and pray before the Virgin. It was a routine I had become used to in London, where he had favourite churches all over the city, and on any journey we always made a detour to visit one to light a candle. 'To remember the dead, and pray for friends who are sick or in need.'

St Multose was also the church, as Brian told it, where he had *triumphed* in his performance playing Augustus in Stephen's play, *Born to be King*. Over dinner one night, Stephen described the occasion in glowing terms: 'You could have been a great actor, Brian, I'm sure.'

'Oh yes. Except, if you remember, I have trouble memorising lines.'

'I remember very well,' Stephen said, smiling. While it had become evident during rehearsals that Brian was every inch an emperor, it was also clear he was an emperor of few words. The lengthy and flowery speeches penned for Augustus became terse and erratic one-liners. The problem was resolved by dressing a good-looking youth in a toga to play a slave, who crouched at Brian's feet with a copy of the play. Every time Augustus dried, he would make an imperial gesture towards the slave, who would quietly prompt him. 'It worked very well,' Stephen said.

'I'm sure nobody noticed.'

'I'm not sure about *that*!'

Brian spoke of previous stage experiences. As an art student in Toronto, he told us, he had appeared as a character called Dreams in a Christmas fantasy entitled *Castles in the Air*. 'Poor Dreams had no costume, but the wardrobe mistress draped tulle around me haphazardly. I had to run on stage to this pool and say, "Greetings to you, fairy of the pool." On my first entrance someone put their foot on the last layer of the delicately pinned tulle. By the time I arrived at the pool the flimsy material had been stripped off me and I was quite naked. It raised such an enormous laugh I repeated the performance every night.' Brian put his hand to his mouth, chuckling at the memory. 'And there was this character in the play called the Enchanter who was surrounded by beautiful girls. I coached him a bit on the delivery of his lines. I had to say to him, "Enchanter, do all these dear little girls belong to you?" He replied, "Yes, Dreams, they do. Not only their dear little bodies but their dear little, ahhh, souls." That rocked Toronto.'

'I had no idea you had spent time in Canada,' Stephen said.

Brian explained that after being demobbed from the British Army, at the end of the First World War, he took a government offer of £100 and free passage to Canada, and took ship for Montreal. He found work running a camp of eighty men constructing a golf course at Tecumseh, a French settlement on Lake St Clair, close to Detroit, and made enough money to go to Ontario College of Art in Toronto. As a painter he felt he needed a shorter name, and became Desmond Hurst. One of the people attracted to his early work was Walter Chrysler, owner of the eponymous automobile company. 'He saw a lake scene of mine for which I was asking eighty dollars. Chrysler said, "If you take that terrible pink cloud out, I'll buy it." I looked at him and replied, "Mr Chrysler, you may be able to get your clothes made to order – though they don't look it – but you can't order your painting from me like that." Later, I heard he asked, "Who is that insolent Irish bastard?"'

'All this going into your book?' Stephen asked.

'If Boswell there can remember any of it. Now listen, talking of that, I want to try out titles on you. I'm bloody annoyed I gave Gerald Hamilton *The Way It Was With Me*. That should have been it. Oh, well. But how about this? I have a very clear memory of an incident during the making of *Riders to the Sea*. I'm normally a non-smoker but I'd had a long day and been given a cigarette and needed a puff. I went up to an old woman standing in the doorway of her cottage, with a fine weathered face and a long red petticoat falling in sculptural folds to the ground. "Could you give me a light, please?" She said she had no matches but would bring me a coal from the fire, and returned blowing on this sod of turf. She held it out with a regal gesture and gave me a light. I might have been somewhat profuse in my thanks, for she then said in the pure language of Synge, "Sure, 'tis nothing at all, sir – wouldn't I like a light, an old widow woman travelling the road alone?"'

There was a respectful silence while we digested these moving and beautiful words, but I could not resist puncturing the poetic mood. 'Surely you're not going to call your autobiography *Old Widow Woman*?'

Brian sighed, and turned to Lady Ursula. 'You see what I am up against with this callow youth – the insensitivity, the vulgarity, the crude humour? No, Christopher – the title I have in mind is *Travelling the Road*.'

I never liked it. It always seemed too top-of-the-morning,

tinker Irish and contrived. Brian was right – it should have been called *The Way It Was With Me*. In the coming months I tried to persuade him to change it but he rejected all alternatives. Even insensitive, vulgar, crude humour failed. How about *Travelling the Road in a Rolls*, I suggested, or *Paddy Takes the Low Road*? At one point, when we were cross with one another, I even proposed *Old Twank*.

Brian would not be moved, so the autobiography became *Travelling the Road*. I scrawled the title in pencil on a cover sheet on top of the growing pile of half-written manuscript and interview transcripts I kept in an old cardboard box. After a while, I reluctantly typed it in capital letters, and that remains the title of the unpublished autobiography.

It was decided that we would fly back to London rather than go by ship, and arrived at Cork airport one morning when it was still dark. We had left Kinsale so early that we had not eaten breakfast, hoping to have some at the airport, but could find no restaurant. Scarcely anyone seemed to be about, except for a figure swabbing the floor of the bar. 'This place opening soon?' Brian asked.

'Open now.'

'Any chance of some breakfast?'

'What does it look like? This is a bar, not a restaurant.'

'I see. Very well – we'll have two Irish coffees.'

The thought of Irish coffee, so early in the morning, made my stomach churn. The man with the bucket and mop went behind the bar, poured two double measures of whiskey into tumblers, and banged them down in front of us. 'My God, I can't drink *that*!' Brian said. 'I want something with coffee in it. That's why I ordered Irish coffees!'

'The coffee's cold and the fockin' cream is off,' the man said, returning to his bucket.

'What an unpleasant individual!' Brian said to me. 'I wonder what hellhole of a country spawned him?'

'Bri, he's Irish.'

'Do you think so? I doubt it very much.' Brian looked across at barman and bucket. 'Perhaps you're right – let's hope the bastard emigrates to America quick!'

'But think about it, Bri – he's the first miserable sod we've met on the whole trip. Except for the Broke Titled Gentleman.'

'Perhaps the government employs this surly barkeep as an educational tool – to prepare the soft-mannered folk of County Cork for the rude assault of London.' Brian smiled. 'Had a nice time in Ireland?'

'Very nice. The natives are not as bad as one's led to believe. Charming and amusing and original, most of them. A special lot – off the evolutionary scale. And they don't seem to hate the English, as advertised, which was a relief. I love the place. Thanks, Bri.'

'No, no, they don't hate the English. Well, in private, of course. Or if intoxicated. But even then, they only hate the English as a race, not as individuals. Mostly, they just think the English odd – a case, even I have to allow, of the pot calling the kettle black.' Brian sighed. 'Ireland – such a little place to be so greatly loved.'

PART V

London

On one of those damp and cheerless mid-winter nights in London, when the cold enters the bones and the spirits slump, I wandered the wet streets with Brian in search of a taxi. But nothing came. We must have walked for half an hour and the only taxis that passed were filled with provocatively warm and comfortable-looking passengers: 'Smug bastards!' Brian muttered. His health was always fragile in winter, when the damp air aggravated a lung condition, and as we went from corner to corner he grew increasingly distressed. I could see that he was slowing down and could scarcely breathe. He stopped, trying to calm himself, and used his inhaler. 'St Thérèse will find a taxi for us,' he said. Finally, he turned towards the railings at the side of the pavement and grabbed them with both hands for support. He lifted his head towards heaven and cried, 'All I want is a bloody taxi! Is that asking too much?'

At that moment, directly on cue, a black taxi came around the corner with its orange 'For Hire' light glowing warmly in the gloom. St Thérèse had heard the call. Brian crossed himself and muttered a small prayer of thanks – and a few words of contrition. Inside the taxi he looked a little shamefaced: 'It was unnecessary to have shouted.'

'Who is St Thérèse?' I asked. 'The patron saint of black taxis?'

'My personal saint. The one I love above all others.'

'More than St Bridget?'

'St Bridget's spread a bit thin looking after all those Irish.'

Later, he explained the reasons for his devotion. 'I had

developed very severe asthma and couldn't go fifty steps without a large inhaler. I was really very ill and told Thérèse, "Life is not worth living as I am living it now." There was no obvious miracle, but slowly I began to get better. Then I had a vision. In the house where Thérèse was brought up, Les Buissonets in Lisieux, there is a panel of plate glass in the front hall on the right of the fireplace through which one can look into the dining room, where the saint sat for her last supper before becoming a nun. In my vision, however – which I experienced in the afternoon, when I was wide awake – I looked through a door on the *left* side of the fireplace. Everyone in the dining room seemed to be made of particles of light and they were turning Thérèse in her chair to face me. I knew that if I blinked, the vision would be over – and, of course, this is what happened. I had to blink and the vision disappeared.

'On my next visit to Lisieux, I went to pray in the house. But I could see no door on the left of the fireplace, just a wall covered with habits and overcoats. Nevertheless, I told the two nuns in charge of the house about my vision. "But there is a door," one said excitedly. "Behind the coats." They opened the door, took me in, and sat me in the seat where Thérèse had sat. Ever since my vision, Thérèse has been my saint and spiritual companion.'

Over the years Brian made regular pilgrimages to the saint's house in Lisieux, and made extravagant contributions to the Carmelite nunnery nearby where she enclosed herself. His intended gifts to the nuns were not always appropriate. On one occasion he was dissuaded by a friend from showing up with a suitcase full of black silk stockings. Brian looked puzzled. 'But nuns wear stockings, don't they?'

'Only in pornographic movies!'

These pilgrimages were greeted with a certain amount of scepticism by his friends. 'Is Brian *really* going on a pilgrimage to Lisieux?'

'Yes.'

'Is he walking?'

'No – but he's kneeling in the Bentley.'

St Thérèse entered Brian's life when he bought Wardrobe's Lodge, a Queen Anne house outside Princes Risborough, near Aylesbury. 'An old Breton priest called Father Dreves showed up in the village, where he administered to eleven Catholics in a tin hut. He prayed for a miracle in order to build a church to St Thérèse – adding to his prayer the practical detail that this would require three thousand pounds. Three different people came to see him in the following months, without knowing his ambition, and each gave him a thousand pounds. So today in the middle of Princes Risborough this curious Byzantine tower rises, with the image of St Thérèse in it, matching the one in Lisieux. I gave the church twelve stained-glass windows by Pilgrim Wetton, depicting the life and family of St Thérèse, dressed in Victorian costume.'

Brian began to read about St Thérèse and was deeply affected by her book, *The Story of a Soul*, with its simple stories of the joy and anguish of a young girl's devotion to God. At a time when enclosed orders practised extreme physical penance, and believed that true holiness was the prerogative of the chosen few, Thérèse rejected physical austerity and advocated the spirituality of the 'little way' – a simple Christian creed suggesting that it is within everyone's reach to do everything in their lives with love. (The saint had an earthly and very human attachment to her foot warmer.) A Carmelite nun at fifteen, Thérèse died of consumption at twenty-four, but was canonised in less than thirty years – an unheard-of occurrence in the Catholic Church. She remains the most popular of modern saints, and Mother Teresa of Calcutta took her name out of devotion to 'The Little Flower'.

'Many miracles were attributed to St Thérèse, including

the cure of a young priest whose lungs were completely gone,' Brian told me. 'And Edith Piaf, the French singer, regained her sight because of her. She had developed a cataract after her birth and was blind for almost three years. Doctors despaired. Her grandmother took her to Lisieux, and afterwards she could see. Piaf always believed this to have been a miracle, and wore a medal of Thérèse around her neck, and had a picture of the Little Flower beside her bed.

After the war, Brian bought the lease on a small Elizabethan house three miles from the Carmelite monastery at Aylesford, which has close connections to St Thérèse. 'I often visited and became a very great friend of Father Malachy Lynch, who had completed the restoration of Aylesford from nothing, turning the Friary into one of the most beautiful in England and a great shrine.' Over the years Brian gave the Carmelites jewels, paintings and sculptures – including a wooden carving of St Anne by Riemenschneider, the only work by this artist still in private hands – and a valuable copy of a Raphael.

Brian assured me in all seriousness that St Thérèse was on board one hundred per cent for the movie and working hard on our behalf. 'I can practically hear her grinding out the miracles in the back room.'

'Presumably, saints are above the line?'*

'*Hovering* above the line. The Little Flower will have a separate card in last position of the opening credits – *Miracles by St Thérèse.*'

Once the first draft of the screenplay actually existed, Brian became promiscuous in its dissemination. While I waited patiently for St Thérèse to work a financial miracle, the script

*A film term in which everyone with credits at the beginning of a movie – principal stars, producer, writer, and director – is said to be 'above the line', and all other credits, technicians, crew and so on, are 'below the line'.

had been copied and sent out to various theatrical types, and I was told to remain open and receptive to whatever comments and notes this brilliant group might make. Brian then telephoned to say that he had recently met a *fascinating* young continental playwright whose extraordinary insights were invaluable, and he was eager for us to meet.

I confess that I did not like Sven from the moment I clapped eyes on him, coiled like a poisonous snake in a chair in Brian's front room. A thin, tubular figure with a long insect head, he sat nursing a cup of tea with his legs tucked beneath him. He was encased from head to foot in a uniform of shabby black, shiny from wear – tight black jeans, black raincoat, and a black V-necked sweater, mottled with age and worn next to the skin. Although only in his early thirties, he was prematurely and patchily bald, a state accentuated by a curtain of long, greasy hair that fell on to narrow shoulders. A sharp goatee beard jutted from beneath a clean-shaven upper lip. Tiny reptilian eyes swam behind bottle-bottom granny glasses, and his smile was a cold baring of yellow saw-teeth. No, I did not like the bastard. My revulsion was instant, a chemical reaction of unreasoned animal prejudice, deadly accurate and just. Sven was the enemy.

Brian introduced us with the voice he adopted to convey the presence of great and original talent. It also meant I was to show respect and be on my best behaviour. Sven was *prominent* among avant-garde political and theatrical circles in Norway, Brian said, and was in London to put on a play at the National Theatre. He had *very generously* consented to read the screenplay and offer ideas. After an exchange of mutually hypocritical pleasantries, I sat down and prepared to do battle.

Unschooled in the numerous treacheries employed in the art of film-making, I had never before been blooded in the brutal ritual, inevitable as nightfall, in which the screenwriter is slowly stripped of power. For months, I had plied my lonely trade and filled blank pages with stuff for people to do and say, while Brian had been reduced to the impotent role of producer-in-waiting. But now that the first draft existed, a campaign was about to be launched to take the script over, page by page and line by line, to regain authority and control.

Sven was merely a dispensable scout sent out ahead of the ruthless army of critics who would follow in his wake, the first dog to lift its leg and make its mark. One after another, director, actors and others would fall on the screenplay like jungle beasts ripping at fresh kill. In due course, lovers, typists, friends, lunch companions, barmen and, in our case, a cross-section of the Brigade of Guards and Ronnie the milkman, would be consulted. Inexperienced as I was, I knew instinctively that Sven had to be defeated.

'To correct a mistake!' Sven announced flatly in a thick Scandinavian accent immediately after Brian's introduction. 'It is not a play we are making – and not at National Theatre, which is government and therefore not correct platform. Our production is gay political statement in dramatic form, from Maoist perspective.'

'I'm Labour,' Brian said, nodding approval.

Sven uncoiled long, bony legs from beneath him to expose thickly socked feet clad in clod-hopping black sandals wide as dinner plates. *Sandals!* I felt a malicious rush of pleasure in the knowledge that Brian had an oft-expressed loathing for grown men moving about the city in sandals, and willed him to look down at the footwear of the Maoist Viking dramaturge.

'Sven is very active in gay rights,' Brian said. 'He is organising a Great Big Riot to be held in Trafalgar Square.'

'*Rally*,' Sven corrected gently. 'I'm involved in organising Scandinavian section of a gay rights *rally*.'

'If you want Brian to be there,' I said, 'be sure to invite the Household Cavalry.'

Sven looked puzzled.

'Sven has read the script and I am eager to hear his thoughts,' Brian said, shooting me a warning look. 'We welcome constructive criticism, don't we, Christopher?'

'Oh, yes,' I said. 'We're *mad* for constructive criticism!'

Sven straightened himself, and placed his tea-cup to one side, ready for business. 'This is objective analysis and critique,' he said, casting a patronising look in my direction. 'Not personal – is understood?'

'Of course,' Brian said, nodding gravely.

'Is understood?' Sven said to me.

'Is understood.'

'To forget the subject matter on its own – I read the script to give objective opinion. Not to comment on religion being opium of people, but for drama and speeches and so on, *ja*? How audience react to this? *Ja*?'

It was not easy to follow Sven's arctic accent, odd syntax, and monotonous delivery, but I nodded. Brian adopted his most serious look.

'It must be said that approach is bourgeois. Using historical plot is conventional – if Bible story can be accepted as history.' Sven sniggered. 'But beginning, middle and ending – three acts like play. This is not interesting structure. No free form. This makes old-fashioned film. Not using devices of Fellini, Antonioni, others.'

Brian looked as if he were beginning to entertain doubts about Sven. The crack about religion being the opium of the people, and innuendo about the questionable historicity of the Bible, would not have gone down well. Furthermore, Brian held strong views on plot and structure, and was lukewarm at best in regard to the work of Fellini and Antonioni. He also objected to overt politics in film, was sensitive to charges of being old-fashioned, and did not consider the Bible bourgeois. And he had not yet noticed the sandals . . .

'Modern audience need shock, surprise – political challenge,'

Sven continued. 'Is necessary to confront them with unusual to attack middle-class values.'

Enough was enough. It was time to take Sven on. 'If I understand you correctly,' I said, placing my fingertips together in a spire and attempting an intellectual squint, 'you are saying that we need a more radical form – that the script needs to be subversive. A film for the people.'

'This is good. *Ja*.'

'Perhaps we could take a more satirical approach?'

Sven looked interested and began to nod.

'Do the whole thing in the style of a *Carry On* film.'

'*Carry On* film?' Sven asked carefully, unsure whether this was some cutting-edge political form unknown to him.

'A classic English movie genre beloved by the proletariat,' I explained. 'We could get Kenneth Williams to play Herod. A disappointment for Sir Michael, no doubt, but he has not previously distinguished himself in this demanding discipline.'

'Kenneth Williams?' Sven said. 'I do not know this actor.'

I rose from my seat and did a camp rendition of Kenneth Williams playing Herod which I hoped Sven would find deeply offensive. I minced across the room, my right arm flapping a limp wrist. 'Infamy, infamy – they've all got it *in for me*!'

'That's enough, Christopher,' Brian said.

But I was not to be stopped. 'How about Barbara Windsor for Mariamne? Miss Windsor is an English actress revered by the working class.' I winked at Sven. '*Big Bristols!*'

'Big Bristols?' Sven repeated blankly.

'Imagine this,' I said, in full imaginative flight. 'Interior, Herod's Bedchamber, Night: Herod pulls Mariamne towards him – "You have the most luscious melons in all Israel!" Mariamne – "Yeah, an' all Lebanon an' all."' I attempted an impersonation of the throaty Windsoresque cluck. 'Miss Windsor has a vulgar and suggestive laugh.'

'*Basta!*' Brian turned to Sven, shaking his head in apology. 'You will have observed that my writer does not always display the gravitas the subject-matter demands. His concentration dissolves around lunchtime – he needs to be given Guinness and sausages. But to be serious, nobody has ever suggested – and I think I know a fair bit about it – that Herod was queer.'

Sven had been reduced to horrified silence by my extravagant fairy routine, but now his eyes burned with anger. His voice was low and dangerous, hissing disapproval. 'I am surprised to hear this word spoken. Here. In this house.'

It was Brian's turn to look puzzled.

'He means the word "queer",' I explained. 'I happen to agree with you, Sven, that "gay" as a term is here to stay. And that queer has a pejorative resonance when used by people like, say, my father. But Brian doesn't think "gay" really does the job. And honestly, it couldn't be a more clumping misnomer for some of the old homos we know – could it, Bri?'

'You wonder how it came about and how it stuck,' Brian said. '*Gay* is such an odd word to adopt. Used to be used of prostitutes, you know. A gay woman was on the game. Then it was just used for fast company. Then for people who were witty or a bit of fun. Now us.' Brian waved a hand between Sven and himself, excluding me with a jerk of his head in my direction. 'That one's *normal*, would you believe?'

The disclosure meant that Sven now regarded me with open hostility.

'You go to a party,' Brian continued, oblivious to his guest's seething disapproval, 'and see some gloomy closet queen from the Foreign Office, or somewhere, standing in the corner dressed in a dozen shades of grey, and somebody says, "That one over there, he's *gay*."'

'When Miserable Sod would probably more accurately describe the gentleman in question.'

'Or Boring Bugger,' Brian said, laughing.

Sven could not believe his ears. 'You talk like this?' He

seemed about to launch a scathing political diatribe but something made him pull back. He changed tack, and turned to me, eyes sparkling with spite. 'One more note on script.'

'*Ja?*'

'The angels.'

'What about them?'

'You have *angels* in script.'

'Yes. But no wings, harps or halos, you notice. We held back on the feathers and accessories. Just simple white smocks. The audience will be made aware that they're angels by their extraordinary, unearthly beauty and physical perfection. Casting here is so important that Brian himself will probably undertake the ordeal.'

'*Angels!*' Sven let out a nasal fart of contempt. Unaware that he had moved into an area of utmost danger, he teetered on the edge of an abyss, his snowshoe sandals skidding and slipping beneath him.

'You don't *like* the angels?' I coaxed him gently towards certain destruction.

'This is for simple people. This is *stupid*.'

'I'm sorry you think so.'

'All aware people will laugh.' Sven had thrown himself into the abyss and was tumbling head over sandals into the bottomless dark, long as the arctic night of his frozen homeland. There was a moment of silence.

'Christopher,' Brian said, in a neutral, measured voice.

'Yes, Brian?'

He had pulled himself upright in his chair, and sat with his hands together in an attitude that signalled the delivery of an important pronouncement. 'Make a note.'

'Yes, Brian.'

'Remove the angels from the script.'

It was my turn for outrage. My anguish was genuine, but my shrill voice sounded horribly like my imitation of Kenneth Williams. '*Take out the angels?*'

'Yes. They will not do.'

Sven smirked in triumph.

'There is great merit in your previous idea to have creatures of unearthly beauty to play the angels,' Brian said. 'It was an idea inspired, I believe, by the *queer* Italian film director Pasolini, who used the device in *The Passion of St Matthew* – a truly *great* religious film our progressive friend here would no doubt find risible. However, on reflection, I would like to return to my original concept.' Brian raised his arms towards the ceiling to illustrate the grandeur of his vision. 'Magnificent angels on high, seen from a great distance against a heavenly cloud formation. Their giant wings of snow-white feathers bathed in an arc of luminous light glinting off unearthly, golden halos. And the sound of a celestial choir made up of a hundred boys with sweet unbroken voices piping divine music. Not symbolic angels played by hunks in nightshirts – but proper angels with wings and harps. A real show!'

'Right you are,' I said happily. 'One Great Big Angel Scene coming up!'

Sven gaped at us, confused and lost.

Brian rose from his chair with great formality, buttoning his jacket. 'It is very good of you to give us your time, Mr Christiansen.'

'Eriksen,' Sven said feebly.

'I wish you every success in your avant-garde efforts,' Brian continued. 'You must understand, however, that we are not undertaking an experiment. Our project is not an improvised indulgence put on for an evening by a group of unemployed actors in the back room of a pub. This is not some free-form political rant in black leather and old Norse. We have assembled a cast of some of Britain's finest actors and are involved in the making of a Major Motion Picture.'

'You ask my opinion!' Sven said, unwisely adopting righteous indignation as a weapon of last resort.

'Yes, I have heard your opinion, such as it is. It differs from the myriad critics – some of them thinking people, you'll be surprised to hear – who over my long career have said many things, but never that I was a simpleton or stupid.'

'I did not mean this personal.'

'And, I might add, that when it comes to homosexual politics, homosexual nomenclature, or good old-fashioned homosexual screwing, I do not need any lectures from you. I have been practising buggery and its related arts since before you were born, and I have reached a level damn near close to perfection. Christopher, be so kind as to show Mr Johannsen the door.'

The fight had gone out of Sven. All the confidence and superiority had drained away, and even outrage had deserted him. He was left silent and off-balance. As I crossed into the hallway he padded obediently after me, his vast sandals making a clownish slapping sound as he moved from carpet to floorboard. Magnanimous in victory, I held open the front door: 'God speed, old fruit!'

Without a word, the routed Norseman hopped across the threshold and scampered away. I returned to the front room to find Brian reading a newspaper as if nothing had happened. 'That was some pair of sandals on that bird!'

Brian lowered his paper: 'What an *utter* shit!'

Work on the Big Bestseller meant that I began to spend even more time at Kinnerton Street than in the early days of the Box Office Blockbuster – three or four mornings a week, on average – and usually stayed on to cook lunch. I began to meet not only those people involved in the film, but every good friend of Brian's. The close female friends tended to be either *grandes dames* or grotesques, both formidable in their different ways. The most magnificent of the *grandes dames* was Baroness Moura Budberg, a character who might have stepped from the pages of Tolstoy, and who grew very fond of my scrambled eggs. Moura lunched regularly at Kinnerton Street, arriving punctually at 12.45 in a black taxi. I was often the cook on these occasions and the first time I asked how she liked her eggs she growled, '*Baveuse*.'

I nodded and looked across to Brian for help as I backed out of the room on my way down to the kitchen. 'Runny!'

Born Countess Zakrevskaya, Moura became Countess Benckendorff by her first marriage, Baroness Budberg by her second, and had known war, revolution, political imprisonment, exile and high-flying literary love as the *maîtresse littéraire* of both Maxim Gorky and H. G. Wells. She also led a strange, parallel secret life in the world of espionage that would not be revealed until long after her death.

Moura's friendship with Brian had been such a long one that after an exchange of small jokes and gossip, they would often sit facing each other in their armchairs for long stretches saying nothing. I once watched Moura disappear for half-hour behind the *Daily Mail* as she studied the racing form. After much deliberation she asked me to phone her bookie and place her 'usual' bet on a certain horse. I made the call and told the bookie somewhat grandly to put on the 'Baroness's Usual', vaguely entertaining visions of diamond tiaras and pre-revolutionary gold roubles at risk. 'Right,' came the brisk reply, 'twenty-five pence each way it is.'

At another lunch I noticed that the baroness's underclothes had slipped halfway down her legs, and threatened to end up around her ankles. I passed close to Brian and discreetly explained the situation. He nodded and I sat back down.

'Moura,' Brian called loudly, for the baroness was somewhat deaf, 'your drawers are coming down.'

Unembarrassed, Moura stood and hiked up the wayward bloomers. She sat down heavily and resumed reading her paper. This stolid display of unconcern was one of the many profound Russian qualities that Moura possessed. 'It means being resilient to the point of absurdity,' I was told later by Peter Ustinov, whose mother was a lifelong friend of Moura's. 'It also means being absolutely unsurprised or unembarrassed by anything.'

He illustrated this quality with an anecdote. 'One day Moura thought she heard somebody at the door of her London flat. She got out of her bath stark-naked and cautiously opened the front door. There was nobody there, so she went out to look over the banisters when the door slammed behind her. Her solution to the problem was very simple and it didn't need much consideration. She emptied sand from a fire bucket, which was on the landing, put it over her head and went out into the street to look for help. The logic is not concerned with personal modesty but with being recognised.'

Forever at the call of Grub Street, when I first met Moura I was writing articles on great historical escapes and extraordinary prison stories – another of the *Observer*'s ideas for a ripping magazine series. 'Moura was banged up in chokey by the Bolsheviks,' Brian said. 'You should write about that.'

'I was imprisoned after the revolution, yes,' Moura said, laughing. 'An interesting experience, but a long time ago.' After some badgering from Brian – 'The boy's got to eat!' – she reluctantly agreed to talk to me about her experiences, and I arranged to go to her flat.

When the baroness had been collected by a black taxi at precisely 2.45, Brian said, 'You'll enjoy chatting with Moura. It's like a Tsarist museum over there. You'll get authentic chunks of Russian history washed down with gallons of vodka. Stories of revolution and Rasputin, all told without a hint of emotion. I have never known Moura to express any external emotion whatsoever, or speak of her feelings. I once brought her back flowers from Gorky Park, in Moscow, and expected a Great Big Russian Emotional Scene as I handed them over. But when I offered my flowers, picked early that same morning, she ignored them and took the bottle of vodka which I had in my hand and said, "Let's have a drink." It was not until long afterwards that Moura confessed she had pressed every single flower between the leaves of a Russian Bible.'

I went to visit Moura in her rambling Victorian flat, rattled by the traffic of the Cromwell Road, later that week. The front door was opened by a uniformed maid and I was led into a room crammed with books, which had spilled from the shelves and lay heaped on the tops of tables and cabinets. The mantelpiece groaned beneath the weight of numerous pieces of jade, antique silver and Japanese ivory *netsuke*, so exquisitely carved that lines on the hands and faces of the small figures could be made out. Various mementoes hung from the wall: a solid gold Russian icon, a Persian carpet depicting the Tsar's wedding breakfast, and various portraits of Wells, Gorky and Moura herself. There was a black and white photograph of her aged eighteen – a full-faced Russian beauty with wide cheekbones and large, intelligent eyes.

Her entrance was heralded by the rhythmic tapping of her silver-topped cane in the corridor. She entertained from the stronghold of a large, comfortable armchair strategically placed by a table with glasses and a bottle of Russian vodka upon it. Moura served it neat, throwing a small, full glass back in one.

'Aldous Huxley once recommended a clairvoyant,' she said. 'The man told me, "You have a much more interesting biography than personality."' Moura laughed. 'I'm afraid it's true. I'm not much of a talker.' To my surprise, I found her a very difficult person to interview. If it had not been for a lurking sense of fun, she would have been daunting. She seemed bored by the past, dismissing great historical events with a shrug, while whole decades tended to be condensed into a single sentence.

Almost everyone of note from her era had sat in this room drinking Moura's Russian vodka: politicians, intellectuals, film magnates, directors, actors, and of course her favourites, the writers – Somerset Maugham, Robert Graves, Ernest Hemingway, Arthur Koestler, Graham Greene, David Garnett, Virginia Woolf – a Who's Who of English literature. But she was reluctant to talk about them, and only gave up the occasional titbit: she heartily disliked George Bernard Shaw, for instance, and described him as possessing a pettiness, 'a nagging quality', and told him to his face that he behaved like a woman; Arnold Bennett, Moura said, lost all inspiration the moment his actress wife made him give up wearing shirts with myosotis flowers on them.

A friend arrived during one of our conversations, and Moura said, 'Come in, you're not interrupting – I'm just telling the story of my life.' The version I was being given had been expurgated and judiciously edited for posterity, and I listened politely and unknowing, and asked no hard questions. As a young nobody I felt excited and privileged to be in the presence of a person who had lived so close to history and its personalities, and was flattered to be treated as a friend. How could I know I was in the presence of the *grande dame* of spin?

Moura was born Marie Zakrevskaya, in 1892, the third and youngest daughter of Count Ignaty Platonovitch Zakrevski, a wealthy Russian senator who had estates near Kiev. The summers were spent in the country and the winters immersed in St Petersburg society. 'My life before the revolution was the usual one of a rather rich family. I remember a herd of governesses.' Her father also surrounded her with an equal number of tutors and encouraged her education. By the time she was thirteen she spoke five languages – English, Italian, German, French and Russian – and was already a voracious reader.

'As a young girl I was very protected and naïve. I remember sitting next to Norman Douglas, the novelist, who liked to shock. He turned to me and said, "Have you ever had syphilis?" I had no idea what he was talking about – was this an exotic food, some eastern spice or type of English marmalade? My reply silenced him when I shrugged and said, "I don't remember.''

After her presentation to the Tsar she fell in love, at the age of eighteen, with a diplomat attached to the Russian Embassy in Berlin, a member of the Von Benckendorff family who owned large estates in Estonia. The young couple pursued a glamorous social round within the stiff corset of diplomatic life, but even at that age Moura had the ability to make herself noticed – 'Who is that Queen of Sheba?' the Kaiser asked when she arrived at an official reception wearing a plum velvet gown with a silver head-dress, and three-yard train embroidered in gold.

At the outbreak of the First World War the couple returned to St Petersburg with a one-year-old son. Despite the war, life remained an elegant entertainment for the aristocracy as they dined and danced, skated on the frozen Neva, and went to the opera. Moura fulfilled the role dictated to her by her position in society, and although her life was cushioned it was also formal and circumscribed.

She met Rasputin a number of times, as he moved in the same circles. The 'mad monk', I discovered, was her least favourite subject. 'It's really boring. Honestly, I'm not trying to make nothing of the story but it's . . . corny. There was nothing about him except that he was a dirty, smelly peasant.' The comment was not that of a reactionary Russian émigré aristocrat, but one of exasperation from someone who was repelled not only by the man himself, but also by the cult and legend that grew up around him. Moura remained staunchly unimpressed by the charismatic villain. 'He was very shrewd and because he had a certain hypnotic power he was able to stop the Tsarevitch bleeding, and this gave him influence over the Tsarina. But in every Russian village we always used to have an old man or woman who would be called to stop a cow bleeding. I asked a doctor here in London about it and he told me that you can stop bleeding by hypnosis but that it doesn't cure anything.'

The revolution of 1917 reduced Moura's comfortable and ordered world to chaos, and she reacted by being tremendously excited – 'I knew at once that it was a great event.' The aristocracy lived by selling what they could – the plum velvet dress and embroidered train which had startled the Kaiser was bought by peasants for two sacks of flour. Her husband remained trapped on his Estonian estates with their two small children.

To make money she took jobs as a translator – a trade that was to last a lifetime, in which she translated around fifty books ranging from the crime novels of Georges Simenon to the memoirs of the Russian socialist writer Alexander Herzen – and, of course, the work of Maxim Gorky. It was during her work as a translator that she met Robert Bruce Lockhart – the unofficial go-between for the British and the Bolsheviks during the revolution – who fell in love with her. It was a very Russian romance, with horse-drawn sled rides through the snow, gypsy music and dancing in smoky restaurants, staying up all night to watch the sun rise over the Kremlin – and the thrill of living in dangerous and historic times. 'A Russian of the Russians,' is how Lockhart described her. 'She had a lofty disregard for all the pettiness of life and a courage which was proof against all cowardice. Her vitality, due perhaps to an iron constitution, was immense and invigorated everybody with whom she came into contact. Where she loved, there was her world, and her philosophy of life made her mistress of all the consequences.'

In August 1918, there was an assassination attempt on Lenin, and Lockhart was immediately suspected of masterminding the plot. He was imprisoned in the Kremlin, reserved for the most serious political prisoners, and lived in the shadow of the firing squad. The betting among the guards that Lockhart would be shot was two-to-one on. Moura took him daily presents of clothes, books, tobacco, ham and coffee.

Lenin recovered, and Lockhart was exchanged for the Russian Ambassador to England, who had been arrested in reprisal. Moura was now arrested, because of her association with Lockhart, and put into a cell with fifty-two female political prisoners. She was interrogated endlessly, slept on the floor and lived off a diet of potato soup. 'Prison was a most beneficial thing for me because I was a very spoilt young person, totally divorced from ordinary life, and the first time I saw what life was like was when I went to prison. It didn't frighten or cow me in any way. I was interested in it, excited by something that was different. I have nothing to complain about. A short time in prison is a very good school.'

After a month of squalid overcrowding, she was put into solitary confinement and found it almost as interesting as the communal cell. Starved of books or conversation, she made friends with a rat and waited for it to appear 'as one would wait for a lover'. Moura was released, but as an aristocrat remained vulnerable to arrest at any time. She spent a further two months in prison when police raided a house where she was living, suspected as a centre for black marketeering. 'At that time one was imprisoned for almost anything. One of my interrogators told me that if you had such a name as mine you were bound to be in prison.'

Moura went to work as a translator at World Literature, the publishing house founded by Maxim Gorky. Twenty-four years his junior, she became his secretary within weeks of meeting him and moved into her own room in his vast twelve-room apartment. The cream of Russian political and literary life flowed through this colony, a place described by Moura as a refuge for intellectuals and stray dogs.

A final four-month spell of imprisonment came when she

Grandest of the grandes dames*, Baroness Moura Budberg, as a young girl in St Petersburg*

was arrested for trying to leave the country without papers. Gorky, who enjoyed tremendous stature with the Bolsheviks, intervened and secured her release. While she had been in prison her husband had been murdered by his own peasants and his estates appropriated, so that at twenty-seven she found herself a widow without money, and estranged from her children.

She had become Gorky's lover and eventually spent eleven years with him and was regarded as his common-law wife – he later dedicated his novel *Klim Samgin* to her. 'Gorky was a wonderful man and probably much more important as a person than he was as a writer. The new regime had to have a figurehead who was not odious to the rest of the world and he fitted that position very well. He was a revolutionary in spirit but he was not at all a political figure. He never liked politics. That was his great point of discord with Lenin. What he liked was civilisation.'

It was through Gorky's influence that Moura was able to

visit her children in Estonia, whom she had not seen in four years. While she was there she met Baron Nicolas Budberg, whom she married under an arrangement to obtain an Estonian passport. The baron proved to be an inveterate gambler and not a lucky one; Gorky bought him a one-way ticket to Argentina where he eked out a living giving bridge lessons.

Moura rejoined Gorky, who had left Russia to live in Berlin, and worked as his secretary translating six books a year from Russian into English at the rate of 4,000 words a day. They moved south to Italy where they found themselves under the constant surveillance of Mussolini's police. Moura arranged a meeting with Il Duce to complain, and Mussolini explained that it was not Gorky they were following but herself. 'I think it is rather strange that you, Baroness Budberg, should be on such close terms with a man of the people like Maxim Gorky.'

'Well, don't people change?' Moura replied. 'You, after all, were the editor of the left-wing journal *Avanti*.' Mussolini rocked with laughter.

Gorky's health was poor, and he returned to Moscow, but Moura refused to accompany him. However, she would continue to see him almost every year until his death. 'He had got hold of my imagination – he was the one I missed the most.' In the meantime she had moved to London and into the arms of H. G. Wells. 'I liked the atmosphere of London and I wanted my children to finish their education there.' She became a literary agent and one of the books she placed was *All Quiet on the Western Front*.

The relationship with Wells, whom she had met when he visited Gorky in the Soviet Union, now became paramount, and their tortured love affair continued until his death. Wells doted on her. He sent her presents accompanied with little cards written in his small, neat hand: 'Dear Moura! Sweet Moura!' He saw the affair as a 'glorious adventure' and wanted to marry her, and even went as far as arranging a dinner party to announce his plans. In the taxi on the way he broke the news to Moura, who absolutely forbade it and said she would prefer to throw herself out of the cab.

Back in London, she also renewed her friendship with Lockhart, who complained in his diary that she was 'expensive to feed, or rather water'. He recorded Moura consuming three double gins at eight shillings each before lunch, and a doubly brandy after it at twelve shillings.

After France fell in 1940, she joined the editorial staff of *La France Libre*, where she worked until the Liberation. She admitted to thoroughly enjoying the war. 'There was such activity and such a remarkable understanding between people. They were much better-tempered than they are now. There were such a lot of interesting events and it showed people up in a better way than anything else.' The death of Wells, in 1946, left a void, and she later said that afterwards no man mattered in her life. (A telegram from Bertrand Russell – 'The place is vacant' – went unanswered.)

During our various conversations, I found her attitude towards the Soviet Union peculiar, particularly for somebody who had lost everything in the revolution. 'I think that on the whole they have succeeded in doing what they wanted to do, because certainly eighty per cent of the population live better than they did, whereas before it was the other way round. They have also succeeded in education.'

This was the sort of guff that many pro-Soviets – Lenin's 'useful idiots' – maintained at the time, but I did not expect to hear it from Moura. Brian certainly went easy on the Soviet Union, but as a (ludicrous) self-proclaimed Man of the Left who had been invited to judge films in Moscow – where he was shamelessly flattered and bribed with caviar – he was, as always, a special and eccentric case.

The clairvoyant recommended by Aldous Huxley had been wrong about Moura's biography being more interesting than her personality – both were equally fantastic and improbable. True, her life had been amazing, but it paled beside the complexities of her character that would perplex and defeat a number of subsequent would-be biographers. A certain mystery was part of her aura and reputation, but she took pains to lay a false trail to confuse and muddle posterity. There was good reason why she glossed over historic moments, telescoped time, and was loath to talk, for after her death it became clear she had much to hide.

Brian came to Moura's flat for drinks one evening after a taping session to pick me up for dinner. He needled her mildly with an account of the religious devotion displayed by Russian Orthodox believers he had witnessed on a visit to Zagorsk, the holy city outside Moscow. 'The Soviets wanted to take me to see the new canal connecting the Moscow river to the Volga. I told them I'd seen the Kiel Canal, the Panama Canal, the Suez Canal and the Regent's Park Canal – and that was quite enough canals for me. So I went to Zagorsk instead and saw hundreds of people taking water from the holy well in the Kremlin there. It was like a scene in Ireland, where there are many holy wells. I was told there was an icon in the church there that made everything wrong with you go away if you kissed it. It was slobbered over by generations of Russian peasants day and night, but after taking a rapid inward glance at everything that was morally and spiritually wrong with me I decided to get in the queue. I pressed my lips to the icon, which was covered with spit and sweat, and kissed fervently. And there was a miracle, Moura – I didn't catch anything!'

Moura grunted, seemingly unamused, but responded with a story Gorky had told her about a priest. It was summer and Gorky was lying in a field resting in the hot sun when a dirty, dust-covered priest in a torn black soutane collapsed by the side of the road, took off his boots and started talking to them. 'There you are, you've been hurting me the whole morning, causing me great pain, but can you go a step without me? No, you can't!' The priest put the boots back on and went off limping down the road.

'That could be an Irish story,' Brian said. 'Russian and Irish stories are virtually interchangeable. But it could never be an English story.'

After we left the flat, he said: 'You didn't mention the shoplifting, did you?'

'What shoplifting?'

'Oh good – I had not told you. How very noble and *unusually* discreet of me. But years ago when I returned from a trip abroad, I found Moura in a rare animated condition – she actually *emphasised* words and raised an eyebrow, which meant she was close to hysteria. "What do you think of this *terrible* shoplifting?" I have never seen the harm in a little light pilfering myself and shrugged the subject off – "Moura, *all* my friends shoplift." She was not to be mollified and shook her cane in irritation. Apparently, she had been in the food hall in Harrods, shopping for a dinner party, and *inadvertently* slipped a couple of tins of *foie gras* into her bag. Easily done, and wholly justifiable in my opinion at the prices they charge. A manager had confronted her and accused her of shoplifting. No amount of lofty posturing could convince him otherwise – not even a sharp whack with an umbrella. She was duly charged and fined five pounds in a highly publicised case, most notable for the fame and grandeur of her supporters in the public gallery. That's the way life is with these old Russian aristos – arrested by Lenin's secret police one day, pinched by a Harrods floor detective the next.'

'How humiliating it must have been for Moura,' I said. 'Surely she isn't short of money – all she has to do is sell one of those heirlooms. Out of all the treasures in that museum of a front room the most beautiful to my mind is that little jade apple on the mantelpiece.'

'Never noticed it.'

'I don't know – maybe it's Fabergé, or Chinese, but it's perfect. A gem.'

'Why don't you steal it?'

'*Steal* it?'

'Yes. Trouser it, if you think it's so beautiful. She'll never notice. She's always complaining how the place is cluttered with stuff. You'd be doing her a favour.'

I sighed and smiled, shaking my head. There were times when I was never quite certain whether Brian was joking or artlessly displaying another facet of his casual amorality. A couple of weeks later, as he climbed out of a taxi that I was taking on, he slipped something into my jacket pocket. 'Present,' he said, slamming the door after him. As the taxi moved off, I fished into my pocket. And there was the jade apple.

Subsequent remonstrations were met with irritation and impatience. 'You said it was one of the most beautiful things you had ever seen!'

'I admired the damn thing. I didn't expect you to go and steal it for me.'

'Ingrate! I thought you'd be tickled pink. Obviously I should never have bothered.'

'My God, Bri – Moura's one of your oldest friends.'

'Call it redistribution of wealth. Moura's all for it late at night after a few drinks. Anyway, the woman's a convicted shoplifter. And she no longer looks at or takes pleasure from all those knick-knacks all over the place. That museum atmosphere is oppressive. You, on the other hand, are desperately in need of the odd knick-knack. I'm sure you have precious little of value or beauty in your tiny flat.'

'I would never steal anything from Moura, for heaven's sake! I go cold and clammy at the thought of it.'

'Spare me this unconvincing display of conscience and morals. *You want that little jade apple!* Anyway, you didn't take it – I did. Go ahead and enjoy it. Only last week you were boasting to me that you collected expenses from two newspapers for the same trip to Scotland.'

'That's different.'

'I see. You seem to have your own highly developed and flexible ethical system, Christopher, so no doubt you'll find a way to accommodate this.'

The subject was closed. Over the next few days the tiny jade apple became an obsession. I fretted over it, dreamed about it, worried myself sick. I placed the apple in a drawer and formulated elaborate plans to return it to the mantelpiece. I dreaded that Moura might already have missed it, and agonised over whether I had ever mentioned my admiration for the wretched thing to her, so that she might already suspect me of being the thief. Every time I thought of this I groaned out loud.

When I next went to Cromwell Road, I arrived with the jade apple in my trouser pocket only to find another guest waiting in the front room. Normally this would have been a pleasure – offering the opportunity to meet one of Moura's fascinating friends – but I was unable to rise to the occasion. I sat in silence, distracted and dull, casting furtive and guilty glances at the mantelpiece. Even if Moura didn't suspect me of being a thief, she was beginning to find me unrewarding company.

My chance came one afternoon a week later when I was led by the maid into an empty front room. I moved quickly to the mantelpiece and dropped the jade back in position among the precious objects. But the moment I put the apple down I began to suffer misgivings about its original position. Had it been more to the left, or more to the right – further forward, or further back? For all I knew, it might have occupied a favourite position for years. Perhaps, when the maid dusted, she moved all the things around – perhaps the maid had already discovered the apple was missing! But at least it was back – that was the important thing.

Usually, Moura took a full five minutes to appear after a guest was announced, tap, tap, tapping along the corridor, but this afternoon I heard no warning sound from the silver-topped cane and the door opened almost immediately. I whirled around, knocking over some ornament or other with a clatter. Moura stood framed in the door, looking directly across the room at me.

'So sorry!' I burbled, picking up the ornament. 'Just admiring these lovely things.'

Moura said nothing but sat heavily in her chair. 'Drink?'

My self-consciousness and sense of guilt were such that I now became convinced that she had not only noticed the jade apple had gone missing, but that the perpetrator had been surprised in another oafish attempt at theft. As I sat down I felt myself blushing. It was not a normal blush of pink, tingling embarrassment, but a pulsating purple glow of guilt and shame. 'Hot in here,' I said weakly, running a finger under my collar. 'Or is it me?'

'It is *not* hot,' Moura said, giving me an odd look as she threw back a vodka. 'It *is* you.'

I wanted to jump from my chair and drag her to the mantelpiece. 'See – nothing missing! It's all there! Every last bit of it! Look at the beautiful jade apple! The maid might have moved it while dusting, and you might have thought it was missing, but it's there. Look!' Instead, I sat and mouthed the sort of empty small talk I knew Moura found unforgivable. Had I told her the whole story, she would probably have thrown back her head and let out a big Russian laugh, but I was too young to think the truth would do. And perhaps even Moura, big-hearted and generous-natured though she was, might have drawn the line at her old friend Brian redistributing her treasured possessions.

Mission accomplished, I fled the apartment. I never mentioned the jade apple to Brian again. He must have assumed, if he thought about it at all, that I had made the appropriate hypocritical accommodation with my conscience that he had suggested was well within my flexible moral system. It was a judgement I was prepared to live with. The real fear was that if he ever found out what I had done, he might steal the apple again out of sheer wickedness, and give it to someone else.

I continued to see Moura until she took the unlikely step, at the age of eighty-two, of emigrating to Florence. Apart from general disenchantment with modern London, the cost of relentless entertaining had become a burden. Her salon was too grand to scale down while the art of boiling eggs was not among Moura's talents. 'I'm quite unable to live without service and now service is almost impossible to get, so in Italy I'm going to live on the top floor of a hotel.'

I suggested an alternative plan: cut down on entertaining and retire to a small flat in Putney. A number of my friends had recently moved to Putney, I said, although why I imagined Moura would be keen to follow in their wake I cannot imagine. '*Putney*,' she said, with magnificent disdain. 'I would rather *die*!'

Her emigration seemed like a dignified retreat from a life that had become overwhelming, but as always with Moura there were other, secret motives. She was tidying up a long and eventful life, stacking her books, arranging her letters, settling her affairs, and methodically preparing for death. She was riddled with cancer and knew she did not have long. The move was a consideration to her friends, relieving them of the need to fuss and worry. There were a series of luncheons and dinner parties, and Moura departed for Italy. Within two months of the uprooting she was dead.

The obituaries were long and respectful, and spoke of her originality and how the mould had been broken, and were full of errors. *Grande dame*, *maîtresse littéraire*, society hostess et cetera, et cetera – the party line that I had been fed and swallowed. She knew she was dying when she granted me the unusual privilege of lengthy interviews, in which she merely promoted the version of her life and character she wished to leave behind.

Since her death, Moura has been written about in numerous books as a part player in the lives of Lockhart, Gorky and Wells, but at least three biographies of her have been abandoned as their writers floundered and sank in the quicksand of her myth. She wove such a skein of truth and untruth into her history, and kept her true character so hidden, that a definitive biography has become virtually impossible. And that is how she wanted it. Even some of the harmless anecdotes she told proved unreliable – according to her daughter she never met Norman Douglas, and the syphilis story happened to a close friend.

Moura has been described as 'blissfully vague', and had good reason to be. Ten years after her death the world began to learn that she was not what she had seemed to be. Anthony West, the son of H. G. Wells and Rebecca West, wrote bluntly in his book on his father, *Aspects of a Life*, that she had been a Soviet agent. Moura had been under surveillance by both the British and French security services for thirty years, suspected of being a Russian spy, and had used and manipulated the men in her life to promote the Soviet cause. Throughout her life she had both spun and been entangled in a fantastic web of espionage and sexual deceit. Robin Lockhart, son of Bruce Lockhart, went further and wrote that she was the most effective Soviet agent ever based in London.

A floodgate had been opened, and a torrent of information followed, suggesting Moura spied for the Germans in the First World War, the British during the early days of the Russian revolution, and the Soviets ever after. Like all great agents, Moura created a legend around herself, so that fact and fiction became so closely intertwined that it was impossible to shake the lies from the truth.

'We have all been deceived by her,' said Nina Berberova, the Russian émigré writer and friend who wrote a biography of Moura in Russian, using as a title the name Gorky gave her – *Woman of Iron*. In Moscow, Berberova wrote, Moura was suspected of being an English spy; in Estonia, a Russian or German spy; in France, Russian émigrés believed she worked for Germany; the French security services saw her as a triple agent – possibly more. The Germans accused her of spying for Russia; the English thought she was a Russian agent; the Nazis intended to arrest her as a British agent following the invasion of Britain. It is possible that at different times in her life she was all of the above.

Yes, everyone was deceived by Moura – myself as a young, awestruck journalist, taking my place at the end of a long line of the gulled. Her own daughter, Tania Alexander, in her book *Memories of a Lost World*, wrote that while all who knew Moura spoke of her courage, charm and self-confidence, and even her sharpest detractors did not deny her good humour, warmth and affection, 'At the same time they also acknowledged the lack of scruple, the disregard for the truth, the insatiable need for admiration and attention . . . I was dragged into her deceptions, used as an accomplice or an alibi, forced into telling lies for her, brought face to face on numerous occasions with the unscrupulous side of her character.' Michael Foot, an ardent admirer who described her as 'one of the most considerable women of this century . . . one of the most intelligent women in Europe of her times . . . an embodiment of true internationalism,' rashly dismissed all charges of espionage as 'monstrous'. Nevertheless, he wrote in *The History of Mr Wells* that Moura displayed 'a chronic incapacity to tell the truth' and admitted her 'reckless readiness to deceive with audacious lies'. Wells himself, doting lover that he was, wrote that Moura was 'swathed in disingenuousness'.

In retrospect, it seems obvious that Moura was a spy. She

enjoyed easy and constant access to Iron Curtain countries and the Soviet Union during the most frozen period of the Cold War, when all movement internally and externally, even for the highest-ranking members of the Communist Party, was tightly controlled by the KGB. Moura entered the world of espionage as a young woman, came under suspicion early on, and remained suspect ever after.

The *Cheka* – the Bolshevik intelligence organisation and political police – had documentary evidence linking Moura to German espionage during the First World War, when she was in her early twenties. The supposition is that Moura's rapid release from prison after her initial arrest, authorised by the deputy chief of the *Cheka*, Jacob Peters – also rumoured to be a lover – was on condition that she work for the Bolsheviks. She was then planted on Lockhart, and later on Gorky, and Wells – and even admitted as much to them, claiming to be disgusted by her role and further earning their trust.

The British Embassy in Moscow considered Moura a very dangerous woman directly after the revolution, and by the 1930s referred to her as an 'illustrious' Soviet agent. After she moved to London, she was kept under constant surveillance until the early 1950s. (One MI5 report admired Moura's capacity for alcohol: 'She can drink an amazing quantity, mostly gin, without showing any apparent slow-up in her mental process.')

The French also compiled a thick file on Moura over the years – there are intelligence reports on her from the Ministry for National Defence and War, numerous secret dossiers from the Deuxième Bureau, and the French Embassy in London. The French identified Moura early on as a member of Petrograd's *Cheka*, and later call her a 'redoubtable agent' and 'a very dangerous spy in the service of the Soviets'.

An especially revealing item in the most recently released MI5 files (November 2002), both in regard to Moura's inside knowledge and the complacency of British intelligence at the time, is that MI5 disregarded information she disclosed about Anthony Blunt, the Soviet master spy. Moura gave a dinner party at her flat on 27 August 1950, where the guests included a publisher, an American diplomat, and an MI5 agent. 'The most startling story Moura told me was that Anthony Blunt – to whom Guy Burgess was so devoted – is a member of the Communist party,' the MI5 agent reported the following day. 'When I said, "The only thing I know about him is that he looks after the king's pictures," Moura retorted, "Such things only happen in England."'

Nine months after this conversation Moura's friend, Guy Burgess – who was not just 'devoted' to Blunt, but his ex-lover, and had recruited him as a Soviet agent – defected to Moscow. The security services failed to uncover Blunt's role as a spy until 1964. He was publicly exposed as a traitor in 1979, stripped of his knighthood and disgraced, but not prosecuted. As Moura remarked, such things could only happen in England.

Naturally, I had no clue of any of Moura's espionage activities when I knew her, and if Brian had heard the rumours or knew anything he kept it to himself. It would probably not have concerned him much. As a homosexual, Anglophile Ulsterman with a strong emotional attachment to the North, yet sympathetic to the Irish Republican cause, and a Protestant who had converted to Catholicism in a country where people consider such an act traitorous and beyond comprehension, he well understood muddled, conflicting loyalties. He often remarked on the shared characteristics of the Irish and the Russians – big-hearted and soulful people whose tortured patriotism ran in their blood, and who carried the weight of their tragic history on their backs; a people with a reputation for escaping reality through the oblivion of drink; who lived in their music and poetry, inventing and mythologising themselves as they went along.

Besides, the bare facts of a human being's life did not much interest Brian, who held biography in low regard: even the best could never truly reveal the secrets of a human heart, scarcely even guess those of the soul. Missing these insights the written story of a life was little more than a crude outline at most, while the worst demeaned and defamed both writer and subject. Brian assessed a person's essence by instinct, and felt that the deepest insights into character were glanced sideways.

My own view of Moura, arrived at from researching her life rather than personal acquaintance, is that the three great loves of her life were genuine – Moura lost her heart to Lockhart, admired and respected Gorky as a great figure, and had a mature love for Wells. Deceit, manipulation and betrayal came with her heart – it was her scorpion nature, the way it was with her.

But the English love a spy, especially a beautiful, strong and mysterious woman of high intelligence and exotic origin with a hearty laugh and a sense of humour, who can drink like a man. Even MI5 – judging by the written record – held Moura Budberg in high regard. The final document in the most recently released files describes her as, 'An unusually intelligent and amusing woman – a quite outstanding personality.' As Brian said to me before I went to interview her for the first time, 'The thing to bear in mind with Moura when you talk to her is that while she is a *grande dame* of great power, style, dignity and presence, she is entirely feminine inside.'

In a rather different category of powerful woman, but another of Brian's great female friends, was the actress Hermione Gingold, the most extreme of the grotesques. I met her when she returned temporarily to London from her home in New York to play in Stephen Sondheim's *A Little Night Music* in the West End. In any gathering she demanded to be the centre of attention, and while she was very funny, she was altogether alarming. I thought her a monster.

One lunchtime at Kinnerton Street, as I hopped from foot to foot by the fireplace, ignoring an empty chair beside La Gingold – as Brian called her – she boomed, 'For heaven's sake sit down, unless you have some ghastly affliction! I don't bite.'

'That's not what I've heard.'

After that, we became quite good friends. I saw her often at the house and enjoyed her heartless, lisping wit. This was original and spontaneous, and of a quality that allowed the world to overlook a host of character flaws. 'Once after a long Sunday lunch at Wardrobe's Lodge,' Brian told me, 'someone asked what we were all going to do that afternoon. Hanging from the wall was a pair of Mexican spurs in bronze and silver, with a hundred points on each wheel. Without a moment's pause, Hermione said: "I'm going to take off all my clothes, except my high-heeled shoes, and I am going to put on those Mexican spurs, go into the kitchen and run around the pastry."'

A friend of Brian's, who was a professional clairvoyant with a reputation for above-average accuracy in his predictions, joined us one day for lunch. He had clearly been ill and was the colour of old parchment. 'Good God, man, what's up with you?' La Gingold exclaimed. 'Have you taken Chinese nationality?' The soothsayer explained that he had recently recovered from a severe bout of jaundice. 'A terrible and debilitating disease,' Hermione sympathised. 'Does it affect your prognostications?'

As far as I could make out, Hermione and Brian used to share military men when she was a regular weekend guest at his various country homes. When La Gingold showed up with a young soldier, Brian remarked that her escort was a 'mere boy'. 'There is nothing "mere",' Hermione shot back, 'about boys.' On another occasion, during the war, Brian had

Hermione Gingold, vicious wit and lifelong friend

decided to rent out his house, Wardrobe's Lodge. 'A brigadier-general and his very correct wife came to look the place over during a weekend party. I opened the door to an upstairs bedroom to find the mother of a scriptwriter feeding her pet canary – completely naked (fortunately with her back to camera). I shut the door quickly. In the next bedroom Hermione was prancing around with nothing on but a Spitfire pilot's cap and high boots, while the Spitfire pilot was naked in one of Hermione's see-through dresses and dancing like a Hottentot. The brigadier-general and his wife fled.'

La Gingold invited me to her show, reserving house seats. She was superb in the part of an an aristocratic, wheelchair-bound Swedish grandmother 'who has numbered kings among her lovers . . . the first, a Croatian Count with the moustache of a brigand . . . and afterwards the beloved of hundreds – regardless of their matrimonial obligations'. She made the lines her own: 'Tonight at dinner I shall tell you amusing stories about my liaison with the Baron de Signac, who was, to put it mildly, peculiar . . . To lose a lover or even a husband or two during the course of one's life can be vexing. But to lose one's teeth is a catastrophe. Bear that in mind, child, as you chomp so recklessly into that ginger snap . . . At the palace of the Duke of Ferrara, who was prematurely deaf but a dear, I acquired some position, plus a Tiny Titian.' And as she orders her footman to fetch a bottle of vintage champagne, she declares, 'One bottle less will not, I hope, diminish the hilarity at my wake.' La Gingold particularly relished bringing down the final curtain on her nightly death. After the show I went to her dressing room and she agreed to be interviewed. 'Pop along one evening with your apparatus and we'll cook up some scandal for the bored and the curious.'

A couple of days later when I called to fix a date, she made an odd request. 'Do you happen to have easy access to sausage rolls?'

'The baker round the corner makes quite good ones.'

'How unbelievably quaint, darling. It makes me quiver with nostalgia. I am all a-flutter. Sausage rolls are not a delicacy the natives of New York have taken up, alas, and I have had to learn to live without them. It is a sacrifice and I suffer, but temper my misery by thinking of all the starving people in the world without a sausage roll between them. Bring half a dozen to the dressing room and we'll sit and scoff them and drink gin. And I'll tell you my secrets.'

We tucked into the sausage rolls and gin, and after a while began the interview. I apologised, saying I knew she must have answered every reporter's question a hundred times, and I was no doubt obliging her to repeat herself. 'What the hell,' Hermione said, 'let's suffer through it together – that's what we're here for, isn't it?'

La Gingold was a philistine and proud of it. 'The only education an actress needs is to learn to write well enough to sign contracts,' she declared. 'I know nothing about politics or world events, or anything else for that matter, but am *very* opinionated. I speak in a loud, commanding voice and bang the table. People are impressed!'

Perhaps it was the gin that opened her up, or some sort of euphoria induced by the sausage rolls, but she made no attempt to gild the grotesque lily. 'I am that strange phenomenon, the ugly woman who is attractive – especially to men.' She described herself as a 'strange and horrid child' afflicted with nightmares and sleep-walking. She said she knew very early on that she was not pretty, and learned not to fish for compliments in that regard. On telling a little boy cast opposite her in *Sleeping Beauty* that she could not imagine why she had been chosen as she was not nearly beautiful enough, the child replied, 'You could wear a mask.' She was, however, recognised as a precocious talent: 'The headmistress of Cricklewood Kindergarten found my Cardinal Wolsey memorable.'

Almost all of La Gingold's friends were male, having made a decision early in life not to have girlfriends. She much preferred men, and greatly favoured her father to her mother. She described her father as a handsome, amusing and completely unscrupulous man, who went through three fortunes, only one of which was his own. A spendthrift with fifty pairs of handmade shoes and twenty pairs of monogrammed silk pyjamas, when he finally ran out of money he very sensibly became a Buddhist.

The father was forgiven all his sins on account of his charm, while the mother was hated for the lack of it. 'You could write all the feelings of love I had for my mother on the head of a pin and still have room for the Lord's Prayer. Mother was a hypochondriac whose only ambition was to be a chronic invalid. She scoured seaside towns searching for residences conducive to nervous breakdowns. She was very proper and extremely boring. Once, to liven things up, my father suggested inviting a neighbour for tea. "I will not have that woman in the house. She dyes her hair."' The Turkish grandmother, on the other hand, was an exotic and used to scandalise St John's Wood, where Hermione was brought up, by sitting cross-legged on the floor smoking a hookah.

La Gingold cheerfully confessed to a chilling degree of selfishness, and said that she married purely out of sexual curiosity. She abandoned her first husband – the publisher, Michael Joseph – with three small children, but took the cat. She admitted to having been a terrible mother with no love for her babies, and never bothered to see her children until they were grown up. 'But you *must* write down that I *adore* animals!'

Towards the end of the interview, which we had both thoroughly enjoyed, I found La Gingold inspecting me with such intensity that it made me uncomfortable. I feared I might have eaten one more sausage roll than my allotment, or was behaving peculiarly from too much gin. 'Forgive me for staring, darling – I was trying to sort out a puzzlement. To establish the connection between yourself and the events leading up to the birth of Christ. You don't *look* like a biblical epic man – you must be the strong, *silent* religious-maniac type.'

The Box Office Blockbuster had in fact become moribund, and even work on the Big Bestseller was sporadic. I was thrown back upon journalism in a Canute-like effort to withstand a tidal wave of debt. Unexpected relief had come in the form of a dozen signed etchings from Salvador Dalí, acquired from the hands of the great man himself over tea in the Hotel Meurice, in Paris. I sold six of them in less than a week, covering their initial cost, and was looking forward to picking up the pure profit from the sale of the second half-dozen.

The folder had been left with a friend of Brian's, a rich theatrical producer named David, who had expressed interest in buying two – maybe even three – of the remaining prints. And then I received a call from Brian. The voice was stern and humourless: 'I want to talk to you.'

The severe demeanour was maintained when I pitched up at the house the following day. 'Christopher, I do not object when you interrogate my closest friends and disseminate their deepest secrets across the public prints, but your present racket goes too far. I really must protest.'

'What racket would that be, Bri?'

'The unprincipled profiteering over these etchings.'

'What are you talking about?' I was instantly angry.

'David may be rich, but he's not a fool.'

'I never supposed he was.'

'Perhaps, then, you can explain this.' Brian handed me a full-page advertisement torn from the *Sunday Times* magazine. It was an offer for a 'genuine' Salvador Dalí print for a fraction of the price I was demanding.

'I would have thought with your background as an artist,' I said stiffly, 'that you would know the difference between an etching produced in a worthless edition of a thousand, and signed in the plate – meaning that the signature on the etching is *printed* – and a limited edition of one hundred and fifty signed and numbered in pencil by the artist himself. However, if David would prefer a cut-price piece of suburban tat to the real thing, he should send his cheque off to the *Sunday Times* art club. In fact,' I concluded grandly, 'I no longer wish to sell them to the ignorant bastard – especially as he is suggesting that I am trying to stitch him up.'

'Do not adopt that tone with me, Christopher.' We were both now very angry. 'I certainly have no wish to be in the middle of this sordid transaction. I am merely acting as unwilling go-between in regard to compensation.'

'Wants them cheap, does he? Tell him to get stuffed.'

'Your attitude is most unfortunate – more like a barrow-boy than an art dealer. And the situation has become complicated. The etchings you left at David's have gone missing. He takes responsibility for their disappearance, and is quite prepared to compensate you – but at a fair price.'

'I don't believe this!' I was livid. 'They've been nicked by some rent boy and I'm supposed to take the loss! I want my bloody money in full!'

'You are being most unreasonable.'

'Your mate David doesn't know what unreasonable is.'

We parted on sour terms. I despaired of ever receiving my money and began to feel very sorry for myself. I muttered dark things about Brian and his friends, and the whole homosexual tribe, and nurtured wild fantasies of revenge.

Two days later Brian called. 'Christopher, it would seem I owe you an apology. I have spoken to an art-dealer friend of mine in Bond Street, and he confirms what you told me – although he says your prices verge on the impertinent. And that this man Dalí has more signed etchings on the market than you can shake a stick at. But he broadly agrees on the price you quoted. I have spoken to David, but have not been able to extract a cheque from him . . .' He paused momentarily with exquisite timing, allowing my spirits to plunge, before restoring them: 'He has given me *cash*.'

'Thanks, Bri,' I said, dripping gratitude.

'I thought it gracious in the circumstances, as David has nothing to show for this large and honourable outlay of the folding stuff, to offer a ten per cent discount on your behalf.'

'Oh, all right.'

'Good. Then we can all be friends, and put this unfortunate incident behind us. Come for lunch tomorrow and I'll give you the money, and you can take me for a Slap-Up Feed at Wheeler's.'

'A pleasure.'

'And we really must get back to work on the Big Bestseller. It has been greatly neglected during this sordid phase of money-grubbing.'

PART VI

Gallipoli

The first time Brian mentioned his service in Gallipoli with the Royal Irish Rifles during the First World War was in a throwaway story told on an airport bus taking us from a terminal to a waiting plane. Brian sat across from myself and Dave, the Welsh Guardsman, and told how he first tried to enlist with a childhood friend. The boys were nineteen years old, but skinny and pale-faced, which made them look years younger. They went to a recruiting office in the centre of Belfast where a sergeant-major regarded them sceptically. 'What do you want?'

'I want to be a soldier,' Brian said.

The sergeant-major winked at a colleague seated beside him. 'Got any hair on it?'

Brian blushed, said nothing, but thought how vulgar the man was. ('I considered it vulgar even to say "belly" then.') The sergeant-major said, 'Come back when you've got a great big bunch on it, lad.' The humiliated young men slunk away, accompanied by a roar of laughter.

And that is how Brian continued to talk about his experiences in the first war – light-hearted anecdotes that pictured war not as hell but as a bit of a lark. I accepted the stories at face value for a long time, and developed the view that, except for bouts of illness, he had enjoyed an amusing and easy war.

One of our favourite private jokes – 'Pleasant, isn't it?' – came out of a seemingly carefree period of convalescence in Egypt. As Brian recovered from jaundice in Cairo – earning from matron the nickname, 'The Daffodil of Ward B11' – he was given the job of hospital postman. This involved daily visits to the capital's main post office to collect the English mail, and one day he met a woman on the tram who asked him in French if he could get hold of some sugar for her 'girls'.

'I returned to the hospital and chatted up Sambo, the Sudanese cook, who gave me seven pounds of sugar which next day I took to the address I'd been given. I thought it was a girl's school or something, but naturally it turned out to be a brothel. Some of the girls were sitting over alum pots, using the fumes to tighten themselves up a bit for the night's work. They all flew at me when they saw the sugar and embraced me.'

Brian became good friends with the woman from the tram, who was the *madame* of the brothel. 'I used to sit in her room, talking and eating iced grapes. I was fascinated by her. When she was seated there were little ridges of fat all down her body, but when she stood up they vanished and she had a beautiful figure. She told me, "I am not like the other girls here. I only have two or three a week. When I've got my *dot* [dowry], I'm going back to Marseilles to get married."'

Reports of the goings-on at the brothel provided welcome entertainment to the matrons and nurses of the Voluntary Aid Detachment, mostly made up of the daughters of generals and senior officers. Brian regaled them with stories, and descriptions of the various girls, and the dignified *madame* herself. A young lieutenant named Langlands, probably no more than nineteen years old, became intrigued. 'I say sergeant, this house you go to sounds rather interesting. Would you take me with you some night?'

At the weekend the two men set off together for the brothel, but as they entered Langlands became nervous. 'You will stay with me? I've never been with a woman before.' The men were offered two young Nubian girls, but were told by the *madame* that because the place was so busy they would have to share a room with two single beds. 'I wasn't charged anything because I had brought a large bag of sugar, but

Langlands had to pay a hundred *piastres*, which was very expensive. We went into the room and stripped off. In the middle of the whole thing, Langlands looked over at me, his face red with pleasure: "I say, sergeant – pleasant, isn't it?"'

This story naturally made the rounds the moment Brian returned to the hospital. 'The next morning a nurse went to give Langlands his liquid quinine. The taste was so terrible that if the nurse liked you, she would give you a bit of chocolate after. Langlands was given his quinine. He made a terrible face and, as the nurse leaned over to give him a piece of chocolate, she whispered, "Pleasant, isn't it?" Then the matron came along. She picked up his chart and, as she was reading it, she looked out of the window and said, "Lovely day, Lieutenant Langlands. Pleasant, isn't it?" He was never allowed to live it down.'

The impression of an easy war was reinforced by an old letter Brian dug up, sent to his sister Patricia, dated 16 August 1916. Written under a fig tree in a vineyard in Macedonia, it was characteristically more concerned with food than combat:

> My dear Pat,
>
> I arrived out here safely and am having a high old time. All the boys were glad to see me again and I am in a bivouac with Bradley in a vineyard. We are in no danger so don't worry about me. Send me a tin of tooth-powder and some soap now and again as I like to keep my teeth and hands in good trim. We can feed all day on these beautiful grapes as the people of the vineyard have fled long ago. There are also figs in abundance. We get rotten grub, very seldom bread, and these army biscuits are horribly plain fare. But we manage to buy an occasional loaf off the villagers – that is, when we are near a village.
>
> All around us is a beautiful plain and a lake in the distance. It is a very beautiful place indeed, somewhere in

Macedonia. For tea tonight we have the eternal Tickler's jam and biscuits and we sometimes need a hammer for the biscuits, but we are used to these little things. On Gallipoli I never saw bread or butter until I was sent on to a hospital ship, and we can get a wash here, which on Gallipoli was pure suicide to even venture near the well or beach so things might be a lot worse than they are.

No more of those ices or cream buns for a while. Don't send me any tins of cocoa or any coffee, it is too hard to prepare and we cannot get sugar or milk, but Oxo cubes are the best. They only need a little salt and they are ready, and I am very fond of toffee and cakes. Don't send chocolate because in these hot climates, when it reaches us it is a mass of pulp. Tins of toffee are much more handy to carry. I suppose I am a greedy beggar wanting all this stuff, but a parcel out here is a veritable godsend. It is fearfully warm here and I am writing this under a fig tree in the vineyard.

Goodbye now my darling sister, love and kisses from your own – Brian.

When I asked Brian what he was doing sitting in the sun in a Greek vineyard, gorging on grapes and figs, he explained that once he had recuperated he had rejoined the 10th Irish Division, which had been taken off Gallipoli to fight in Macedonia and Serbia. 'We went everywhere and fought battles all over the place, and became known as the Balkan Harriers.'

Fought battles all over the place. It still sounded like a breeze, and even when Brian spoke of hardship he would usually cap it with a joke. He told me the regiment had advanced into Serbia but was checked by the enemy and forced to retreat to Lake Dorian, between Serbia and Macedonia, where it stopped for the night to prepare for a dawn crossing. 'Our clothes froze and we couldn't get into them in the morning.

The boat in which I crossed the lake was loaded to the gunwales with Irish Riflemen – the Catholics were telling their beads, and the Protestants cursing the pope. The water was literally one inch below the gunwales and had any of us moved the boat would have sunk. The battalion sergeant-major encouraged us to keep very still and drew his revolver: "If one of you moves, I'll blow his fucking head off!"

'As we straggled ashore on the other side in rags, blankets and every conceivable sort of garment, we were greeted by the band of the Essex Regiment, gleaming with shiny brass buttons and clean new uniforms, playing "Father O'Flynn, You've A Wonderful Way With You".'

On the retreat, Brian was again stricken with malaria, and ordered back to Britain. 'I was sent from the line on a mule with a basket on either side, as I couldn't walk properly. If you were put in one of these baskets and the man in the other basket was lighter than you, you ended up under the mule's arse.'

And that is how the talk went, so perhaps I can be forgiven for believing Brian had an amusing little war out there in the Eastern Mediterranean. At some stage in our early conversations about the First World War I told Brian of my own family's sad history, which I considered infinitely more dramatic. My grandfather, George – on my mother's side – survived almost four years of the war, only to be killed weeks before the armistice. He had been awarded the Military Medal for valour in March 1918, and was allowed to return home on leave that month, when my mother, Georgina, was conceived. My great aunt Liz told me that during this time George would crawl from the bed and slither across the floor in the grip of hideous nightmares, and awake from them shaking and bathed in sweat. This gentle, decent man in his early twenties, religious by nature, had been assigned a Bren gun. He told his sisters that as he mowed down the enemy emerging from their trenches, he felt like a murderer. My mother was seven months in the womb when he disappeared along with hundreds of his comrades from the Light Surrey Infantry. The body was never found and there is no grave, only a memorial plaque on the wall of a churchyard in France.

A bleak family photograph shows his unsmiling widow dressed in black posing with her first-born, my mother at eight weeks old. There is something unnatural about the photo, something horribly wrong. Instead of a mother's joy there is a blank expression in the eyes, which are disconnected and distant, as if bemused by grief. The mood is mirrored in the expressionless calm of the infant. Many years later my grandmother committed suicide by drowning herself in the river Avon. My great-grandfather was destroyed by the loss of his son, who was supposed to inherit and run the family building business in Weymouth. He sank into black depression, retreated to his study and sat in silence with the curtains drawn, year after year. My mother spent a lifetime in the company of mediums and theosophists, attempting to contact her dead, unknown father.

'That is very sad,' Brian said. 'I would like to see that photo. Perhaps you would bring it over.'

'I'll dig it out.'

'You should make a pilgrimage to the memorial in France – touch the name of your grandfather George engraved there. Honour his memory and his sacrifice. Take the time to remember. I went with Jack Ford and John Wayne to the American war cemetery near the beaches of Normandy. They wanted to find the grave of John Wayne's cameraman's son to photograph it for the boy's father. John Wayne was a big lumbering fellow with a big lumbering heart, and he was overcome with emotion as we knelt to pray by the grave. I withdrew to give him privacy and sat on the steps of the great monument erected there. I thought of these American boys lying so far from home, buried in the soil of

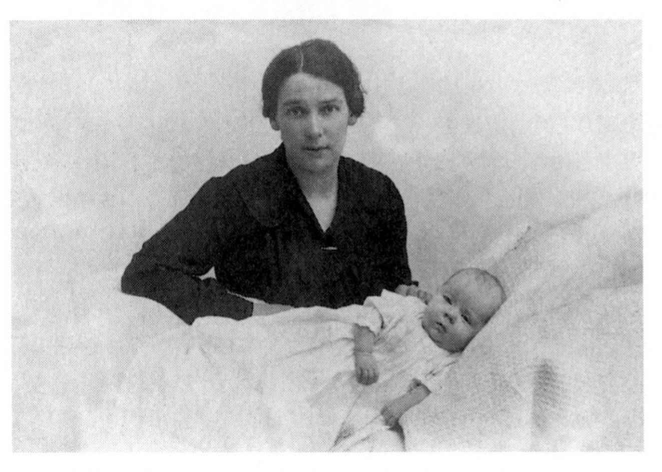

The photograph of the author's grandmother three months after the death of her husband

France. And I thought of war cemeteries all over the world – and my dead comrades left in the gorse and rock of Gallipoli, and the epitaph to a young gunner, killed there in 1916: "Only a boy but a British boy,/The son of a thousand years." And I remembered the words of Pericles: "For the whole earth is a sepulchre of heroes. Monuments will rise and be set up to them, but on far-off shores a more abiding memorial shall be kept. It is graven not on brass, not on stone, but on the living heart of all humanity."'

Although it was obvious that Brian was very moved as he said this, I was ignorant of the memories going through his mind. I thought him a little sentimental and dramatic. After all, his own war had been unencumbered by hardship or tragedy. 'At least you were in the Mediterranean in the sun among fig trees and vineyards, and not in the cold and wet of northern France,' I said. 'Not in the trenches in all that mud with rats the size of dogs.'

'No. Not in northern France.' There was a silence. 'You know about the Gallipoli campaign, do you?'

'Oh, yes.'

'Do tell.'

I trotted out more family history. 'My great aunt Win's first husband – she had three – was killed on one of the battleships that tried to force the Dardanelles and was sunk. Auntie Win was a bit of a chatterbox and never shut up. My father always maintained that her husband had not in fact drowned, but swam to an island, met a beautiful native girl who was quiet and loving, and lived happily ever after on coconuts. But I know that because the battleships failed to get through, what might have been achieved in a few days became a stalemate. It was a bit of a disaster, with nothing much gained on either side.'

I cringe that I could ever have made such a stupid and shallow statement to a veteran of Gallipoli, but had no idea at the time how crass my remarks were. As a child I believed my father's silly story about Auntie Win's husband, and must somehow have carried into adulthood an unmodified and unexamined view of the Gallipoli campaign as something exotic and not altogether unpleasant.

Whatever emotions I awakened in Brian, he kept them under remarkable control. 'We'll need a little time to talk about this in some detail,' he said. 'Come tomorrow with that infernal tape machine of yours. I'll tell you about Gallipoli. As you say, it was indeed a bit of a disaster.'

On the following day I returned to the house for the beginning of my education on the Gallipoli campaign.

'Your Country Needs YOU!' All over Belfast posters of Field Marshal Lord Kitchener, fierce and heavily moustachioed, fixed the youth of Ulster with gimlet eye and commanding forefinger, impelling them to heed the call to war. Brian was transfixed by the image, as if summoned by Mars, God of War, himself. 'Let's enlist,' he said to his great boyhood friend, Robert McKenzie.

'All right. *Anything* to get away from Belfast.'

Brian and Bobby McKenzie returned to a different recruiting office than the one where they had been humiliated, wearing suits borrowed from older brothers, and this time were signed up. In due course they were marched, together with a large group of recruits, on to the square of Belfast's Victoria Barracks, and given broom handles as there were not enough rifles to go around. A year of hard training followed, a life for which Brian was particularly ill-suited. He complained to his sister, Patricia, that because he was called Hans everyone suspected he was German. 'Call yourself Brian,' Patricia said, in her practical way. 'It's a family name.'

The regiment moved to England and final training took place at Hackwood Park near Basingstoke, a country house of Lord Curzon. According to Brian, his lordship is said to have looked out of his window one morning and asked, 'Who are those people bathing in my ponds?'

'Those, my lord, are the men of the Royal Irish Rifles.'

'I never knew the lower classes had such white skins.'

The regiment was issued with embarkation orders, and sent to join HMS *Transylvania* in Liverpool – destination unknown. Along with most young men of his generation, Brian believed in the glamour of war, and longed for action and adventure to replace the tedium of endless drill on the barracks square. Patricia, who had moved to London by this time, took the train up to Liverpool to say goodbye. A shrewd and worldly woman, she seemed instinctively to understand more of the reality of war, and to know her brother better than he knew himself. 'Do you want to desert? Come and hide with me in London.'

'No. I don't want to leave my friends.'

Brian sailed that night, together with more than a thousand comrades-in-arms of the sixth battalion of the Royal Irish Rifles. HMS *Transylvania* steered a course out into the Irish Sea, and headed south bound for Gallipoli.

*

It is difficult to imagine today, after being steeped in the images of a century of modern warfare, the extreme romanticism that war engendered in young men at the beginning of the First World War. It was not principally a belief in the moral rightness of the cause – 'A war to end war' – but the thrill and excitement in the adventure of it all. And the most romantic aspect of the entire war was the campaign against Turkey, known initially as the Constantinople Expedition.

The embodiment of the youthful, romantic vision of war against the Turk was the poet Rupert Brooke, who at the age of twenty-seven was something of an old man for the First World War. He was handsome, charming and gifted, knew everybody and had travelled everywhere. To do battle in the classical Aegean, the 'fabulous coast' of myth, in the footsteps of the heroes of antiquity, thrilled Brooke to his poetic core. The Turks actually had a machine-gun post among the archaeological excavations of the site of Troy.

At the outset of the campaign, Brooke wrote as if in the grip of a fever, imagining the wine-dark sea of classical poetry. 'It's too wonderful for belief. I had not imagined fate could be so kind . . . Oh my God! I've never been quite so happy in my life I think. Never quite so pervasively happy; like a stream flowing entirely to one end. I suddenly realised that the ambition of my life has been – since I was two – to go on a military expedition against Constantinople.' The poet was not alone in these feelings, as numerous other young men described similar yearnings for excitement and adventure in diaries and letters. As a nineteen-year-old boy from Ulster, who had never previously been out of Ireland, Brian certainly shared them in a less extravagant and unarticulated form.

The Commander-in-Chief of the Gallipoli campaign, General Sir Ian Hamilton, then sixty-two years old, was a sensitive and highly intelligent man, who was also a gifted writer and poet. He was of mixed Irish and Highland descent, and was described by one contemporary war correspondent to be 'deeply tinged with *Celtic charm* – that glamour of mind and courtesy of behaviour which creates suspicion among people endowed with neither'. General Hamilton, the Celt, had early presentiments of doom about Gallipoli. A superstitious man, like most great soldiers, he was sensitive to bad omens. As his train left Charing Cross station at the outset of his journey to the Dardanelles, he remarked to a young officer: 'This is going to be an unlucky show. I kissed my wife through her veil.'

The general understood that war seemed to offer the younger generation a release from the ordinary, an opportunity to banish the trivial, and dignify life through danger. He wrote in his diary, kept in an invented French shorthand: 'Once in a generation a mysterious wish for war passes through the people. Their instinct tells them *there is no other way* of progress and of escape from habits that no longer fit them. Whole generations of statesmen will fumble over reforms for a lifetime, which are put into full-blooded execution within a week of a declaration of war. There is *no other way*. Only by intense sufferings can the nations grow . . . Should the fates decree the whole brave Army may disappear during the night at least we shall have lived, acted, dared.'

The yearning for suffering, and the death-wish embodied in this martial romanticism, was repeatedly expressed in Brooke's poetry, and is encapsulated in his most famous lines:

If I should die, think only this of me:
That there's some corner of a foreign field
That is for ever England.

The sentiment provoked bitterness in Brian: 'The rocky earth of Gallipoli is stuffed with Irish, Scots, Welsh, Gurkhas, Australians, New Zealanders and Indians as well.' Rupert Brooke died of blood poisoning before he even reached Gallipoli, his illusions intact. In old age Brian did not quote

British soldiers and their horses in the harsh and inhospitable terrain of the Gallipoli peninsula

Brooke, who wrote of the romance and adventure of war, but Wilfred Owen, the poet who chronicled the slaughter and horror of it: 'What passing-bells for these who die as cattle?'

It had been expected by both the Allies and the Central Powers that Turkey would remain neutral and sit the war out, but the country had entered the hostilities on Germany's side. At best, the decision seemed foolhardy. Turkey was not threatened, and was certainly not ready for war. The Ottoman Empire was in an advanced state of disintegration, domestic politics were chaotic, the treasury was empty, the government unpopular, and the army had suffered a decade of defeat in the Balkans. Its soldiers were unpaid, hungry, poorly equipped and on the point of mutiny. The navy was obsolete. Allied military strategists agreed that the ancient defences of the Dardanelles could not possibly withstand serious attack.

At the other end of the scale was the might of the British Empire. The Royal Navy was the most powerful force on earth, a mighty armada that had gone from victory to victory for two hundred years. Faced with Turkey as an enemy,

Winston Churchill, First Sea Lord, ordered British and French battleships to smash through the Dardanelles, take control of the straits and Constantinople, and thus immobilise the country.

A defeatist Turkish government prepared to abandon Constantinople, and the state archives and gold reserves were removed. The city began to empty, as women and children fled to the interior. A seven-hour bombardment pounded Turkish gun emplacements and at the end of it the Turks were down to just thirty armour-piercing shells, the only effective ammunition against battleships. Then one of the French battleships was hit by a heavy shell that detonated her magazine, and within two minutes the mighty ship had sunk – a witness who saw her capsize and go under said the ship 'just slithered down as a saucer slithers down in a bath'. A British battleship struck a mine and was forced to withdraw, and then a second was hit . . . then a third.

The naval attack was called off in favour of a full-scale landing of troops on the Gallipoli peninsula. Previous Allied military estimates calculated that it would take 150,000 men to invade Gallipoli, but Kitchener thought half the number could do the job, convinced that a wave of the Union Jack would send the cowardly Turks into terrified flight. The opposite proved to be the case. The initial failure to take Constantinople had bolstered the enemy's courage, and the Turks had shown great bravery under long bombardment, exposing themselves to danger with indifference. They were also emboldened by their faith in Islam, and the Imams took their places beside soldiers in the dug-outs, inciting them to fight in the name of Allah and Mohammed to defend their country against foreign infidels intent on launching a new Christian invasion from the west.

The Allied invasion force was the largest amphibious operation in the entire history of warfare up to that time, although its formation and planning took only three weeks (the landing at Normandy was two years in the planning). General Hamilton wrote: 'The landing of an army upon a theatre of operation strongly garrisoned throughout and prepared for any such attempt involved difficulties for which no precedent was forthcoming in military history, except possibly in the sinister legends of Xerxes.' The classically educated general was referring to Xerxes I, king of Persia, who 2,300 years earlier had constructed a pontoon bridge of three hundred ships across the Dardanelles which was swept away in a storm. When Xerxes reviewed his army before battle, he wept at the thought of the slaughter about to take place. 'Of all this multitude, who shall say how many will return?' General Sir Aylmer Hunter-Weston, one of the British brigade's commanders, was cut from coarser cloth: 'Casualties, what do I care for casualties?'

The initial landing was a bloodbath. An aerial spotter reported the 'horrible sight' of a blood-red sea for a distance of fifty yards from the shore. The men landed on terrain that was unmapped and unknown, a wasteland that seemed abandoned even by nature: scrub-covered ridges dropped sheer into the sea, precipices and deadly ravines criss-crossed the peninsula, itself a muddle of hills and dead-end valleys. As troops advanced they found themselves surrounded by the enemy, and forced into hand-to-hand fighting with bayonets. Individual soldiers became cut off from their battalions, and these in turn lost touch with their HQ. No front line was established, Allied troops were exposed to snipers' bullets as much as a mile inland, and the entire force became bogged down.

It was decided that considerably more men were needed to take the peninsula. A large force was assembled – which included Brian's regiment – for a second invasion. The men reached the isle of Lemnos, their base for the eventual landing on Gallipoli, and instead of the sun-bleached Mediterranean of antiquity, found themselves housed in a transit camp as squalid as any slum. 'We were trained in everything, including climbing up and down mountains – everything except landing. Because there weren't any barges available.'

The war on the peninsula, which had previously been starved of sufficient troops, ammunition and modern equipment, was now suddenly bolstered by thirteen new divisions – approximately 120,000 men. Brian was part of a 25,000-man force delineated to go ashore at Suvla Bay, an ideal place for a landing in theory: the terrain was low and undulating, it offered a safe anchorage, and was reported to be lightly defended. 'We finally embarked for Gallipoli in all kinds of craft. I drew a coal boat, and we left in the dark.'

General Hamilton watched the men depart, full of foreboding. 'This empty harbour frightens me. Nothing in legend is stranger or more terrible than the silent departure of this silent army.'

A great yellowish cloud of dust could be seen from five miles out to sea. At three miles the men became aware of the unfamiliar, pungent, rotting-carrion smell of human dead. The silent craft nudged aside the bloated carcasses of mules and horses floating out to sea from the beachhead. As they came within range of the guns, an order was shouted to extinguish all cigarettes and lights.

'We were given an army mug full of rum, which we knocked back so that we were all nearly drunk, and were transferred to barges pulled by a tug. Sitting in the barge, I thought, "Shall I put my hand on the edge of the barge and get it smashed against the hull of the coal boat?" But I didn't do it. I was really very excited at the thought of landing.'

As the force neared the shore, the tug swung outwards and set the barges free to be taken towards the beach by the tide. Close to the beach the troops began to jump into the sea to wade ashore, but the Turks had put barbed wire under the water and men became entangled. 'They clung to the wire under fire, the short ones drowning. I was the next person to jump when the word came down the line, "Nobody else land!"'

The barges were pulled away by the tugs, and monitors came in to shell away the barbed wire. 'Those of our men who were still caught on it, struggling to get off, were all killed.'

The second landing attempt was successful and the troops advanced up the gullies. 'There was a fellow there kneeling down and I said, "Don't stay there, you'll be shot." Somebody yelled, "Come on – he's dead!" The enemy was throwing down everything they could at us and a dead donkey just missed me. I hadn't come all the way from Belfast to Gallipoli to be killed by a dead donkey.'

In addition to a determined enemy, the attacking troops had to contend with bad luck and administrative chaos. Orders were issued, then countermanded or cancelled, and a sudden thunderstorm prevented the landing of artillery and horses. Two of the navy's water-lighters were grounded, leaving the men severely short of water. The Turks had poisoned many of the wells, and men became crazed with thirst, their tongues swelled and blackened, and some waded into the sea and drank salt water. Hidden reefs continued to hamper the landing, but eventually two divisions got ashore although nobody was where he was supposed to be. Twenty-five thousand men now found themselves pinned down by fifteen hundred Turks.

Exhausted, the men from the Irish Rifles fought up the gullies. 'I witnessed an act of murder,' Brian said. 'I saw a second lieutenant shoot three soldiers. One of them had dysentery flowing down his legs from under his shorts and was unable to move. The other two could not or would not move, either from shell-shock or exhaustion.'

During an uphill charge with fixed bayonets, Brian was confronted by a large Turkish soldier. 'I wasn't too frightened but really very excited. He lunged with his bayonet at my guts and I went by instinct to the "on guard" position. His rifle slid along mine and the bayonet went into my arm.' Something rushed past Brian's head, and then a hot, wet mass hit him between the eyes. 'I thought my face had been blown off and started yelling in panic for stretcher-bearers. A sergeant got hold of me and steadied me.'

Out of ammunition, the sergeant had taken his rifle by the barrel and swung it at the Turk who had bayoneted Brian. It was the rush of the rifle's path that he had felt, just before the contents of the enemy soldier's crushed skull hit him between the eyes. The sergeant laid him down, and cleaned the human brains from his face. Brian lost so much blood that he blacked out.

'When I came to, a medical orderly was tenderly binding my wound. The cut was not deep, but the bayonet had severed a vein, although the wound wasn't bad enough to get me on to the hospital ship. I was very sorry for myself about that. Our one idea of heaven was to get on to a hospital ship, and we used to gaze longingly at the red and green lights out to sea. Nearly every soldier's wish after landing was to get off. I discovered early on that I was not of the heroic mould.'

The Turks were pushed back and their trenches occupied. 'The dug-outs were deep and safe. They were facing in the wrong direction, but we soon changed all that. The battle had been furious with bayonets thudding into bodies. Men, whose ammunition was spent, tried to strangle and bite one another.' The fighting on Gallipoli was not war as anyone had previously known it and chroniclers of the conflict have described it as the activity of a disturbed ant heap – frantic movement without apparent plan or meaning. The hand-to-hand combat resembled an urban riot with all the hallmarks of a vicious form of street fighting.

A Turkish counter-attack annihilated one brigade within minutes, killing all its officers and scattering the men into the thick scrub. Many of the wounded and dying were stranded in the gorse of no-man's-land. 'This caught fire and the blaze was so ferocious the men were burned to death. The screaming was absolutely terrible and drove us mad, because there was nothing we could do. My friend Bobbie McKenzie was distraught and desperately tried to run back into the red-hot gorse to save somebody. In anguish I held him to me. I used all my strength to stop him because he would have burned his feet off. We just sat there, helpless and useless, and watched. Clouds of smoke rose from the burning gorse into that merciless blue sky, carrying with it the souls of our comrades.'

General Hamilton witnessed the rout and wrote in his diary: 'My heart has grown tough amidst the struggles of the peninsula but the misery of this scene well nigh broke it.'

'The sixth battalion of the Royal Irish Rifles landed on that Thursday in August with one thousand, one hundred and thirteen men,' Brian said. 'By the following Monday, we were just two hundred and eighty. What was left of my battalion became attached to the Eighth Australian Light Horse, which had also been decimated. We were quite happy to be attached to the Australians, because their rations included chocolate.'

Brian often spoke of the 'beauty' of the Australian troops, and I smiled to myself, attributing his extravagant description of the 'Antipodean gods' to his nature. But the good looks and physical perfection of the Dominion soldiers – the Colonials – was remarked upon by almost everyone who came across them. They were seen as classical heroes, beautiful of body and fearless of spirit in the face of death. General Hamilton wrote of them as 'magnificent specimens'. The novelist Compton Mackenzie, who spent time on Gallipoli, wrote: 'There was not one of the glorious young men who might not himself have been Ajax, Diomed, Hector or Achilles. Their almost complete nudity, their tallness and majestic simplicity of line, their rose-brown flesh burnt by the sun and purged of all grossness by the ordeal through which they were passing, all these united to create something as near

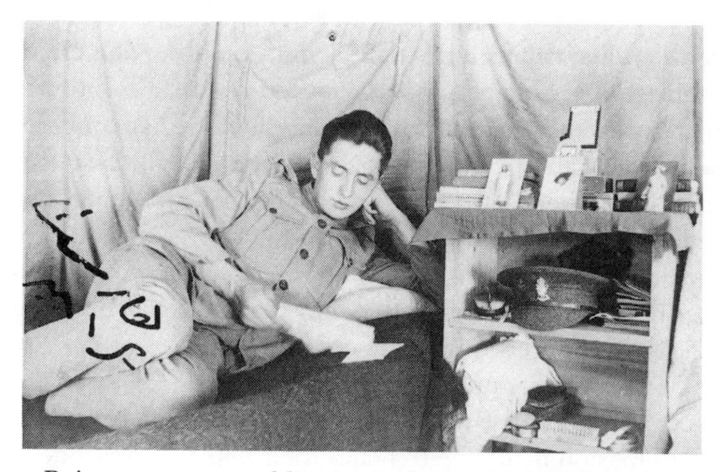

Brian as a young soldier in the Royal Irish Rifles, 1916

to absolute beauty as I shall ever hope to see in the world.'

Like Brian's battalion, the Australian Light Horse had been chopped to pieces. An officer had accurately informed his men, as they waited to mount a frontal attack on Turkish trenches: 'You have ten minutes to live.' The Turks proceeded to kill 650 of the 1,250 soldiers who went over the top, as wave upon wave were shot down and the living clambered over the dead.

At best, corpses were buried in shallow graves amid rock and scrub, but when the heavy rains came even these meagre resting places were washed out. 'We had to rebury them. It was an awful job. Many of the bodies were in an advanced state of decomposition and we had to creep forward at night, handkerchiefs fixed over our faces, and tie puttees round the bodies and pull them into newly dug, deeper graves.'

Turkish casualties were also appalling. The Constantinople Director of Railways, on a chance visit to the front, found himself placed in charge of a position because so many senior officers had been killed. An entire regiment was massacred after being told by its commanding officer, 'I don't order you to attack, I order you to die. In the time which passes until we die other troops and commanders can take our places.' Soldiers were ordered to charge with unloaded rifles to force them to advance right up to the Allied trenches and use their bayonets. Many of the Turkish troops were illiterate conscripts who were harshly treated by their officers and lived under a regime of strict discipline. Poorly fed, and often unpaid for months, outgunned and outnumbered, their enemies respectfully conceded that they remained cool under fire and displayed great bravery in combat.

This previously uninhabited, broiling and benighted peninsula now became Brian's small world, as troops of the 10th Irish Division made the trenches their home. It was a desert landscape of brown rock, dust and gorse bushes, and the only wildlife consisted of lizards, spiders and scorpions. From four in the morning until eight at night, the temperatures were in the high eighties so that cans and tin plates became too hot to touch. Troops forced to live in the rock-lined trenches compared the experience to being baked slowly in a bread oven. The army, with the same lack of planning and foresight it employed in everything to do with Gallipoli, had kitted out the men fighting in this hellish heat for war in northern France – thick serge uniforms, breeches, puttees and heavy boots. (Summer uniforms arrived in time for winter.)

Bloated flies, gorged upon human excrement and rotting corpses, settled thickly upon the men and their food. The troops came to hate the flies as much as the war itself. The food was terrible – bully beef, jam, black tea and the occasional ration of rum. The wounded faced a terrible time, as there were few doctors and limited drugs. There were no dentists at all.

After the initial bloodletting of the landings, the war settled into the dreary and deadly trench warfare that had become so familiar in France. There would be bombardment, followed by infantry attacks on trenches, which sometimes changed hands. Mule teams forever made their way from the beach, winding up rocky paths to the strange cities of trenches and caves dug out of the cliffs. They carried ammunition, food and water – shipped seven hundred miles from the Egyptian Nile. The cicadas were deafening, while the sound of gunfire and artillery from the gullies, ridges and valleys rang out constantly. But no major objectives were gained by either side, and the conflict became a wearying stalemate. Enforced idleness in the baking trenches proved as great a trial as battle, and an even greater sap to morale.

Occasional bombardment enlivened the tedium of trench life. 'A shell landed near our dug-out. I was completely buried in the debris, except for my legs. My companions tried to pull me out but they nearly strangled me because there was a beam right under my chin. I kicked wildly because they were nearly pulling my head off. They stopped pulling and began to dig me out. By this time, I was nearly dead.' Brian was carried a little way along the trench where he was propped against sandbags, given a canteen of water and left to recover.

Men risked their lives for water. One well, close to Brian's section of trench, was rank but unpoisoned, and the Turks landed a shell near it every ten minutes to keep thirsty troops at bay. 'We would rush forward in between shells with our canteens tied to our puttees and run back if a shell came. I was bringing up a lovely canteen of foul water using my puttee as a rope when it broke. I tied the canteen to the thick part of my puttee and lowered it down again. But the spill had thrown my timing off and a shell came a little too soon and I was blown into the well. Floundering around at the bottom, I found I had a dead donkey for company. The first thing I did was to fill myself with this foul water, which I found delicious. Captain Lawrie came over to the edge of the well to see if I was all right. "Stay put. We can't get you out until dark." So I stayed down in the well with the dead donkey until nightfall, when they came and let a rope down to get me up.'

Trenches and positions often exchanged hands several

times, where the corpses of both sides were left exposed until they could be buried, and men grew inured to the close company of the dead. Brian was sent to the ammunition dump for a case of bullets and blithely stepped over the bloated corpse of a dead Turkish soldier lying in a communication trench. 'Coming back, the box of bullets was enormously heavy. I couldn't step over him so I stepped on him. All the wind that had been in his stomach came roaring out of both ends. I dropped the box of bullets and fled back to our position.' He was white and shaking when he arrived, dumb from shock. Fellow soldiers calmed him and tried to find out what had happened. '*The dead Turk is alive!*'

On one occasion, Lord Kitchener himself visited the trenches, the first time Brian had seen a general officer in the front-line trenches during his time on Gallipoli. 'Kitchener came along, a very imposing figure, just like the poster that had snared us all into the army.' The great general's verdict on the peninsula concurred with that of his men: 'An awful place!'

'There were many Gurkhas fighting alongside us at Gallipoli,' Brian said. 'Without doubt the greatest soldiers in the world – and fanatically clean. Each man had two little brass pots, one to wash his genitals and rectum, the other to cook in. They had their own latrine in a separate part of the gully – the usual long pole on trestles over a deep trench. One day there were so many sitting on the pole that it cracked and they all fell in, which was for them the supreme tragedy. Climbing out, they went wild and dashed screaming into the sea impervious to danger. They tore their uniforms off and scrubbed and scrubbed and scrubbed.'

Everyone suffered from dysentery, a scourge endured by Xerxes' soldiers on their return march in the fifth century BC. A thousand men a week were being evacuated from Gallipoli because of it, and many of those who were left were too tired to haul themselves to the latrines. 'Sixty per cent of the fighting forces were immobilised by dysentery at any one time. I had it too but the doctor told me, "I can't send you away, sergeant, anybody who can walk must stay." All of us soldiers who could move had a big army biscuit tin with a round hole in the top and we used that to relieve ourselves in. After stand-to one morning, I went down to the main latrine in Shrapnel Gully to empty my pot. Every morning it was usual to find ten to fifteen men, gripping the ground with their faces in agonised death masks, lying in the mucus and excrement.

'Sitting on the pole that day was a young Australian, his shorts down to his ankles – the Australians fought practically naked, with shorts as short as could be. The dysentery was pouring from him. He said, "Give us a hand up, Pat." (Anybody with the harp badge on their uniform was automatically 'Pat'.) I went to him and cleaned him up as best I could with a dirty old handkerchief he had and his field dressing. Then I carried him through the dead and dying to where there was some shade. I held him in my arms. The skin was drawn tight over his gaunt face, and he opened his eyes and said, "Pat, there's some water in my bottle." A soldier's gift. He knew he was dying and that water was infinitely precious. "There's some chocolate in my haversack – take it." And then he died.'

At that moment two stretcher-bearers came down the gully – a Welsh Fusilier and a Connaught Ranger – with an empty stretcher. 'Put this boy on the stretcher and take him along to Australian headquarters for burial,' Brian said, handing them the soldier's identity disc. A group of some twenty Turkish prisoners stood nearby under guard, and as he helped the stretcher-bearers cover the dead Australian with a groundsheet, one of them gestured for permission to cross over to them. A guard nodded. The prisoner broke off a piece of wild thyme and laid it in the hands of the dead man. 'Then the Welshman said, "Let's pray for him." The three of us knelt down. The Welshman said the Lord's Prayer in Welsh, and the Connaught Ranger in Irish. I had no Irish, so I said it in English. They carried him away to Australian headquarters for burial at night. As I watched him go I thought of the lines by Yeats: "And he had known at last some tenderness / Before earth took him to her stony care."'

In the early stages of the Gallipoli campaign there was intense hatred of the Turks. The army propaganda machine carefully fed an image of an enemy that was cruel and fanatical, and whose vices and bestial practices were scarcely human. The wholesale murder of Christian Armenians inside Turkey lent a sinister reality to the Turks' reputation for cruelty. The Armenian population had long cherished a hope to set up an independent state within Turkey, and at the outbreak of war they were bitterly resented throughout the country as an infidel minority that wished for the defeat of the nation to achieve their own selfish political aims. Turkey planned the genocide of every one of the two million Armenians in the country, and at the beginning of the war ruthlessly exterminated three-quarters of a million men, women and children. The slaughter was appalling. As one contemporary writer described it, 'The Turk, in rage and blind anger, poured out death in a bucket.'

For their part, the Turkish soldiers on Gallipoli believed all foreigners to be inferior. Christians were seen as unclean infidels and natural slaves, lower than dogs. An inferiority complex bred out of the long decline of the Ottoman Empire, endless defeat in battle, together with xenophobia fed by Islam, led the Turk to thirst for revenge on the invaders.

Turkish snipers, who took a heavy toll, were particularly hated by the Allies. 'They had been very active and effective in Shrapnel Gully, and the company sergeant-major was ordered to put together a strong patrol to deal with them,' Brian said. 'He selected twenty riflemen and three sergeants, including me. We advanced slowly and began to make our way under cover up the gully. There was a shot. One soldier fell dead, a bullet between the eyes. We lifted him into the shade and pushed forward. Then there was another crack and a second soldier got hit, this time in the shoulder. But one of the patrol had spotted the flash of the rifle, and we were able to close in, surround the position and capture the sniper.'

The prisoner was roughly manhandled and taken to a secluded part of the gully. The mood among the men was ugly, not least because in recent days a position at Lone Pine had been retaken, and the bodies of Allied officers found obscenely bayoneted to death. The entire patrol gathered around the sniper, and several of the men clutched bayonets. It was reward enough to kill a sniper, but to capture one alive offered an opportunity for brute revenge difficult to resist for men with their blood up.

The sergeant-major pulled off the sniper's woollen cap to expose a bronzed, shaven head. Then he ripped open the prisoner's jacket. Close to a dozen identification discs hung around the sniper's neck, trophies retrieved from soldiers who had been shot. The sergeant-major read out one or two names, then stopped, unable to continue. 'He tore the sniper's shirt open to expose two white breasts with dark brown nipples. The sniper was a woman.'

Four bayonets were driven into the ground, and the sniper was stripped naked and tied to the bayonets with puttees. 'She lay there spread-eagled, and the sun was beating down on her – a white marble statue with bronze head and hands. The sergeant-major told the patrol to fall back slightly. He lay down and went up into her. She gave a low moan and turned her head away. One of the sergeants went up her next, then the other. And then it was my turn. I had never seen a naked woman before, but as a sergeant I had to pretend to do it. She had beautiful dark eyes, half closed. She didn't look at me.'

Most of the patrol took part in the rape, urged on by hatred and a desire for revenge, although several men refused to touch the sniper and looked away. Afterwards, the sergeant-major told the patrol to fall back, adding that the three sergeants were to stay close. There was a shot. The sergeant-major called the sergeants back. 'He had pulled the woollen cap back down over the sniper's shorn head, covering her face and the bullet wound. The three of us carried her over to a ditch at the side of the gully, laid her uniform on her and covered her with gorse. The sergeant-major handed me the bunch of identity discs and her gun. "Take these down to the captain. Tell him the sniper has been dealt with. Don't say anything else."'

Brian returned to the line and stood at the entrance to the captain's tent. 'Come in, sergeant.'

Brian reported the sergeant-major's words, laid the identification discs on the table and handed over the gun. Captain Lawrie examined it and put it aside. 'I began to feel faint and thought I was going to vomit. I grabbed hold of the tent pole.'

The captain moved quickly to Brian's side and put an arm round his shoulders: 'Steady, sergeant.'

As Brian left the tent, he looked back through the open flap to see the captain examining the identification discs and making notes. 'I felt sick. I ran behind a rock and vomited until I thought my soul was coming out of my body.' A passing soldier gave him a drink from a canteen of water and helped him clean up. This small act of tenderness overwhelmed Brian in his emotional state, and he felt as if he were the beneficiary of the greatest kindness on earth. 'I will never forget that soldier.'

Strangely, in the long, hot months in which men killed and maimed one another, these attitudes of hatred softened rather than hardened, and were transmuted into something approaching mutual respect and sympathy. An understanding arose that, as soldiers, the men shared the same hardships, emotions and possible fate. In the lulls between battles, troops often threw small presents into one another's trenches: grapes and sweets from the Turks; tinned food and cigarettes from the Allies. Among the Allies, hatred of the Turk was replaced by deep loathing and contempt for the politicians who had committed them to the killing field. The view developed that the campaign need never have been fought if politicians on both sides had shown more intelligence and imagination.

After the worst encounters, armistices would be declared to allow each army to bury its dead. As the soldiers worked side by side, digging communal graves for both Turkish and Allied dead, a bond grew between them. The carrion stench of death stayed in the nostrils of the men for days, and neither thyme, lavender nor rosemary could remove it. The Turks handed their enemies antiseptic wool to hold under their noses, cigarettes were exchanged, and unit badges swapped as souvenirs. Brian liked to quote a line from Wilfred Owen's poem 'Strange Meeting' to describe this temporary bond bordering on the mystical: 'I am the enemy you killed, my friend . . .'

As the gravediggers prepared to return to their respective trenches, they bade each other farewell in broken phrases of Arabic and English. One Allied soldier joked that he would probably be shot by them the following day. The Turks replied as one man: 'Allah forbid!'

'Goodbye, mate,' the Australians called out. 'Good luck!'

'Smiling may you go,' the Turks replied, 'and smiling may you go again.'

The enemies climbed back into their trenches. The minute the armistice ended, the world returned to what had become normal: the rattle of rifle fire and the crump of artillery, and the routine business of killing.

One night Brian had drawn outpost duty with his close friend Jimmy Willis, and they took up position a thousand yards in advance of Allied lines. 'Jimmy had a lovely singing voice. He used to sing the old ballads of Ulster for us, "My Lagan Love" and "The Banks of the Bann". Yeats later told me that "My Lagan Love" is the oldest song in Ireland. Jimmy also knew all the old Irish legends and told us about the children of Lir, the Irish princes and princesses, who were changed by enchantment into black and white swans and doomed to fly for ever over stormy Lough Foyle.

'I couldn't keep Jimmy awake, although I knew if he was caught sleeping he would be severely punished. Finally, I gave up and turned away from him, and began to think about things to drink. It was a hot, stifling night and we were desperately short of water. My head filled with visions of every cooling drink and ice-cream in the world. I heard a moan. A soft sound, nothing dramatic. I turned to see that a dumdum bullet, which explodes when it hits someone, had entered Jimmy's chest. There was no noise or fuss.

'I took out his field dressing and put it into the wound. Then I added my own, although it was forbidden to give it away. They were instantly sodden and sank into the wound. Jimmy murmured faintly, "Give us a drink, sarge." Before I could get my water-bottle to his lips, the blood came gushing up his throat and he was gone. His lovely voice, with which he sang the old ballads of Ulster, stilled.'

Panic and confusion overtook Brian, as he lowered his friend's body to the ground. He was alone, a long way from his own line, and became filled with dread. Recklessly, he stood and began to move through the gorse in an attempt to get back to the Allied trenches, thrashing about in the spiny bushes until he became thoroughly disoriented, and lost all sense of time. He ran down one gully that led into a dead end and heard voices. Turkish voices.

A soldier rose from the gorse nearby and signalled him to be still. 'The two of us stood for a moment, listening. I then understood that I had been heading straight into the Turkish lines. The presence of the other soldier completely calmed me and I was no longer afraid. I looked across at him and his face seemed familiar. He made me feel safe, and when I got another look at him I somehow recognised the face, but couldn't place it. Although we never said a word to each other, we seemed to be carrying on a conversation. He turned about and I followed him.

'We came to a deep ditch torn out of the earth by the previous torrential rains, which was not the way I had come. This particular ditch was about twelve to fifteen feet deep, narrow and very steep. Along the bottom on either side were lines of dead men, head to toe, waiting for burial. In some cases their helmets had fallen from their faces and their dead eyes were staring. We walked together between the dead men.'

They emerged from the ravine and Brian saw that he was in familiar territory. The soldier raised an arm and pointed towards the tent of Captain Lawrie in the distance. 'I took one step – no more – and realised where I had seen the face before. It was the face of my mother in an old family photograph. I turned quickly, but the soldier had disappeared. I was alone.'

The Gallipoli campaign had become locked in stalemate, and back in London it was debated whether there should be a renewed attack with a strengthened force, or if the Allies should cut their losses and evacuate. This called for some cold-blooded calculation: the army first estimated that withdrawal might leave 40,000 dead on the beaches. General Hamilton was completely opposed to the idea: 'If they do this they make the Dardanelles the bloodiest tragedy in the world.'

The general was supported by an articulate and powerful ally in London in the person of Lord Curzon, a member of the War Committee. He described for the Cabinet a fearsome scene as the trenches slowly emptied: 'A disorganised crowd will press in despairing tumult on to the shore and into the boats. Shells will be falling and bullets ploughing their way into the mass of retreating humanity . . . Conceive the crowding into boats of thousands of half-crazy men, the swamping of craft, the nocturnal panic, the agony of the wounded, the hecatombs of slain.'

Field Marshal Kitchener refused to accept this apocalyptic view and dismissed the army's casualty estimates – even though they had been obligingly scaled down to a possible 25,000 dead. 'You'll just step off without losing a man,' he declared, 'and without the Turks knowing anything about it.' This was nothing more than an old soldier's hunch, voiced by the man who had previously said the Turks would be a pushover. It was a view opposed by commanders in the field, military intelligence and common sense.

But Kitchener won the day, and the decision was taken to spirit the army away in the night. The logistical problems of lifting 100,000 men off Gallipoli were enormous – half the force was medically unfit for a start – without the added fantasy requirement that the Turks should not notice (a number of the Allied trenches were no more than *ten yards* from the enemy). It was also a practical impossibility to evacuate such a large number of men in a single night because there was not enough room on the beaches.

And in addition there was the complication of appalling weather. The hell of summer had given way to the misery of winter, and the men had already suffered the worst blizzard in forty years. Twenty-four hours of torrential rain had turned into a hurricane-force wind, followed by two days of sleet and snow, and a further two nights of frost. At Suvla Bay, where there was little protection, survival itself became a struggle. Wet blankets and bedding froze solid, and icicles formed hard as steel. The dry gullies of summer were turned into raging torrents, dislodging the rotting corpses that had been hastily buried in shallow, stony graves, and sweeping the cadavers into trenches. Rifles jammed from the cold, dug-outs became knee-deep in slush, and the men suffered through it all with no winter kit. Two hundred men *drowned* – a further 5,000 suffered frostbite, and there were another 5,000 mixed casualties. The army calculated it had lost a tenth of its strength as a result of the weather.

Despite these conditions, a plan for secret evacuation was drawn up, which called for 20,000 men a night to be lifted off the beaches. Blankets were to be placed on the piers to deaden the noise, boots to be wrapped in sacking. No tents were to be struck, and troops left behind were to fire twice as many rounds and light twice as many camp fires. An ingenious self-firing rifle was devised that fired a bullet every half-hour. Finally, a small rearguard of the 'bravest and steadiest' men would remain to take their chances of getting away before the Turks poured into the empty trenches. It took courage of a special order to volunteer for this doomed band, but men came forward in their hundreds demanding to be the last to leave the shore. There were so many that there had to be a selection from the volunteers.

One task that profoundly disturbed the men was cutting the throats of those horses that could not be taken away. The slaughter seemed a betrayal of the animals' loyalty and service, and for this job the men did not volunteer. A skeleton crew of medical staff was to be left behind with the seriously wounded, with a letter in French requesting the Turkish commander-in-chief to let them disembark later in a British hospital ship (the bravery of certain of the medical orderlies had bordered on inhuman recklessness – a French doctor wrote of his 'sublime stretcher-bearers'). Twelve thousand hospital beds were made available in Cairo, and fifty-six hospital ships assembled.

After the endless bloodletting and tens of thousands of deaths, the soldiers were embittered to be ordered to run away in the night. Brian had already been transferred to a hospital ship, he had become so ill, and transferred to Cairo. Despite the brutalising months of hardship and combat the soldiers remained remarkably tender and true to one another. The thought of leaving dead friends behind was particularly upsetting. 'I hope *they* won't hear us going down to the beaches.'

On the first night swarms of craft of all sizes arrived after dark, and troops, animals and guns were duly taken aboard. Men followed white trails of flour and sugar through newly laid minefields and booby traps down to the beaches, and twenty thousand disappeared into the dark without the enemy knowing. And so it went, night after night. With fewer and fewer men left behind on the peninsula, the tension for those remaining was close to unbearable. When there were only 35,000 men left – four divisions to defend themselves against twenty-one of the enemy – a rumour ran through the trenches that the Turks planned to castrate the captured.

Close to the end, when the Allies were down to 17,000 men, the Turks launched an attack preceded by a four-and-half-hour bombardment, and then advanced across the few hundred yards to the British trenches. They were met with murderous defensive fire, and not a single Turkish soldier broke through the lines to discover the Allied secret. There was no subsequent attack.

The remaining troops had to face bad weather and persistent shelling, but by the early hours of the last morning only 3,200 men remained. They left their trenches and marched down to the beach and boarded the ships waiting for them. Two hundred men who had moved to an isolated landing place found their lighter had run aground, and as they began a forced two-mile march to the tip of the peninsula in search of another ship, their commanding officer discovered he had left behind his valise containing important documents. He returned with a fellow officer to retrieve it. Meanwhile, the men made contact with a ship and successfully boarded it. The ship's captain was anxious to cast off, but the men refused to abandon their officers, and waited. Ten minutes before the main ammo dump on the peninsula was timed to explode, they reappeared.

The Allies and the Turks had committed a million men between them to the brutal conflict of Gallipoli, and although they suffered a quarter of a million casualties each, the front line never shifted more than half a mile. It was a costly, whole-hearted defeat for the Allies, which perhaps explains the disgraceful fact that no special medal was awarded to the men who fought in the Gallipoli campaign. No veteran of Gallipoli came away with a romantic vision of war, and yet the departure of the army from the peninsula really was the stuff of legend. Not a man was left behind.

'Sorry about the stupid things I said about war on the beach.' I hope my tone conveyed the shame I felt.

'Let's just say I've known better times on Mediterranean shores.'

Even after evacuating Gallipoli in a hospital ship Brian had suffered terribly, and the amusing anecdotes of convalescence masked the truth that the 'Daffodil of B11' almost died. As a result of his time on the peninsula, Brian had contracted chronic dysentery, malignant malaria and yellow jaundice. In addition, his wounded arm had begun to fester, threatening gangrene. He was dangerously ill, on the point of death, for twenty-three days. 'I recovered but was still too weak to go back to the front. Early in 1916, when the Turks were approaching the Suez Canal and it looked as if they would capture Cairo, every walking patient was given extra duties to do. I drew night orderly in a dysentery ward with a hundred patients. The men were so ill that they couldn't even have a bedpan, and we had to put wads of cotton wool under them. Twenty-five soldiers died in a single night.'

The Gallipoli tapings had proved almost as painful for Brian as those of childhood. 'I'm really *exhausted* by going over this again,' he said at last. 'Let's call it a day on the First World War. It's so disturbing to go back into your past and dredge all these memories up. Strange to find how raw one's emotions remain so many years on.'

Brian sat for a moment, lost in thought. 'How could that man in hand-to-hand combat with a bayonet have been me?

The capture of the sniper remains vivid today . . . too vivid. And the visitation from the mother-soldier has stayed with me all my life. And yet, do you know what haunts me – the thing that pains me most when I think of it? The horrible shooting and death of Jimmy Willis. I can hear his voice – his beautiful tenor voice with all of Ulster in it.'

Brian began to murmur, part song and part recitation, half-remembered snatches from 'My Lagan Love', Ireland's oldest song – the ballad that Jimmy Willis sang to entertain his Irish mates in the trenches of Gallipoli:

Where Lagan stream sings lullaby, there blows a lily fair
The twilight gleam is in her eyes, the night is on her hair
And like a lovesick lenanshee she hath my heart in thrall
Nor life I own, nor liberty for love is lord of all

And often when the beetle's horn hath lulled the eye to sleep
I steal unto her shieling lorn and thro' the dooring peep
There on the cricket's singing stone, she stirs the bogwood fire
And hums in sad, sweet undertone the song of heart's desire

Her welcome like her love for me is from the heart within
Her warm kiss is felicity, that knows no taint or sin
When she was only fairy small her gentle mother died
But true love keeps her memory warm, by Lagan's silver side.

PART VII

Malta

Movement towards the production of the film, such as it was, tended to happen in sudden, unannounced lurches that I found out about when I showed up at Command Central, in Kinnerton Street. Somewhere along the line Brian had decided he only wanted to produce the film. I now discovered a director had been recruited, in the person of Roy Ward Baker, and that in the near future we would all be going to Malta for a location scout.

Roy was something of a catch. Among a score of movies he had made was the 1958 classic *A Night to Remember*, about the sinking of the *Titanic*. Except for special effects, the film was infinitely superior to the later *Titanic*, and was both factually accurate and emotionally moving. Roy's film cost a little over half a million pounds – a large sum for the time – but even allowing for conversion to present values, a tenth of the budget of its vaudevillian successor.

My first encounter with Mr Baker was somewhat intimidating. Roy sat by the table, with the script on his lap in the midst of a furious session with a red crayon. This continued for fifteen minutes, and there seemed scarcely a page that did not attract the speed-reading director's attention. Eventually, Roy handed the script back to me. I opened it in trepidation. Every camera direction – tracking, crane, dolly, close-up – had a thick red line through it. 'You write the film – I'll direct it,' Roy said. 'And we'll get on like a house on fire.'

The plan was for Brian and myself to fly out to Malta in advance for a few days, after which Roy would join us. I

Brian with Roy Ward Baker, the director of A Night to Remember *who was also slated to direct* Darkness Before Dawn

worked hard and pulled strings with the tourist office for the trip, so that we were given free air tickets by Air Malta. 'Well done, Christopher,' Brian said. 'So much better to go to these places as VIPs. Sets the right tone straight away – disguises the begging bowl.' I had also found a copy of *Who's Who in Malta*, a slim volume that listed all the noble families and important people on the island. Brian was pleased to see that despite the passage of time since he had made *Malta Story*, he still knew a good number of these VIPs, and marked them with large crosses in blue biro.

Malta itself had been the star of Brian's movie. Although only twenty-one miles long by twelve miles wide, the island has been of enormous strategic importance throughout history because of its location in the Mediterranean between Sicily and North Africa. In the Second World War it became an essential Allied base between enemy-occupied Europe and the German armies in the deserts of North Africa, and Hitler ordered it to be obliterated. From June 1940 until the end of

1942, Malta was put under siege and became the most heavily bombed place on earth. Its inhabitants were forced to undergo appalling privations, but the island held. As a result Malta was awarded the George Cross – second only to the Victoria Cross as a military decoration – for 'acts of the greatest heroism or of the most conspicuous courage in circumstances of extreme danger'. This valiant stand against the odds formed the basis of *Malta Story*.

On the journey to the airport I tried to bring Brian up to date on the political situation. This had changed radically since he had last been on the island. The current Prime Minister, Dom Mintoff, had led the Maltese Liberation Movement, which spearheaded the drive for independence, achieved in 1964. Since then he had become increasingly nationalistic and anti-British, pushing for the removal of military bases and developing close relations with China, Libya and Algeria. It was important, I explained, to emphasise the economic advantages of making the film on the island, while downplaying the subject matter – Mintoff was the bitter enemy of Archbishop Gonzi, head of the island's Catholic Church, and in perpetual conflict with the Knights of Malta, both of whom he saw as forces of reaction. Brian said nothing, a silence I should have interpreted as ominous.

At the airport he demanded to be taken to the VIP lounge, but we were told there was no time, and so went straight to the plane. Once on board, Brian was scandalised to find we had been placed in the economy section. He summoned the stewardess, claiming a serious mistake had been made. 'We are guests of the government, Dom whoever it is – how is this possible?'

The stewardess checked the tickets and said she was sorry, but those were the seats we had been assigned and there was nothing she could do about it. 'Extraordinary!' Brian snorted.

'No point making a fuss, Bri,' I said. 'I mean, they are *free*.'

'This man Dom Wotzisname is a fucking communist

cheapskate. Thinks he's a revolutionary by punishing his erstwhile masters by depriving them of a couple of drinks and a bag of nuts. But to do this to *me*! The man who made the film celebrating the heroism of his people. I am appalled!'

We settled into our seats. After a couple of minutes Brian nudged me and gave me one of his big, exaggerated winks. His mood had changed from noisy outrage to silent mischief, an infinitely more dangerous state. A rapid metamorphosis occurred as he turned into a wheezing Little Old Man. 'Miss, miss!' he called pitifully, as the stewardess passed.

'Yes, sir?'

'My doctor made me promise to inform you – I have a dicky heart. I may need oxygen on the flight. You might tell the captain.'

The stewardess looked alarmed and hurried off, while Brian turned and gave me another enormous wink. She returned within a couple of minutes. 'I've spoken to the captain, sir. He suggests you might be more comfortable at the front of the plane in First Class, where there is more room if we need to administer oxygen.'

'Whatever you say, miss,' Brian said. 'Anything to help.' He pointed at me. 'This is Mr Robbins, my travelling companion. He is a qualified male nurse. Can he come with me?'

'I'm sure that will be all right,' the stewardess said, relieved not to have the sole responsibility of a sickly old man on her hands. We made our way into First Class where we were greeted by a steward. 'Good morning, sir.'

'Hiya, handsome!' Brian nudged me again – he had marked the steward as gay, a potential victim. He demanded a bottle of champagne, and the steward returned with two miniatures. 'This Dom fellow imposed rationing on the island?'

'This is how the champagne comes, sir.'

'You are a tease! How many of those things make up a proper bottle?'

'Five or six.'

'Bring us six – it's not the same but . . .'

'. . . *it'll do*,' we said in unison.

I was not much in the mood for drink, but Brian began to open and consume the tiny bottles at a fantastic rate. I assumed he was celebrating his triumph in being moved into First Class. I read a book in my nice, wide seat, looked out of the window and snoozed. About an hour or more into the flight I heard a theatrical wheezing on my right. I turned with a joke on my lips – 'Time for your oxygen, Mr Hurst!' – but Brian was not play-acting. His face had gone bright red, his eyes bulged, and his mouth was wide open, exposing a lolling tongue as he gasped for air like a landed fish. He seemed scarcely conscious.

The steward appeared in the aisle, greatly concerned, and looked to me for instructions. After all, I was a qualified male nurse. I felt close to panic as I saw Brian begin to turn purple. *Oh my God*, I thought, *he's had a heart attack!*

'What shall I do?' the steward asked.

'Undo his tie!' The steward fumbled to loosen Brian's tie, while the stewardess appeared toting a small canister of oxygen.

'Shall I give him oxygen?'

'Good idea.' The mask was applied and Brian began to breathe the pure oxygen in large, gulping breaths.

'The captain will radio through for a doctor and ambulance to be available when we land,' the steward said. 'It's only forty minutes or so.'

I sat there terrified. *Please God, don't let him die, don't let him die, don't let him die! St Thérèse, don't let him die!* For ten minutes I beseeched Brian's God and patron saint to come to his aid. He must have had a hotline to Heaven, for he began to breathe more easily, and his colour returned to normal. 'Had a bit of a funny turn,' he said. 'Better now.'

Apart from seeming shaken, Brian was pretty much his normal self when we landed. He said he did not need the ambulance and refused to go to hospital, but did talk to a doctor who awaited us. 'Any idea what might have triggered this?' the doctor asked.

'No, doctor. No idea at all.'

'He drank the best part of a bottle of champagne in half an hour,' I interjected. 'That's what triggered it.' Brian gave me the kind of look a schoolboy gives another when he has been betrayed to a master. I stared him down.

'Not very clever,' the doctor said. 'Pretty silly to drink like that on the ground, but you do know that on an airplane at high altitudes alcohol works very quickly with extra potency?'

'I had no idea,' Brian said, amazed. 'You'd think they'd warn you.'

'You seem all right now,' the doctor said. 'But you should rest – and not drink. Or at least,' he said with a grin, 'less and more slowly. Good luck – and welcome to Malta.'

'Thank you, doctor,' Brian said.

As we waited for a taxi, Brian said: 'Why did you tell the doctor about the champagne? Dropping me in it like that!'

'In a question of life and death I thought even you might not object to the truth. After all, the man isn't a policeman, but a doctor concerned with your health and welfare.'

'Never tell doctors *anything*! They only store the information up and use it against you. They've oversold the whole medical bandwagon as a science, when really it's a dubious art form, the province of quacks and charlatans. Most of the time it's guesswork dressed up with lots of long words – a mystification delivered by a man in a white coat with a long, serious face and a stethoscope, instead of a witch doctor in a feathered headdress with a juju stick. If you had said much more to this fellow, the next thing you know he'd have me on a trolley giving me a transplant. I do wish you'd *think*.'

Brian was subdued on the drive to our hotel in Mdina, the ancient Roman and Saracen city in the centre of the island. 'Please don't pull a stunt like that again, Bri,' I said. 'It scared

Bomb damage from the Second World War in Valletta harbour, Malta

me to death. Pleading with St Thérèse, I was, making all sorts of promises and deals. Another ten minutes and I would have become a Catholic.'

'I'm touched. But it wasn't a stunt – I really am an old man with a weak heart.'

'Yes, but I'm *not* a qualified male nurse!'

We began to giggle. 'The scrapes we get into,' Brian said, nudging me. We began to laugh hard all the way to the hotel, so hard that we infected our driver, who began to bark like a hyena and had to mop his eyes with a handkerchief on arrival. 'They like a laugh, these Maltese,' Brian said.

The old walled city of Mdina was an enchanting, sleepy place reached by driving across a stone bridge and passing through a monumental, stone entranceway. Our hotel, the shabby but delightful Xarah Palace, was built into the ramparts and faced a quiet, dusty square. This establishment was owned by an old friend known as the uncrowned Queen of Malta. I had become so conditioned to Brian's world that it came as a surprise to find the queen was a woman. Mabel Strickland had once been an active political force on the island and still owned the *Times of Malta*, steadfast in its opposition to Prime Minister Dom Mintoff. The Xarah Palace, therefore, was not the most politic choice as an HQ to launch an appeal for government funds and support.

Brian was installed in a suite that was virtually a small house on the roof of the hotel, while I had a room that looked along the city's butter-coloured walls. As I leaned out of the window on the first morning, I could see into the gardens of the bishop's palace, and saw Archbishop Gonzi himself in black robes and scarlet skull cap, walking along a path trailed by a gaggle of gesticulating priests.

We had been invited to lunch by Queen Mabel, and around midday made our way to her private dining room. Brian, who had gone to bed early, seemed completely recovered from the previous day's adventure. 'Walk in,' Mabel commanded as we appeared at the door. 'Come here and sit you!'

We did as were told. Mabel was that sort of person – a booming, daunting giant of a woman who was as imperial and structurally imposing as the Royal Naval battleships that once dropped anchor in Valletta harbour. Instead of eighteen-inch guns on the foredeck, Mabel boasted a massive bosom proudly thrust before her, seemingly lashed in place by some seafaring contrivance of canvas and rope. She would have much preferred artillery. 'But for these,' she would boom over lunch, placing her arms before her with fingers splayed wide to symbolise the great mass of her breasts, 'I'd be prime minister of this island.'

There was something very likeable about Mabel, however, a girlish innocence and enthusiasm beneath the formidable veneer. I was encouraged to shout details about myself, as she was mildly deaf, and was questioned closely about the film.

Her dated English fascinated me. 'I hope you don't repent you of your decision to make the film here.'

'I hope we don't repent us too,' Brian said.

We were joined for lunch by a friend of Mabel's, the equally intimidating Baroness Emmett, then deputy speaker of the House of Lords, who had come to Malta for a holiday. On being told that we were on the island to scout locations for a film, the baroness said, 'Movies? Never go to 'em!' I found myself seated next to her and was ordered to repeat my name slowly and clearly. 'Stage name is it – Christopher Robin?'

'No, it's my real name – but with two Bs and an S.'

'Good God,' the baroness said. 'The names some parents inflict upon their children!'

'It wasn't my parents,' I said loyally, 'it was a bureaucrat who worked in the Orange Juice Office in Bristol.'

'Orange Juice Office?'

'Yes. My father had planned to call me Amanda, so it could have been worse.'

'*Amanda*?' The baroness was growing impatient for an explanation.

'My father desperately wanted a girl and was heartbroken when I turned out to be a boy. He just couldn't accept the fact. My parents had settled on a girl's name, but had not given any thought to naming a boy. So I stayed Amanda for a bit. But as I was born just after the war, orange juice was rationed, or kept back for babies or something. To get it you had to go to this office and fill out a form and put down the baby's name. My father explained how I was called Amanda and everything, and he hadn't come up with a good boy's name yet, and asked if he couldn't just put down Baby Robbins. The bureaucrat said it was out of the question – no name, no orange juice. My father couldn't think of anything off the cuff, so the bureaucrat jumped in with, "Why don't you call him Christopher? Christopher Robin and Winnie the Pooh, ha, ha, ha!" So I was called Christopher, and presumably received my ration of orange juice.'

The baroness had listened to what was supposed to be a mildly amusing anecdote without a flicker of a smile, and stared hard at me as I spoke, with a look of the utmost seriousness. I felt like a stand-up comic whose routine falls flat in front of an unforgiving audience, and when I had finished I lowered my eyes, and awkwardly pushed a potato around my plate. 'Did the silly name blight your childhood?' the baroness asked.

'It wasn't much fun at school. I was at boarding school from seven, and there was always some wag who sent in a request to the BBC's *Children's Favourites* on a Saturday morning for "Christopher Robin is Saying His Prayers" or "They're Changing Guard at Buckingham Palace". So I spent most Saturday mornings hiding in cupboards. And today at cocktail parties I groan inwardly when I see some wit's eyes light up as they prepare to spring the old Christopher Robin jokes on me, as if I'd never heard them in my life.'

The baroness nodded as she digested and analysed the facts laid before her. 'So that,' she said in thoughtful conclusion, 'is how you became muddled in the post?'

'I beg your pardon?'

'Put you on the road to being a woofter?'

The authority and certainty with which this psychological diagnosis was delivered left me momentarily speechless. It was clear that Mabel must have mentioned something to the baroness about Brian's sexual orientation, and that my story had led her to jump to conclusions. 'Actually . . .'

'Quite understandable, *quite* understandable,' the baroness said, magisterial in her tolerance. 'Your father wants a girl and never forgives you for being male. All your life you try to win his love and please him. On top of that he allows you to be given a silly name by a complete stranger that leads you to being mocked at school. Naturally, confusion and inversion follow.

It's all *quite* understandable.' She added that she was fascinated by this sort of thing because a son, nephew, cousin or friend – I can't remember which – was studying psychology at Oxford. She was sure he would be much interested to hear about my 'case'. Before I could respond, the baroness had turned away and was talking to someone else.

After lunch Brian said, 'I didn't know you were called Amanda. What a pretty name!'

'Did you hear her call me a woofter – is she really that rude and humourless?'

'I'd say so. You have just experienced the breathtaking insensitivity displayed by certain members of the English upper class. It comes from a sense of absolute superiority and total indifference to the thoughts and feelings of lesser mortals. Without humour and grace this can be a bruising combination. Still, every cloud has a silver lining and the baroness has unwittingly provided a most original title for *your* autobiography – *Muddled in the Post*.'

The afternoon was spent in our respective rooms on the telephone. My list was made up of practical people involved in the film business, while Brian concentrated on religious and social connections. We met for dinner, taken at a modest restaurant close to the hotel. 'I had forgotten how sour and astringent the local wine is,' Brian said. '*Most* unpleasant! What are we to do?'

'We could drink beer.'

'Don't be absurd!' We made the most of a bad carafe. 'Jacket and tie, tomorrow. We have important meetings.'

'Where are we going?'

'The Archbishop has graciously agreed to receive us in the morning. So good of him at such short notice, and such a busy man. And after lunch we are going over to the head office of the Knights of Malta. Everyone is very excited about our project.'

As I had painstakingly explained, it was not good politics

to go about our business this way around. It was bad enough to be staying in the fastness of the prime minister's belligerent political opponent, the Queen of Malta, without actively courting his declared enemies. I muttered that, rather than obtaining the government's co-operation and cash, Brian's priority seemed to be cultivating the island's religious establishment. 'Of course!'

He proved to be adept at handling archbishops, a master of the art. A scheduled twenty-minute audience stretched into well over an hour, and Archbishop Gonzi listened enthralled as Brian explained how he was fulfilling a lifelong ambition by making *Darkness Before Dawn* – the first time I had heard it so described – and seemed to suggest that St Thérèse was part of the production team. He spoke of visions and miracles, and presented Gonzi with a copy of the script as if delivering a holy relic to the Pope. As we said goodbye, the archbishop extended his right hand to Brian who bowed low, sank on to one knee and kissed the massive ruby ring. Gonzi then turned to me and did the same. Uncertain what the non-aligned response should be, I clumsily shook the proffered hand.

As we walked away from the palace, Brian criticised my ignorance of religious etiquette. 'When an archbishop offers you a personal blessing, you don't pump his hand like an American politician running for re-election. You bend – if you're too high and mighty to kneel – and lightly kiss the holy ring.'

'But I'm not a Catholic!'

'It would have been good manners and you wouldn't have looked such a bloody fool.' I made some crack about being more interested in raising money for the movie than collecting archbishops' blessings. 'I would have thought you need all the blessings you can get. But no doubt you'll make a splendid job of kissing Dom Mintoff's arse.'

The meeting with the Knights of Malta, in Valletta, was

interesting and similarly unproductive. I harboured some schoolboy image of the knights in ceremonial chainmail and white smocks emblazoned with big red crosses, but we were received by two small, smiling men in dark suits, who nonetheless wielded great power within the organisation. Brian told them all about the making of *Malta Story*, and they asked dozens of questions and pumped him for anecdotes over coffee and cake. 'Money was so short at the end that we used shots from newsreels taken at the time,' Brian told the Knights. 'I sat through over a hundred thousand feet of film at the Admiralty, captured from the Germans, as well as everything shot by our own war cameramen. There is quite a lot of genuine newsreel in the film, some of it taken during the actual siege, showing planes crashing and houses being blown up.

'Alec Guinness came to me and asked if he could play the straight lead in the picture. "I am fed up with playing funny little men." I studied him carefully, and as a portrait painter had learned how to look at a face. I knew that if I kept him looking camera left the whole time he had a very good profile and a very good three-quarter shot. However, when I proposed him to the studio heads they didn't want him and said that he wouldn't do the picture any good at all. I pointed out that he was a very fine actor and that the story was not about one particular person but about Malta and its siege during the Second World War, and eventually they agreed. With Alec there was an absolutely top cast including Jack Hawkins.'

'Every time I see the film,' one of the Knights said, 'it moves me to tears. It is very realistic.'

'Thank you. If pride were not a sin, I should be extremely proud of it. We worked in very close collaboration with the navy. At one point we needed thirty officers on a Saturday for a scene in which they were briefed by Jack Hawkins, but were told the officers didn't like working at weekends. So I told

Alec Guinness and Brian share a joke on the set of Malta Story

them just to give me the uniforms and I would put them on ratings. They threw up their hands in absolute horror, but I got my naval officers.

'We were only able to find three Spitfires, which had been cocooned for preservation, to use in the aerial shots. I used them coming in over Malta from every conceivable direction, in threes, twos and ones. But it was always the same Spitfires. In one scene Alec Guinness was seated in a cockpit against a back-projection of a sky full of enemy planes. "What do I do when these bullets strike me?" he asked. "What you do not do is clutch your guts." "Thank God for that," Alec said. I told him to look faintly surprised and lower his eyelids slightly, and that I'd move the camera gently forward until his face filled the screen, then cut into a shot of the plane falling at ever increasing speed to the earth and crashing.

'While on Malta we found out about a ship called the *Ohio*, given or loaned to Britain by the Americans. She had a terrible time as part of a convoy bringing vital supplies of oil from England. The ship was bombed and bombed and bombed. If she hadn't got through, the articles of surrender would have had to have been signed. The ship was ablaze but the crew managed to control the fire and the *Ohio* limped in to Malta harbour with her decks burned and a large hole in her bow. We decided to include this episode and wanted to have a scene with people watching the ship come into the harbour. We had only £500 left in the budget for 1,000 extras at ten bob a time, and I was scared the crowd would look a bit thin, but need not have worried. Over 7,000 locals turned up free of charge.' (When I later saw the film it looked to me more like five hundred, if that, but the story pleased the Knights.)

For their part, the Knights told us of their history on the island. Legend has it that St Paul was shipwrecked in Malta in AD 60 and personally converted the inhabitants, who boast a history of uninterrupted Christianity ever since. The island was ceded to the religious and military Catholic Order of the Hospital of St John of Jerusalem (the Knights Hospitaller) in 1530. Under the Grand Master, Jean de la Valette, the Knights successfully withstood the Ottoman siege of 1565, and afterwards built fabulous public buildings and palaces. At the end of the afternoon, Brian was so enraptured by the story that he assured the Knights that his next film – after *Darkness Before Dawn* – would be the story of the original siege, and that I would be set to work on the research immediately. Our current project had scarcely been mentioned. As we said goodbye Brian placed his hand on his heart and said, '"Malta, my dear sirs, is in my thoughts sleeping or waking." The words of Horatio Nelson. As it was for Lord Nelson, gentlemen, so it is with me.' Perhaps it was humbug, but it was humbug from the heart and moved the Knights close to tears. We came away with their blessing.

*

In *Malta Story*, Brian took the time in a sub-plot to show sympathy for a young Maltese who supports the enemy, the Italian fascists. It was Brian's view, often expressed in conversation – albeit obliquely, or through anecdote – and played out in scenes in a number of his films, that men who honestly take a contrary position, however misguided, deserve respect and fair treatment. One of the characters in the film, the brother of the Maltese woman with whom Alec Guinness falls in love, is arrested as a traitor. The man has been living in Italy and sincerely believes the best course for Malta is to free itself from the British. He is dropped off by an Italian submarine with the mission of reporting on gasoline dumps, but captured by the British who treat him as a traitor because of his Maltese nationality. The way these scenes are handled is an insight into how Brian, an Ulsterman who fought for the British in the First World War, but still believed in an independent Ireland, sympathised and identified with those condemned for misplaced loyalties. 'I'm not a traitor, I'm not a traitor,' the man insists. 'This is my country – not yours. You have no right here!'

The man's mother goes to visit him in prison, knowing that her son will not even be granted the dignity of being shot as a spy, but will be hanged as a traitor. 'They may hang me but that doesn't make me a traitor. Malta is my country. And all I wanted to do was save her from this suffering and misery . . . You do see, mother? You do see what I was trying to do was the best for Malta and all of you?'

'You chose your side as we have all had to do,' the mother replies.

'But my side was the right side, the sensible side that would bring peace!'

'You chose as you thought right, my son, we have done the same. The choices were different, that is all.'

No doubt Brian felt a need to explain and defend his own choices. In his film *Dangerous Moonlight*, about an exiled

Polish pianist who volunteers to fly for the Royal Air Force, there is tongue-in-cheek dialogue which pretty much expresses Brian's view of the English. An Irish airman, who is a friend of the hero, leaves New York to fly with the British against Germany, and a woman friend seeing him off says, 'I don't understand you. After all you've told me about what Cromwell did to your ancestors in Ireland and what you thought of the English, doesn't it seem funny to be going back to fight for them?'

'Well, the English are all right, some of them. I don't mind the Irish taking a crack at them, that doesn't count, but when somebody else butts in that's different. Beside, we must preserve the English so there's someone to fight against when this war's over.' Although I never heard Brian comment directly on Ireland's neutrality in the face of the Nazis, perhaps the Irish flyer speaks for him when he is offered the easy option of sitting out the war: 'I'd die of shame.'

This view of the Troubles between the Irish and the English as a family quarrel, where outsiders are an unwelcome complication, was Brian's lifelong belief. He often quoted his father's remark on the Orange Marches in Belfast, to commemorate the Battle of the Boyne in 1690 and the victory of Protestant Ulstermen over the Catholic forces of James II – 'When the Irish celebrate the defeat of themselves by themselves.'

He did not even seem bitter when he spoke of English troops stationed in Cairo, who had yet to see combat, turning on Irish veterans of Gallipoli at the time of the 1916 Easter Rising in Dublin. 'An Irish nurse, Sister McNulty, came rushing up to me and said: "Oh Brian, they're shooting us down in Dublin." A lot of the English soldiers began to attack various Irishmen in the hospital dining hall, and one jumped up on a table and kicked an Irish patient in the head. The colonel in charge of the hospital had all these soldiers, who were members of the Royal Army Medical Corps, lined up in the square. "These Irishmen are veterans of Gallipoli, and you are nothing but Medical Corps wallahs, so behave yourselves."

'James Connolly, one of the leaders of the rebellion, was sentenced to death. As he had been badly wounded in the leg and was suffering from gangrene, he was carried in a chair to the place of execution at Portobello Barracks, in Dublin. The young officer in charge offered to bandage his eyes but he refused. The sergeant of the firing squad spoke to the officer who was seen to nod. He then went over to Connolly and said, "Sir, the firing squad asks if you will forgive them." Connolly replied: "I forgive all brave men everywhere who do their duty."'

It had always been Brian's ambition to make a film of Sean O'Casey's play, *The Shadow of a Gunman*, about the British Black and Tans in Ireland at the time of the Troubles. Brian went down to Torquay, in Devon, where O'Casey lived in self-imposed exile, to negotiate the rights. 'Sean was there wearing an embroidered skull cap, with all the Russian newspapers laid out on the table. "I'm a communist, you know." I remained silent. He was charming and his mind was sparkling, and he went into a tirade for an hour or so on how terrible motion pictures were and how they debased public taste. And then we negotiated the rights to the movie – he demanded a considerable sum, and insisted on control over casting as he didn't want anyone from the Abbey Theatre in the film because he'd had a row with them.'

Over tea, O'Casey spoke of his own experiences with the British. 'He and some friends had dressed up as British soldiers and gone into Portobello Barracks to "lift" an Irishman who was imprisoned there. They got him, and as they came to the barracks' gates a sentry became suspicious. "We had to shoot him," O'Casey said. "It was such a pity because he seemed a nice young fellow."'

There was something chilling in the tolerance Brian dis-

Dirk Bogarde and Brian during the filming of Simba, *1954*

played towards murder in what he considered the right cause. He remained provocatively open-minded when he made *Simba* in Kenya at the height of the Mau Mau crisis, when the Kikuyu waged a campaign of sabotage and assassination against the British administration. Four years of ruthless military operations killed 11,000 rebels and placed more than 20,000 Kikuyu in detention centres. In the circumstances, the studio would not allow Brian to take any of the stars – Dirk Bogarde, Virginia McKenna and Donald Sinden – to Africa. Brian went alone with his camera crew to film background shots.

Again, his loyalties were divided, but the Irishman in him made him sympathetic to the rebels. 'We stayed in the Hotel Stanley, in Nairobi, and found British settlers shouting at the top of their voices, "Gather all the Kikuyu together, drive them into the jungle and gas them." There were other settlers who thought better of the Kikuyu, but the tribe was seen as little more than a source of cheap labour. I discovered my driver was a member of the Mau Mau, a fact I kept to myself. I said to him, "Why don't you stop killing isolated settlers on their outlying farms – which they have torn out of the jungle through hard work – and shoot the Governor-General" (who was a friend of mine) "or the senior military officer? Otherwise, you're going to bring discredit on your movement for freedom."'

Brian was well aware that everything he said was going back to the Mau Mau, and that he was greatly out of favour with the British authorities. The security of his unit came under a certain Captain Fox, a Dubliner serving in the Kenyan police force. One day, as they shot scenes in Nairobi, a lorry went by full of caged Kikuyu. 'Captain Fox, this must remind you of Dublin,' Brian said, 'when the people in the caged lorries were Irish Republicans.' The captain turned abruptly and marched away.

I once sat through one of Brian's anti-English tirades – always mocking, rather than savage: 'That irresistibly and unconsciously funny tribe, the English' – while a young American nodded in enthusiastic agreement. The American took up the argument, and went on to add a few derogatory remarks of his own. 'If you are going to be gratuitously rude about the English in my house, I really must ask you to leave.'

The American was confounded. 'But you just said . . .'

'An Irishman has a *right* to say what he likes about the English. You are a guest here in England among my English friends, who accept this sort of thing from an Irishman, but are understandably irritated when they hear it mouthed by foreigners. I suggest you contemplate the blood on the hands of your forefathers who so ruthlessly massacred the original natives of your own young country.'

Not all Englishmen accepted Brian's right to criticise them at will, however, and one or two challenged what they considered to be self-indulgent hypocrisy. 'If Ireland and the Irish are so wonderful, and England and the English are so terrible, I wonder why you don't go and live in Ireland?'

'What,' Brian exclaimed in mock horror, 'surrounded by all those Irish?'

It was impossible to debate Brian in the usual way – he just didn't follow the rules. It was the same with his politics – on the surface they didn't seem to make any sense or hold a position, but actually they were entirely consistent, despite the apparent illogic. On one election day I was walking with him through Belgravia to the polling booth when we came across a Rolls-Royce stuck in traffic. Brian tapped on the window. The driver looked him over and then lowered it with a smile. 'Going to vote?' Brian asked.

'Yes,' the plutocrat in the car replied.

'Me too. Don't forget – vote Labour!' Brian skipped away, snickering with glee.

It must be said that he carried his socialism lightly, although the purchase of the *New Statesman* – then the liveliest and best-written magazine around – was a weekly ritual. It remained mostly unread. Apart from voting Labour, Brian's commitment to the class struggle was little more than mischievous ankle-biting. When Vanessa Redgrave, an earnest and humourless Trotskyite, once asked him what political causes he felt strongly enough to march for, he replied: 'That would depend on the weather.' And when a studio undergoing labour unrest suggested it might be diplomatic if he stopped driving to the set in a Rolls-Royce, he responded by showing up the next day in a Bentley. Yet, as an Irishman, he felt drawn to the underdog, and as a homosexual knew what it was to be a scorned and criminalised outsider. His friends were of every political persuasion, and while he knew he could never be a member of the Establishment – and would not have wanted to be – he was at ease among its most august members. In the process of becoming a self-made man – an original and fabulous creation – he had become a highly idiosyncratic snob. Most of all, he enjoyed the role of Bad Boy.

His international politics also seemed contradictory. A Libyan journalist once showed up in Kinnerton Street to interview him about *Black Tent*, a film he had made in Libya. Brian sat with an enormous pile of papers on his lap and insisted the reporter make note of the annual box-office receipts going back twenty years. He then lectured the Libyan on Jesus as a revered Islamic prophet, recited snatches of the Koran in Arabic, before making a strange little speech about Gaddafi being the strong man of Arabia. After the journalist had left I said, 'Why didn't you tell him about giving blood to the Jews during the Six-Day War?'

'Do you think he would have been interested?' There was no irony in the response at all.

'It would have been interesting,' I said, 'to see how he worked it into his article about Gaddafi being the strong man of Arabia.'

But in Brian's mind there was no contradiction. Israel had been threatened, and his natural instinct was to side with her and show his support. He liked and admired the Jews, both inside and outside Israel, and spoke of Jewish writers, philosophers, artists and musicians as the salt and pepper of English intellectual life. Without the Celts and the Jews, he suggested, the island's culture would be heavy, unseasoned stodge. He also liked and respected Arabs – quite apart from the Tangier beach boys – and was particularly interested in Egyptian history and culture, which he thought superior even to that of the Ancient Greeks. What seemed like pure hypocrisy on the surface, proved on closer inspection to be honestly held views.

It had been left to me to call the Maltese Prime Minister. Not surprisingly, I was referred to the film office. I knew this would not satisfy Brian, so bullied my contacts on the *Observer* to help arrange a meeting with Mintoff himself. Although this resulted in a personal call from a senior official telling me that the Prime Minister's schedule was hectic, it did not bring about the desired *tête à tête*. I explained to Brian how polite and helpful everybody had been, but that Mintoff was simply too busy with affairs of state to see us. Naturally, Brian was outraged. 'Extraordinary! The Archbishop has the grace to see us immediately, as do the Knights, but this nobody is *too busy*! How can he be? It's not a very *big* island.'

'He is the Prime Minister, Bri. Clearly he doesn't get involved in film production. After all, we are just a couple of hustlers with a dog-eared script, trying to get money out of him.'

'Sometimes your vulgarity flabbergasts me. I resent being characterised as a hustler. I am no such thing. I am offering Malta, this most Catholic country, the opportunity to collaborate in the making of a Major Motion Picture with a religious theme. They provide facilities, and accommodation and so on, we bring in the outside money. An excellent economic opportunity for the island, if only this blinkered and self-important ideologue could put aside his dreams of world domination. If we were a couple of Libyan arms dealers this joke Napoleon would be all over us.'

In fact, the government's film office, Malta Film Facilities, proved to be enormously helpful, providing us with scouts for locations, access to everyone we needed to meet, and the opportunity to look over the sound stages at the studio. I arranged for all of these meetings to coincide with the arrival of our director, Roy Ward Baker, who flew out from London to join us for a few days on his way to Hong Kong. The surreal nature of our enterprise had so much become the norm that it did not strike me in the least odd that Brian's choice to direct his religious masterwork, the culmination of his career, was about to make a horror exploitation movie for the Chinese called *The Legend of the Seven Golden Vampires*.

Although Roy and Brian did not know each other well, they had both worked in the small world of London film and knew many of the same people. Roy spoke of their first meeting at Denham Studios, when he asked Brian what film he was working on. 'A bag of shit,' Brian replied. He raised his right hand, as if conducting an orchestra. 'But the most *bee-yoo-tee-ful* bag of shit you will ever see.'

They had both worked for a producer called George Minter and cheerfully agreed that the man was a terrible crook. 'He owed me more than £40,000 from the profits of *Tom Brown's Schooldays* and *A Christmas Carol*,' Brian said, 'and it became clear I would never see a penny. I took every opportunity to humiliate George in public, and would shout across the room in restaurants, "Pay me my money, you crook!" But as you know, Roy, I am sorry to say George developed ulcers and died when he was just over fifty – while I am now over eighty and have never had a single ulcer.'

'I didn't know you worked on *Tom Brown's Schooldays*,' Roy said.

'After my contract with Rank ended, George asked me to produce it. I looked at the early rushes, and it was apparent that the story was not getting through, and the director was paid off. I took over, and ended up directing seventy-five per cent of the movie, although I refused to take off the director's original credit. We spent several weeks at Rugby School, shooting exteriors, and I was pleased to upstage the English master who was unwise enough to quote from Yeats' "Byzantium". They had been rather patronising to me, no doubt thinking that film directors were an uneducated lot. So when the English master made a mistake, I recited the entire poem, which I loved and knew by heart. They were rather more careful of me after that.'

A number of the boys who were to be used as extras in the

Brian at the première of Tom Brown's Schooldays, *with its young star John Howard Davies*

film were encouraged to introduce themselves. 'An extremely handsome rugger player said, "Sir, I'm Ferguson – Head of Games." I said, "What kind of games, Fergie?" The next day I saw him limping across the quadrangle after we had shot the great sixty-a-side rugger match. "What's up, Fergie – fallen off a fag?"'

Both men had worked with Roger Moore, Dirk Bogarde and Alexander Korda, and swapped stories over dinner while I sat and listened. Roy told of his disastrous experience with Bogarde on *The Singer Not the Song*. 'It was a Western and I allowed Dirk to dress all in black, with black leather trousers. What was I thinking? He looked camp as Christmas! The press were merciless, and every paper slaughtered us in the reviews. And yet at the première I was convinced it would be well received, and waited up at the Dorchester with a large party for the early editions of the papers. It was terrible. My father had always told me not to mind bad reviews – just so long they didn't undermine your confidence. But the roasting over that film shook my confidence badly.'

'In *Simba,*' Brian said, 'Dirk had to play a love scene with Virginia McKenna against a back-projection of a mountain-top in Kenya. Considerable tension had already grown between us after I repeatedly attempted to get him to stretch his abilities and take risks. "I'm a pop actor," Dirk kept saying. "I can't do that sort of acting." In one of the love scenes I was exasperated to find that, despite take after take, there was no passion or chemistry between the two supposed lovers. "Dirk, could you look at Miss McKenna just once as if you would like to fuck her?" This was reported to the studio heads and I was asked to apologise. And I did apologise – to Virginia McKenna.'

Brian could be hard on actors, it became clear. In a film with Clive Brook, *On Approval*, he was impatient to get going after endless delays. On the first take of the first scene, the actor entered as he had done during the interminable rehearsals. But as the camera began to roll, Brook turned and said, 'This is the wrong side of my face. I shall have to come in the door on the right and exit left.'

Brian stared at the actor in silence for a full minute, before slowly and very deliberately saying, 'Go and fuck yourself.' There was a stunned silence and the actor walked off the set. 'I shouldn't have said it – but I couldn't stand the clacking of his false teeth in the love scenes.'

The stories about Alexander Korda mostly highlighted his extravagance. Roy remembered the suite that Korda lived in at Claridge's, where he had his own antique furniture and original impressionist paintings on the wall. Korda was lavish in every way, and rewarded the talent contracted to him accordingly. When he wanted Brian to join him he offered very generous terms. 'I went to see him and we immediately liked each other. He then staggered me by a proposition he made to direct three films. For the first I was to get £3,500, for the second £5,000, and £10,000 for the third. All in one year.'

Brian signed, and waited. After six weeks on a large salary he had done nothing. Korda told him to be patient. 'A wave of economy then hit Denham Studios. This manifested itself in a coarser grade of toilet paper and the decision that windows were not to be cleaned. So all these people on fantastic salaries ended up bringing in their own toilet paper and moving about in a fug. Meanwhile, Alex was filming *Knight Without Armour* for which he was paying Marlene Dietrich £70,000.'

Another six weeks of inactivity passed. 'Relax,' Korda said. 'Have a little rest.' Four more weeks went by. 'This is absurd,' Brian complained. 'You're paying me all this money and I haven't done a thing.' Korda suggested a holiday in the South of France, and Brian departed for Cannes.

Eventually, he was assigned the plum job of the year – *Lawrence of Arabia*, starring Leslie Howard. 'We had great difficulties getting the film set up. After several false starts, I was at last sitting in a great seaplane waiting to go to Palestine to start work. As I was sitting there, I saw a launch racing towards me. I thought, "Oh no, here we go again!" I was asked to go ashore and speak to Korda, who told me that the Governor of Palestine would not countenance any large gathering of Arabs anywhere in the country. So that put paid to *Lawrence of Arabia* for me.'

Brian said he had been chosen for the project because of his knowledge of the Middle East, and his ability to speak Arabic. As far as I could make out, his Arabic comprised of a dozen or so phrases, and the first paragraph of the Koran learned by rote (which greatly impressed Tangier taxi drivers). True, he had taught me how to deal with the relentless and exhausting tradesmen, hustlers and beggars of the Kasbah – '*La*,' spoken harshly, followed by '*Min fadlak*.' An emphatic – as I understood it – 'No, thank you.' This worked every time, although it was precisely wrong. I was actually saying a stern, 'No, please!'

Both men knew Roger Moore well, and liked him – Roy had directed many episodes of the TV series *The Saint*, while Brian had given the actor his very first job in film. 'I was co-directing, in a secondary capacity, *Caesar and Cleopatra* with Gabriel Pascal,' Brian said, 'and was watching Vivien Leigh rehearsing coming out of her palace to say goodbye to Claude Rains as he left for Rome. A man came across to me in one of the innumerable lulls between rehearsals accompanied by a tall and very handsome young man. He said, "You don't remember me, sir, but I'm Detective Sergeant Moore and I came to investigate one of your many robberies. This is my son, Roger, who wants to be an actor." I called over the first assistant and told him to make the young man a centurion at eight pounds a day. When I found out Roger was serious about being an actor I told Pascal, and we persuaded his father to send him to RADA.'

'Good-looking man, Roger Moore,' I said later when Brian and I were alone.

'Think so, do you?'

'Must have been *extraordinarily* handsome as a young man,' I said, sly and probing.

'It is evident why you were so attracted to journalism,' Brian said with a sigh. 'You are a natural for the profession with your tart's appetite for low gossip and sensation. Many reporters over the years have questioned me about Roger's background, hoping to be told some snide story about him. I have never been able to supply them because I don't know any. Since the day I met Roger he has always been surrounded by the most beautiful women – and part of the reason for his success is his tremendous sex magnetism for women. I'm sorry to be unable to provide you with any scandal, but Roger Moore is *not* like that.'

'Oh, well.'

'You sound disappointed.'

'It would be fun if James Bond turned out to be gay.'

During the daytime on Malta, we scouted the island for locations, and found splendid palaces and rocky wastes. At one location Roy found the terrain a bit *too* sparse and ruminated about the possibility of introducing plastic boulders. '*Plastic boulders!*' Brian muttered to me in a low voice. 'Over my dead body!'

We took the ferry across to Gozo, an island to the north of Malta half its size. It was a beautiful, barren place, scarcely developed in those days. Brian was very pleased to be introduced to a shy priest named Father Joseph, known as the unofficial governor of the island. He joined us for lunch in a fish restaurant, and brought two bottles of his own home-made wine contained in old whisky bottles. Afterwards we visited a local church. As usual, Brian was magnificent in his piety, crossing himself theatrically, lighting candles before the Virgin, and kneeling in lengthy prayer. 'Is he really this religious?' Father Joseph whispered to me. 'I'll have to watch him.'

We returned to Malta on a flat, clear sea, in preparation for a meeting with the Maltese Film Censor the following day. Naturally, as film-makers involved in the production of a movie based on the events leading up to the birth of Christ, we did not anticipate trouble. The censor, a tall, scholarly man genuinely interested in film, proved to be a fan of Brian's and had seen most of his work. In the course of our conversation, however, he explained that Malta, as a Catholic country, was seriously concerned in restricting two areas of film – violence and explicit sexuality. He confided that he personally found the introduction of homosexual themes particularly offensive, and mentioned John Schlesinger's *Midnight Cowboy* and *Sunday, Bloody Sunday* as unacceptable. The censor found the sight of men openly kissing one another on the screen profoundly disturbing, and feared there might be worse to come.

'Don't particularly like seeing men kissing on the screen,' Roy said lightly. 'But you won't have to worry about that sort of thing with our film, will he, Christopher?'

'Certainly not!'

Brian said nothing, heavily silent. I found it wonderfully ironic that a declared fan of his movies should be a religious homophobe with the power to ban work with even the mildest gay content. It was simply too good an opportunity not to exploit. 'It's disgusting,' I said. 'These people are everywhere – it's sometimes difficult to tell them apart from decent folk. Some of them look quite normal. And no doubt they would be only too pleased to put their vile and abominable practices on the screen if it were allowed.'

The censor seemed surprised by my outburst, and almost inclined to object. Brian continued to say nothing, pursing his lips. I was highly amused by my little joke, and further elaborated on the theme of the despicable nature of such a dreadful perversion, and the damned souls who indulged in it. Actually, I rather overdid it.

After lunch, we left the restaurant through a revolving glass door. Roy went first, followed by the censor, and Brian gestured that I should go next. As I began to exit I felt a sudden sharp pain between my shoulder blades. Brian had punched me in the back. Hard. I was almost propelled through the glass.

'You all right?' Roy asked in alarm, as I shot groaning from the revolving door.

'Wrenched my back,' I said. 'Don't ask me how.'

'Hurt your back?' Brian said, coming through the door. 'You poor boy!'

I was still in pain when we arrived back at the hotel, and complained bitterly to Brian once we were alone. 'What did you do that for? I was only joking!'

'Hurt you, did I?'

'Bloody did!'

'Remember – this Old Pervert packs a punch! To inflict maximum suffering when delivering a single sharp jab to the backbone of an irritating and impertinent Clever Boots, extend the middle knuckle of the right fist.'

'I'll bear that in mind – next time I punch somebody *in the back*!'

'Punishment for gratuitous collaboration with the enemy.' This was said with good humour, but the punch was real enough – a reminder that even by the relaxed standards of those times, before political correctness imposed rigid neo-Victorian hypocrisy and self-censorship on speech and thought, I had gone too far. Brian had not felt inclined to engage in aimless argument with the censor, but was not amused by my flippant exploitation of the situation. This was serious business, he was saying, the foundation of his being and focus of his life, and not to be taken lightly.

It was not Brian's style to join marches or committees, or agitate politically for gay rights, but his whole homosexual life had been led openly and fearlessly in an era when to do so was dangerous and illegal. He had the courage of his sexual convictions at a time when open homosexuality invited violence, blackmail, and the perpetual threat of criminal prosecution and personal ruin. His friend, Lord Montagu of Beaulieu – first chairman of English Heritage and founder of the National Motor Museum – was sent to prison at the height of Brian's career, convicted of 'gross' offences with two RAF men. As a result the homosexual world of London went even deeper underground, but Brian continued his life without change. He was unable to explain the mystery of why he had never been prosecuted. Could the chaste and unworldly, and no doubt blushing, St Thérèse really have had the old sinner under her protection?

I once asked Brian how he could be a Catholic when his

church was so strongly and outspokenly opposed to homosexuality. 'Fortunately, I am a member of a faith that is unshockable. The pronouncements of God's minions are subject to fashion and politics – Jesus preached love and forgiveness, and never condemns or comments on sexual love between men, or even sex outside of marriage for that matter. And even if this natural state were a sin – which I have never believed to be the case, and have therefore never felt any guilt – Jesus had a soft spot for sinners. Remember Christ's words to Simon the Pharisee, "To whom less is forgiven, he loveth less." Jesus seemed to prefer the company of flawed humanity to the stuffed shirts of authority, and offered the worst of sinners everlasting life through redemption. *You* might take note and investigate the benefits. My own belief is that a soul finds Hell through acts of unkindness and cruelty, not sexual peccadilloes. God is Love, Christopher, not some sexually repressed hanging judge.'

The openness of Brian's homosexuality and his outspokenness naturally made him vulnerable throughout his career. Before he was offered a contract with the Rank Organisation, he was invited to lunch at the country home of Arthur Rank, known as 'The Miller' because the fortune funding the giant film production company came from flour mills in the north of England. Rank was a down-to-earth man, a lay preacher in the Methodist Church, and a strict teetotaller. His views on homosexuals can be imagined.

'After lunch Arthur took me for a walk in his garden and showed me a beautiful bank of daffodils,' Brian said. 'He asked me how many I thought there were, and thinking to be flattering I said sixteen thousand. "Twenty-six thousand!" Arthur then told me about the sermon he had preached to the boys at Bible class that morning. I was admiring the espaliered trees along the garden walls when he suddenly swung around to face me, blocking my path. He said in his slight North Country accent, "I've heard some peculiar things about you, lad!"'

Brian stood before the decent but narrow-minded miller, his career in the balance. He stretched out his arms – 'Arthur, I am as God made me!' It was the right, and possibly the only answer that would have satisfied Arthur Rank. The next day he signed a three-year contract with the studio, where he was to work for seventeen years.

When Brian was under contract to Alexander Korda, he was also persistently undermined by homophobic senior executives in the company, although Korda himself was a broad-minded and tolerant man. At a meeting to determine a replacement director for *Prison Without Bars*, a remake of a French film about an open prison for women, Brian's name was put forward. One of the executives said, 'A fine director – isn't he a bugger?'

The story got back to Brian, who characteristically was not about to let it pass without comment. He waited for the right opportunity to confront the man in question, which came when he saw the executive walking with the studio heads, including Korda, in front of Denham Studios. He stopped them and directly addressed his adversary. 'I have been told that you said at a public meeting that I was a bugger. That may or may not be true. To find out, ask your brother what happened between us a week ago.'

Some time later Korda asked Brian to see him in private. 'You are a *terrible* young man to talk like that to one of my senior executives,' he said. He then laughed, and gave Brian the assignment to direct *Prison Without Bars*. 'When Korda showed me the work that had already been done, I told him it wasn't a story about a prison, but a finishing school for young ladies. We did a lot of work on the script – Korda had a habit of holding up a scenario in both hands and saying, "This will need a lot of alterations." It was well known that he was having an affair with Corinne Luchaire, the star of the original

The movie mogul Sir Alexander Korda, who put Brian under contract at Denham Studios

French version. During the making of the picture, I said to Korda, "Would you please not make love to my leading lady tonight, because I want to do her close-ups in the morning and I don't want her to come on the set with big bags under those French eyes of hers." He laid a hand on my shoulder and said, "For you, my boy, tonight I will sleep with my wife."'

In the evenings after Roy had gone on to Hong Kong, Brian and I talked at length about the many different films he had made, and I was particularly interested in those that dealt with war. Those concerning the Second World War – after, perhaps, *Scrooge* – make up the best of his body of work, conceived from deep experience and sympathy for men in combat. They are mostly concerned not with action and derring-do but the cold courage of men in hopeless situations, and the tenderness that soldiers have for one another amidst brutality and death.

When the Second World War broke out, Brian could easily have retreated with honour to his country home near Oxford to escape the bombs, but he chose to stay in his glass-fronted studio in Bradbrooke House, Studio Place, around the corner from Kinnerton Street. He was to make a slew of propaganda films both for British studios and Crown Films, a unit of the Ministry of Information. 'One short film, *A Call to Arms*, was aimed at recruiting women for the munitions factories. I went down to Woolwich Arsenal to do research for the script, and watched as the women left the factory at the end of a shift. As two young girls passed, I heard one say to the other, "Jesus, Alice – I could soften a couple tonight."'

The first full-length propaganda feature, *The Lion Has Wings*, was co-directed with Michael Powell and Adrian Brunel in 1939, aimed at bolstering British confidence in the RAF. The intervention of civil servants anxious not to upset the status of the 'phoney war' rendered it ludicrous, and its reception by the public was derisory. The Germans were even said to have obtained a print and shown it in theatres as an example of British naïveté. Graham Greene, then film critic of the *Spectator*, wrote, 'As a statement of war aims, one feels this leaves the world beyond Roedean still expectant.'

'I directed all the scenes with Ralph Richardson and Merle Oberon and many of the air scenes,' Brian said. 'I took a film unit out to Hatfield aerodrome where we had been promised that Spitfires would come and dive right down into our cameras. We waited and waited but they didn't arrive. Hours went by. I became impatient and cross – "Where the hell are those Spitfires?" I was put properly in my place by an RAF officer who had been assigned to us. "They'll be over as soon as possible, sir, but at the moment they're fighting over France."'

The next project, *A Gift for the King*, was a film about a tramp steamer sinking a German submarine in the Indian Ocean. One of Brian's assistants, Terence Young, came to him with a script he had written called *Dangerous Moonlight*, the story of a Polish pilot flying with the RAF. 'It was so much better that I convinced RKO to scrap the film we had already started and go to work on Terence's scenario instead. I got him a hefty sum for the script – £2,000 – and he gave me a Rolls-Royce.' I must have looked suspicious. 'No, Christopher, Terence was not *like that* – even though when I first saw him in the Footlights revue at Cambridge University he was singing a song dressed as a cowboy.'

Terence Young became a lifelong friend of Brian's, almost outstripping him in extravagance and excess, a man proudly and recklessly dedicated to living beyond his means. Later, I often saw him hand over fistfuls of pound notes to Brian to pay outstanding milk bills and the like. After working for Brian as an assistant and screenwriter, Terence Young went on to become a director in his own right, directing the first three of the James Bond movies. ('When he was casting for Bond he brought this young actor in an ill-fitting suit around who seemed very ill at ease and kept calling Terence "Sir". Imagine calling Terence "Sir"! I looked the young man over, whom Terence assured me had great presence on screen in various film tests he had shot, and said: "Take him to your tailor, run a lawnmower over his eyebrows and you have a star."' The young actor was Sir Sean Connery.)

While making *Dangerous Moonlight*, Brian promised the producer that under no condition would he go to London for the weekend, which was then suffering through the worst of the Blitz. Inevitably, he disobeyed. 'I went up with Terence and Sally Gray, one of the stars of the film, to have dinner at the Ritz. We were in the downstairs dining room when the bomb fell that destroyed Green Park station. A sort of fuzz came through the ventilators and people panicked, thinking it was gas. The dead and dying from the station were carried into the foyer of the hotel, which was soon awash with blood. The women were tearing their dresses and their underwear to make bandages for the wounded. We finally got everyone away in ambulances and the three of us came out of the Ritz and into Piccadilly. Long Acre was burning in the background and all the shattered glass was lying in the gutters with moonlight shining on it. As we stood there, some thirty or forty ranks of young people, ten deep, in uniform and out of uniform, moved towards us up Piccadilly from the Circus. They were singing, and at first we couldn't make out what, and then we heard it – "There'll Always Be an England."

'We went across to the Mayfair Hotel, where we stayed the night. The next morning we went back to Denham Studios to discover fire bombs had burned all our offices and dressing rooms and they were searching for our bodies. We continued work, although we were always getting bombed – sometimes six times in one day. When the sirens went, I have never seen electricians come down from the gantry so fast!

'The lead in *Dangerous Moonlight* was played by Anton Walbrook, who had been a concert pianist. We needed a concerto for him to play and I had written to Rachmaninov, who was in America. He sent back a very polite letter saying he would be delighted to do it but he was a slow composer and a concerto would take him two years. I replied in an equally polite letter that unfortunately we couldn't wait two years as we needed the music in six weeks. I went instead to see Richard Addinsell, who looked a bit like a sad pelican, and took Rachmaninov's *Second Piano Concerto* under my arm. "Don't exactly steal – add a little Tchaikovsky. That's the sort of thing I want." Two weeks later he rang me up and said he had a couple of ideas. He played me one theme and it didn't move me at all. Then he played the second theme – "That's it!" So he wrote the *Warsaw Concerto*.

'The day before we started shooting, the authorities took away Walbrook's car and radio, because he was German, and sent his Norwegian boyfriend to Canada. On top of all this poor Walbrook had a boil on his bum throughout the shoot. In one scene he had to say, "I'm handsome, full of charm and a wonderful musician." I thought he was doing this in an extremely feminine way and tried every word I could think of to explain this to him diplomatically – the term "camp" had not yet been invented. Walbrook pretended not to understand. The cameraman hid himself in the black cloth as I tied myself in knots trying to get through to him, but he refused to take the point. Finally, I lost patience: "Anton, it's just too damned sissy!"

'When the film was finished, I said to RKO, "This piece of music, as film music goes, is rather good." They weren't interested. Then when the film came out, people started wanting to buy a record of the *Warsaw Concerto*. In spite of the demand, no gramophone company would make one. Luckily, there was one long take involving the music and we were able to get a tape from the movie and when this was transferred on to wax it was charming. It had the scrape of a chair now and then, and the occasional cough, but 100,000 copies were sold in the first week. RKO hadn't bothered to secure the rights to the music so Addinsell made an enormous sum of money.'

Another propaganda film made with Terence Young took Brian back to Ulster. 'Eire, of course, was neutral but the Germans at the embassy in Dublin were spreading rumours that the Americans stationed in Ulster were behaving like an army of occupation. Our film was called *Letter from Ulster*, and the basis of the screenplay was to be a series of letters from a Catholic and a Protestant GI, writing home to show how splendidly they were getting along with the people of Ulster.

'The first thing I did on arrival was to get over the border fast to Dublin so I could have a huge steak, and see a city lit up after the drab blackout of London. Before I got back to Belfast, an ordinary Irish bus got itself entangled one day with a large convoy of American tanks, and one of the GIs lost his head and shot the bus driver in the arm. That night the man's two brothers went into the American camp and shot an officer very deliberately in the arm. "If you shoot any more of us, we shoot you." It was in this atmosphere that I arrived to make a goodwill documentary.'

The unit visited the American Camp Tynan, in Enniskillen, and many of the eleven-man crew were dressed in safari jackets and sandals. They were prevented from entering by a surly sergeant who was not expecting them. 'I'm not letting in a bunch of fucking draft-dodgers,' he growled. 'Hope I'm the hell out of here before you start messing around.'

'I can arrange for that,' Brian said, glaring at the sentry. 'You'll not be here tomorrow.'

'It was a curse,' said William McQuitty, who witnessed the incident. (McQuitty, who went on to produce Brian's film *Black Tent* in Libya, and also Roy Ward Baker's movie *A Night to Remember*, was then a neophyte assistant director.) 'And that sentry was not there the following day. He was in hospital. There were those who thought Brian was gifted with extra-sensory perception, and some who said he possessed the evil eye. He wouldn't stand any sort of subterfuge. He had developed an instinct that made him able to visualise the reality of situations. He could pick out the core of things – a very penetrating eye.'

No GIs were available for a final scene in St Mary's Church, Belfast, and prisoners were used instead. When the scene was ready to be shot, McQuitty quietly informed Brian, who was kneeling in the front row of the church. 'You direct it,' Brian said, closing his eyes. 'I'm praying.'

Out of all his films, Brian's favourite was *Theirs is the Glory*, a story of a disastrous defeat in which the British 1st Airborne Division – more than 10,000 men – was destroyed. The intention of Operation Market Garden was to take key bridges behind enemy lines along the Rhine to open a back door into Germany, and bring the war in Western Europe to a speedy conclusion. The plan was for British and American paratroopers and glider-borne troops to land in German-occupied Holland to take the bridge across the Rhine at Arnhem – the notorious 'Bridge Too Far'. At the same time tanks from the Guards' Armoured Division were to make a sixty-mile dash along the road known as Hell's Highway to link up with the airborne troops. Brilliant in concept, the plan proved to be a catastrophe in execution.

The first drop of paratroops landed successfully and captured the bridge, but bad weather delayed the second drop. Poor planning, faulty intelligence and pure bad luck followed. A German Panzer division got between the two Allied forces and cut off the paras at the bridge, who were either killed or captured. 'Having my memories of Gallipoli, I knew how the men felt having to abandon their comrades,' Brian told me. 'I very much wanted to make the film, but when I heard how the studio proposed to do it – with a story using stock shots and a few jokes – I said to myself, "This is not on!" It was also suggested to me by the Rank Organisation that we should use their most popular male star. I absolutely refused – "He doesn't know one end of the rifle from another!"'

Brian's concept was to make a docudrama using the soldiers who had survived the battle, and he went to Arnhem to do research for the script. 'I learned there were 250 paratroopers who had fought at Arnhem resting in Norway and had them flown to Salisbury Plain. I selected the men for the film very carefully and we had to pay the army three pounds a day for each paratrooper. There was nobody who appeared in the film, officer or soldier, who had not fought at Arnhem. It was great working with these men because they were accustomed to discipline – although the young soldier I had selected to play the lead didn't turn up one morning. I found out he was back in the barracks scrubbing the floors – old military habits and priorities died hard! But on set I would lock the soldiers into a close-up so they couldn't move and say, "Just think what you felt at the time when the RAF accidentally dropped the desperately needed supplies on the German lines."

'The results were superb. The film is my favourite because of the wonderful experience of working with the soldiers, and because it is a true documentary reconstruction of the event, and the scenario simply follows the battle day by day. We also used the newspapermen who had reported the battle on the spot. There is not one foot of film shot in the studio. Most of the filming was done on location at Arnhem, but I couldn't ask the men to swim across the Rhine because, in 1945, there were still dead bodies floating down and it was full of typhus. We shot the Rhine crossing in the Wraysbury gravel pits, just outside London, and the lighting was done by the Pioneer Corps and the explosions by the Royal Engineers.

'At Arnhem, the paratroops spent hours of their spare time searching for the graves of their comrades who had been buried where they fell, so that they could photograph them and send the pictures back to the dead men's parents in England. Most of the townspeople had not yet returned, and since many of the houses were badly damaged and scheduled for demolition, we were able to get wonderful shots of them being blown up. There was an old man – one of the few inhabitants who had stayed throughout – sheltering in a cellar and practically starving. We used to give him army rations to eat. In gratitude, he brought me a present of the first of a crop of tomatoes he had managed to grow. The most beautiful gift I have ever received.

'I had heard about a woman, Madame van Horst, who hid about fifty of the seriously wounded who had to be left behind. The doctors and the padres stayed with them in this cellar ankle-deep in blood. Madame van Horst went down to the cellar and said, "There's nothing I can give you. I have just read the 91st Psalm to my children. Would you like me to read it for you?" One of the soldiers nodded. She stood on the stairs and read, "For he shall give his angels charge over thee to keep thee in all thy days."

'I sought her out and asked her to play this scene for us. Strangely, she refused, but said she would think about it after I told her that every mother in England would like to see her read to the seriously wounded boys. She came to me that night, having talked it over with her husband. She agreed to do it only if I kept her face in deep shadow. I had no intention of doing any such thing! The next morning we shot the scene in her cellar and by the end of the day we had become quite good friends, and I asked why she had wanted me to keep her face in shadow. "I'm a member of the Arnhem Atheists' Society and I don't want my friends to see me reading the Bible."

'When the film was finished, the king saw it at a special command performance at Balmoral. The same evening it had simultaneous premières in Ottawa – because of all the brave Canadians at Arnhem – and at the Gaumont, Haymarket, in London. I went to the London showing which was stuffed with VIPs, including the Prime Minister, Clement Attlee. I don't know why, but I was terribly nervous over this film – I felt like turning and running away. I think I wanted it to be a success for the soldiers – for what they had done and suffered. At the end of the film, there was complete silence in the cinema. I thought – "My God, it's a terrible flop!" Then after an endless minute of silence there was thunderous applause. I say without modesty it is one of the best war films ever made.'

The most extreme example of Brian's sympathy for soldiers was his friendship with Otto Skorzeny, the six-feet-four-inch-tall Waffen SS colonel, and favourite of Adolf Hitler, who personally awarded him the Knight's Cross in gold. He saw combat in the invasion of Holland and France, and later in the Balkans and Russia. Sent back from the Eastern Front with a serious shrapnel wound, he was ordered on his recovery to form an elite SS commando unit.

Skorzeny became world-famous during his daring 1943 rescue of the deposed Italian dictator, Benito Mussolini. Mussolini had been imprisoned at Campo Imperatore in the Abruzzi mountains, and Hitler personally ordered Skorzeny to come up with a plan to free him. This called for a small group of commandos – expected to suffer an 80 per cent loss – to crash-land gliders on to the steep, rocky slopes surrounding the hotel and take it by force. The daring plan went without a hitch and Mussolini was liberated within four minutes without a shot being fired. Skorzeny flew away with his prize in a Fiesler Storch short-take-off-and-landing aircraft, barely surviving being launched over a cliff into a chasm.

Later, Skorzeny was ordered to prevent the Hungarian regent, Admiral Miklos Horthy, from signing a separate peace with Stalin in 1944. In a similarly brazen plan, Skorzeny kidnapped the admiral's pro-Soviet son – wrapping him in a carpet – before encircling and storming Burgberg castle in Budapest. A few months later he was put in charge of Operation Greif, during the Battle of the Bulge in the Ardennes, when hundreds of English-speaking SS commandos, dressed in United States uniforms and driving American military vehicles, were infiltrated behind Allied lines to cause chaos and confusion.

After the defeat of Germany, there was a vast manhunt for Skorzeny, hyperbolically named 'The Most Dangerous Man in Europe'. He eventually gave himself up to the Americans and was put on trial for war crimes before escaping to live in Spain. British Lion wanted to make a film about this extraordinary man and his daredevil life, and sent Brian to Madrid to spend time with him. 'I became great friends with Otto, who was living quietly and styled himself an engineer-diplomat, and had set up a business selling sheet metal and cement and suchlike.'

Since his escape from prison camp, the sensational British press had turned Skorzeny into a Nazi monster. He was supposed to have masterminded an international Nazi mafia known as Der Spinne – the spider – and organised the escape of thousands of Nazi war criminals. Over the years he was said to have planned to kidnap Castro, liberate Rudolf Hess from Spandau prison, organise torture teams in Argentina, train assassins in Egypt . . . and so on. 'There were thousands of newspaper and magazine articles about his activities, all of them rubbish. Skorzeny successfully sued the *Daily Sketch* for libel over the Egyptian story and won £10,000 and costs – he donated half of this award to the British Red Cross for veterans seriously wounded in the war, and the other half to the German war disabled.'

Brian and Skorzeny spoke to one another as soldier to soldier, and the German talked at length of his admiration for Russian troops on the Eastern Front, and wondered at their dogged, almost inhuman resilience and courage. He described how his elite SS unit studied and imitated the techniques of British commandos – and how the testimony of one of the bravest saved his life. 'He also told me of his dream to raise sheep in Ireland – but it was the story of a mutual friend, the White Rabbit, and his surprise appearance as a defence witness at his war crimes trial that really interested me.'

Wing-Commander Forrest Yeo-Thomas was an unlikely man to give evidence in defence of a Waffen SS officer accused of war crimes. A short, stocky man, he appeared at Skorzeny's trial, held in Dachau concentration camp, dressed in the uniform of the Royal Air Force, beribboned with numerous decorations for gallantry, including French medals and the George Cross. He was one of the most famous British commandos of the war, known throughout the French underground as the White Rabbit, his *nom de guerre* used in radio messages from London. He frequently parachuted into German-occupied France on missions, until he was betrayed and captured by the Gestapo. He was sent to Buchenwald concentration camp in Germany, where he refused to talk under torture and was condemned to death. He escaped by placing a corpse in his bunk, and walked across Germany until he reached Allied lines. His subsequent testimony at the Buchenwald war crimes trial resulted in the death sentence for twenty-two guards and doctors. And yet at Skorzeny's trial, he appeared for the defence.

'Yeo-Thomas shook the court with his very first words, saying that from all he had heard about Skorzeny he had behaved like a gentleman throughout the war. An extraordinary opening statement. He went on to describe how British commandos had worn German uniforms and insignia and killed German officers to get papers. And how they killed guards when they were unable to take prisoners. When asked how they prevented the danger of discovery, he answered bluntly, "Bump off the other guy."

'In other words, the British had done everything Skorzeny was accused of. The defence questioned the White Rabbit closely: "And did you garrotte people with thin wire?" "Yes." "And did you knife men in the back?" "Yes." After he had described all the various activities of the British commandos, the judge asked if he might ask a personal question and enquire what profession the White Rabbit followed in peacetime. "I am a dress designer for Molyneux."'

As Yeo-Thomas left the stand, Skorzeny stood and bowed his head in gratitude. His life had been saved by his enemy. All the charges of war crimes against the German commando were dropped, but as a member of the Waffen SS he remained under the category of automatic arrestee, and was interned in a prison camp in Darmstadt. Skorzeny was not allowed to communicate with the White Rabbit in person, but sent him a letter of thanks. He received a reply on Molyneux business stationery, addressed rue Royale, Paris. 'You did a jolly good job during the war! If you are looking for a place to lie up I have a flat in Paris . . . Escape!'

Skorzeny had been imprisoned for more than three years and was ready to take the advice. He hid in the boot of a car from the camp motor pool about to drive into town to pick up provisions, and was driven through all of the checkpoints without incident. He spent some time in Germany, moving about at will, and then slipped into France. Finally, he made his way to Spain where he was allowed to take up legal residence.

'When we were together in Madrid I asked Otto if there was anything funny he could tell me. He said two GIs came to his cell one morning and told him they had been ordered to take him out for exercise. "Come on, Skorzeny, you're going for a swim." Otto thought they were going to shoot him trying to escape. When he was in the river, he dived and swam underwater for a long way. The GIs ran along the bank with their rifles, trying to keep up. Otto surfaced, saw they were still with him, and dived again. He repeated this three times. Eventually, he was exhausted and staggered ashore. The sweating GIs said, "Jesus, Skorzeny, we thought you were going to drown. We were scared for you."

'Otto was a very valuable prisoner and everywhere he was moved, there would be a tank in front and back, and a tank on either side of him. An American sergeant came to him during a halt and said, "There's a sergeant of mine who has a German grandmother living nearby. Would you mind if we made a slight detour so he can see her?" Otto agreed and they all went and had lunch with the sergeant's granny. I thought this would make a strange and touching scene.'

Brian arrived back in London enthused about the project but ran into strong political opposition. 'British Lion were independent producers but partly financed by the govern-

Brian in Malta during the early 1950s

ment, which decided that it wasn't a very good idea to use taxpayers' money to make a hero out of a German commando. Naturally, I made the argument that the war was over and it was time to show people the difference between brutes and brave men, but I was talking to bureaucrats, not soldiers, so my argument fell on deaf ears.'

After a couple of weeks on Malta, I felt that I had met everyone on the island at least twice, and the same faces appeared over and over at the various cocktail parties we suffered through. The island did, however, have its ration of eccentrics. One of the friends Brian had made on the island while making *Malta Story* was the Noble Marquis Joseph Scicluna, a likeable but highly peculiar man with a fixation on all things military. Whatever the occasion, Joe preferred to dress in a Castro-style uniform, and his everyday conversation was translated into military parlance and peppered with words of war. Lunch was taken at thirteen hundred hours, a policeman on point duty was said to be a 'bandit at three o'clock', while I was designated 'the rear-gunner' because of my seat in the back of the car. (An unfortunate appellation, particularly when amended softly by Brian to '*Amanda*, the rear-gunner'.)

Joe's sister, Baroness Mignon Scicluna, was one of the wealthiest women on the island and lived in the Palacio Pariseo, at Naxxar, one of three palaces built by the corsair Pariseo. (Mabel Strickland lived in a second, while the third was the national post office in Valletta.) 'Pariseo is supposed to have had a black lover of whom he tired,' Brian told me, 'so he walled him up alive somewhere in the palace. The maid hears him screaming from time to time, drops her bucket and runs.'

The baroness invited us to the palace for a grand party to celebrate the annual fiesta in the village. The Palacio Pariseo was quite something, fronting on to the town's main street, with formal gardens in the rear stretching into the distance, and an avenue of cypresses bordering a mile-long stone path to the sea. We wandered through set after set of sumptuous rooms until we arrived at the ballroom, a splendid example of wedding-cake rococo, where the mirrored walls reflected enormous crystal chandeliers into infinity. We were introduced to an Italian prince and princess, and the prince explained in the course of conversation that he was a professor of psychiatry at the Sorbonne. As they moved away, Brian said, 'A *psychiatrist*! The depths to which the Italian aristocracy has sunk!'

After we had eaten, the guests crowded on to balconies at the front of the palace to watch the fiesta procession and firework display. The exterior of the church was brilliantly lit for the occasion, and the Virgin was carried through the streets by the locals at the head of a ragged and noisy band. The high-spirited crowd playfully grabbed their priest and threw him laughing into the air, and swooned in ecstasy before the

Virgin. It struck me that we must have seemed a stiff-necked assembly, as we stood on the balconies clutching our drinks, looking down on the scene with patrician condescension.

Among the guests was a tipsy retired British diplomat, accompanied by his wife and pretty young daughter. The diplomat seemed to know Brian quite well and was very amusing. 'Want a game of billiards?' he asked me suddenly. 'I'm not very good,' I replied. 'I'm hopeless – but what the hell!' he said. We made our way to a vast, deserted snooker room. I thought the diplomat might secretly be a serious player, as he carefully closed the door behind us, took off his coat, and rolled up his sleeves in preparation for the game. But when we began it was obvious he was so drunk he could hardly cue his own ball, let alone pocket and cannon off others. After missing everything, he exclaimed, 'Oh, f— . . . fair weather!'

As I leaned across the table to take a shot all the lights suddenly died and the room went dark. I heard a noise directly behind me and sensed a presence. A voice said, 'This is more of a game,' and a hand clamped itself gently but firmly on to my right buttock. I threw the cue on to the table and fled the room.

'Having a good time?' Brian asked, when I found him a little later.

'No I'm fucking not!'

'Whatever's the matter? I would have thought there's ample free food and drink to induce a state close to bliss. Perhaps you should go and talk to that charming girl you just met – ruby red lips and nice knockers. I'm sure she's a goer!'

'Yes, and all of twelve years old – and it's her father who's the goer!' I related my recent experience in the snooker room.

Brian put his hand to his mouth, cackling with laughter. 'Oh dear, dear, dear! How *dreadful* – how absolutely dreadful!'

'The man's a creep,' I said. 'His wife and daughter out

here, and he's doing a dirty old man drunken queer fumble in the other room!'

'An outrage!' Brian said, choking with laughter. '*Dirty old man drunken queer fumble!* I must say, you do have a colourful turn of phrase. No doubt, the rumour about Amanda the rear-gunner being muddled in the post has got around the island, confusing this wretched Foreign Office type and maddening him with desire. What a carry-on! I doubt if the Palacio Pariseo has ever seen the like. I've a good mind to remonstrate with our hostess . . .'

'Don't you dare!'

'As you wish. It'll remain our little secret, then.'

I was silent on the taxi ride home, while Brian sat muttering and chuckling beside me in pure delight. He nudged me playfully, but I was not to be coaxed from my grumpy mood. At the hotel we took our room keys, and entered the lift together. I got out on my floor and said good night. As the elevator resumed its clanking journey to the roof, Brian called out from the ascending open metal cage – 'Billiards, darling?' His laughter rang through the sleeping hotel. 'Sweet dreams, Amanda!'

Brian never made a film in Hollywood, although he accidentally began his career when he arrived there intending to be a painter rather than a director. His stories of Tinseltown in the 1920s sounded romantic, very different from the dull, driven place I would later find it to be. 'Hollywood sounds fun in those days – almost elegant.'

'Hollywood has never been fun, certainly not elegant. It doesn't attract witty or elegant people. There was then, and always has been, a small nucleus of highly overpaid but genuinely talented people who act as a powerful magnet for workaholic, money-grubbing mediocrities with ice-water in their veins.

'I was art-directing a film for one such director who came

on to the set I had designed and said, "Whaddya got the fucking door over there for? I wanna fucking door over there!" I explained patiently that my design matched the exterior architecture of the house. "I don't give a fuck – I wanna door over there!" I said to the construction manager, "Take the door from the correct place and put it in the incorrect place as the director wishes."'

Brian first moved to Los Angeles after a year in New York painting murals in the style of Louis XVI, the decorating fad of the time. 'My first job was for an architect, painting biblical scenes in the Rabbis' library in the great synagogue on Wilshire Boulevard.' One commission followed another, and he was employed to paint murals for a Pasadena palace under construction for a multi-millionairess who owned a chain of restaurants in Chicago. 'English hunting scenes were to decorate the study, Boticcelli's Venus was to be reborn in the bathroom, and the bedroom was once again to be the domain of Louis XVI. What Louis XVI and Marie Antoinette are doing all over the walls of that Pasadena palace is quite remarkable. But after that, I'd had it with Louis XVI.'

Brian retired to his small, rented house in Hollywood's Laurel Canyon, and painted a religious screen of the Madonna, surrounded by two angels and two saints. The screen was displayed in a bookshop window before Christmas, where it was seen by Charlie Chaplin, who bought it at a very high price for his banker friend Harry Crocker of San Francisco. Someone else who admired the screen was John Ford, who hunted Brian down and invited him home for dinner. It was the beginning of their close, lifelong friendship.

'Jack was delighted to meet someone from Ireland who wasn't either a policeman or a domestic servant. Although he was born in America, he was of Irish descent and loved everything Irish. When he introduced me to Sam Goldwyn I heard him say as I turned away, "Brian speaks French." We

Brian in his first days in Hollywood, in front of the religious screen he painted and which was later bought by Charlie Chaplin

became very close and soon he called me "cousin".'

Brian started to paint for the movies, and one of his first jobs was executing backdrops of Normandy fishing villages for Warner Brothers. 'The usual overturned boat in the foreground and the row of Utrillo houses along the quayside. It's important for Americans that abroad has the familiarity of a postcard. In those days art directors were nearly all ex-window dressers, so I was immediately promoted to art director. I acquired a big yellow Mercedes with red upholstery and great pipes coming up the sides – very vulgar – as well as an enormous studio on Sunset Boulevard, near the Catholic church.'

Ford then hired him as an assistant director – at less money, and he had to sell the magnificent Mercedes. It was the custom in Hollywood then that when an assistant director was not working, their fellow ADs employed them as extras. Brian was eager to study other great directors at work, and especially wanted to see Joseph von Sternberg directing Marlene Dietrich in *Shanghai Express*. Ford was not impressed: 'What do you think you're going to learn from *him*?'

'My Hollywood screen debut was as an extra in John Ford's last silent film, an Irish story called *Hangman's House*. I put on a big black hat and a long cloak and led a donkey along a road. But I also watched Jack direct, and most interesting of all to me, as I was a painter at the time, saw how the cameraman lit the set. It was the study of the use of lighting that first attracted me to movies.'

The close relationship with Ford engendered great jealousy in Hollywood, and after Brian had been in the country for four years without permission, someone reported him to the Immigration Department. He was arrested, but immediately bailed out by Ford. Meanwhile, he received a letter informing him that permission had been granted to depart the country voluntarily, a polite form of deportation.

Before the departure, he was invited to Hawaii by Jack and Mary Ford, who took an entire deck on an ocean liner for the trip. Ford, who was at the height of his fame, received a rapturous welcome to the islands. The party established themselves in suites in the Royal Hawaiian Hotel, on Honolulu, the most luxurious accommodation then available. Another guest at the time was the fabulously wealthy Standard Oil heiress and outrageous eccentric, Betty 'Joe' Carstairs, known everywhere as 'The Admiral' – and from whom Brian was to buy his first Rolls-Royce. Joe dressed as a man, swore horribly, spat in public, smoked cheroots and had her arms covered in seafaring tattoos. She was on Hawaii in a lesbian *ménage à trois* with her 'wife', Ruth Baldwin, and mistress, Mabs Jenkins.

Ruth Baldwin was promiscuous, liked cocaine and drank

heavily – even her Pekinese dog displayed a taste for brandy. Mabs Jenkins was originally a manicurist with a green scorpion tattooed on her thigh, but her rich lover enabled her to indulge a passion for big-game hunting, particularly crocodiles. Although each of the women was perpetually in the throes of multiple affairs, they all displayed jealous and possessive traits over one another, resulting in dramatic public displays of emotion. The girls were not shy of making scenes. Brian naturally found this trio of eccentric lesbians to his taste, but for Jack Ford they were altogether *too* exotic. He referred to them, with heavy irony, as 'Your *swell* friends.'

Joe was obsessed with motorboats, and would become the fastest female speedboat racer in the world (she gave Malcolm Campbell £10,000 towards the construction of *Bluebell*, the car in which he broke the land speed record. Her verdict on Campbell's technique: 'He drives like a woman.') Joe would also later found a colony of 500 blacks in the Bahamas on a private island, earning herself the title 'The Queen of Whale Cay'.

Joe inherited her vast fortune from her mother, while her father was an officer in the Royal Irish Rifles – Brian's old regiment. He took no interest in his daughter whatsoever from her birth on, and rarely saw her. 'I was never a little girl,' Joe said. 'I came out of the womb queer.' She claimed that her only childhood memory was of eating sugarcubes dipped in her mother's scent. At age sixteen she had an affair with Dolly Wilde, who claimed to be possessed by the spirit of her uncle, Oscar.

Joe returned to London, after driving an ambulance at the front in the First World War, and sought out her father at his club in Pall Mall. 'Well, young man? What do you want?' her father asked when she approached.

'I'm your daughter, sir.'

Her father bought her a drink and gave her a cigar, and in the brief conversation that followed Joe voiced a suspicion that her mother had been murdered by the last of her husbands. The advice she received was not to pursue the matter in case it led to trouble. And that was the last time father and daughter met or spoke.

'Ruth Baldwin had fallen in love with Princess Cappiolani of the Royal House of Hawaii,' Brian said. 'We used to see "Cappi" every day when she came to the hotel to visit Ruth. She was always attended by two tiny Japanese ladies-in-waiting, incessantly fanning themselves. They would sit patiently for hours outside Ruth's bedroom. After a big party one night, Cappi left very drunk supported by the two ladies. A little later there was a tapping at my door and the trio was back. "Brian, give me an enormous brandy," Cappi said. "I must be so drunk that I won't care when the watchmen at my mother's palace see me being dragged across the lawn."'*

Although Jack Ford knew of Brian's nature, and extended a wry but mute tolerance, the friends never openly discussed the subject. If anything, Ford was suspicious of homosexuals and usually kept his distance. 'While in Hollywood, I had become friendly with George Cukor, whose sexual orientation was well known. I was staying with Jack once and told him I was going over to George's for dinner. "What do you want to go there for? There's a perfectly good steak waiting for you in the kitchen." When I came back, Jack was waiting up for me, and peppered me with questions. "Who was there?" "Spencer Tracy." "What's Spence doing over there? Who else?" "The Garson Kanins." "Oh, they'll go anywhere for a free dinner." "And Clifton Webb." "Oh, you might expect *that*. What's the house like?" I described the great swimming pool, the drawing room with the hand-painted chinoiserie wallpaper, the painting by Manet over the fireplace, and the panelled study where George kept his Oscar. "I

*Ruth Baldwin died at the age of thirty-two of a heroin overdose; Mabs Jenkins also died young of excess; Joe Carstairs lived to be ninety-three.

The legendary director, John Ford,
Brian's 'most valued and loved friend'

can't give you any information about the bedroom, Jack, because I didn't go upstairs." Jack gave me one of his looks. "Brian, I'm proud of you." It was the first time that he had ever mentioned that side of my life.'

Brian gave a party for Jack when he was in London during the war, filming for the US Navy's Psychological Warfare Unit. 'I invited the whole of film and theatrical London. La Gingold was there, appearing in the revue *Sweet and Low* alongside a beautiful black actress, Elizabeth Welch, who was seated on a sofa surrounded by the chorus. Jack asked, "Who is that beautiful coloured girl up to her arse in pansies?"'

As Brian grew older, he spoke of John Ford more and more, and always declared him to be the greatest friend of his life. We were working on the Big Bestseller one morning when the call came through to Kinnerton Street, from Ford's daughter Barbara, that her father was dying: 'If you want to see Pappy, you'd better come soon.'

Brian flew immediately to Los Angeles, where he stayed

for several weeks, visiting Ford at his home every day. 'One day Jack was in bed drinking Guinness with a big box of cigars on his lap, and he asked me to sing "The Rose of Tralee". It was a song we both loved, although I don't have much of a voice. The Fords had bought a new house in Palm Desert, and there were several men about packing books into cases, and while I croaked out the song they stopped to listen.

'I asked the doctors: "What is it with my cousin? I've come all the way from London to see him." They said he had six months to live – two years at the most. Soon after this he was taken into hospital and that is where I said goodbye to him.' Ford died six months later and it hit Brian hard. 'Jack Ford was my most valued and loved friend on this planet. His impact on world cinema has been profound, and there is hardly a major director anywhere who has not been influenced by him. It is impossible for me to accept that this great genius is ended by dissolution. I am certain that angels watch over him in other dimensions.'

Early on in our stay on Malta, after only a few days on the island, I pulled off something of a coup. I solved the problem regarding the thin, vinegary local wine. I had embarked upon an emotional and troublesome romance with an Italian–English girl, whose parents Brian described as 'sixpenny settlers' – those who settled in Malta for tax reasons, paying sixpence on the pound in income tax. During our courtship I discovered a charming little restaurant tucked away in the side streets of Mdina, with a pretty garden, perfect for romantic dinners in the open air under a trellis of vines. The food was decent enough, but what was truly remarkable was the wine list. Hidden at the back, on a couple of faded, typed pages, was a selection of First Growth clarets. Although I only knew these wines by name and reputation, I recognised that the prices being asked were a generation out of date. I reported my find to Brian, and told him of some of the wines and their bargain prices. 'Not possible,' Brian said sadly. 'I doubt if there is a cache of fine wine like that anywhere on the island – and nowhere in the world at the prices you suggest.'

'I saw the list, Bri – there in black and white.'

'Did you order one?'

'No. We had a carafe of the house wine.'

'How was it?'

'Nasty.'

It was with deep scepticism that Brian accompanied me to the restaurant that night, impatiently demanding the wine list before we even sat down. He began to look through it. 'The usual motley collection,' he said. 'Nothing to write home about.'

'Look in the back. There is a two-page list under Collection.'

He turned to the back and began to read. There was a sharp intake of breath. 'My God, this is unbelievable!'

'See – I told you they had some good gear!'

'Excellent gear, ambrosial gear – gear to make angels weep! Twenty-year-old Lafite, Latour, and Haut-Brion at a fiver! Vintage Krug, six pounds ten. My God – they have a half bottle of thirty-year-old Château-d'Yquem for four pounds! Must be some sort of cruel joke. Unless the owner is three halfpence short of a shilling!'

Brian ordered a bottle of vintage Krug, to be followed by Château Haut-Brion. The waiter then asked for our food order. 'Who cares!'

The champagne arrived and was delicious, and put us in a superb mood. The Haut-Brion was opened and allowed to breathe. 'Thank God,' Brian said, 'they haven't brought it lying down in one of those fucking baskets! Usually, I would ask them to decant an old wine of this pedigree, but the waiter looks a bit brutal. Better leave it as it is. Anyway, nice to have the bottle on the table – I like its distinctive shape and the nice big label. Old Samuel Pepys, the great snail of

English literature, used to enjoy this wine more than three hundred years ago, referring to it as O'Brien. No doubt a hogshead or two of the stuff helped get him through the Great Plague and the Fire of London, and lubricated the composition of his endless, pettifogging diary.'

The waiter poured the wine for Brian to taste. He lifted the glass to his lips, took a sip and closed his eyes in pleasure. '*It'll do!*'

I lifted my own glass and drank my first mouthful of the fabled wine. 'Blimey!'

Brian closed his eyes once more, this time in pain. 'Christopher, although I abhor wine snobs, and all their mouth-swishing and snorting rituals, and fatuous jabbering of raspberry jam, sandalwood and old leather, as they vainly try to fix the ethereal and spiritual experience of fleeting taste with demented jargon – I do take exception to "blimey". Although no doubt conveying sincere appreciation, it is not equal to the occasion. An eyebrow raised an inch or so would be sufficient to signal appreciation to a fellow epicurean.'

I raised my left eyebrow, but must have looked more like a vaudeville villain than a connoisseur of fine wines. 'Never mind.' Brian said. 'But as you seem to appreciate these things in your own strange way, I'll order a half-bottle of Yquem for our pudding.'

The sweet wine was a revelation, and as it touched my lips I vowed to work hard, make a lot of money and live a long life so that I could drink lots of the stuff again and again. And I could not resist the temptation to show off my oenophile sophistication, quoting the words of continental aristocracy in the form of Count Wilhelm von Platz (who had long since disappeared). 'Some smooth shit! First class!'

Brian laughed. '*Pleasant, isn't it?*'

We returned to the little restaurant as often as possible for lunch and dinner. I had never tasted wine like it, and became so spoilt I heard myself voicing disappointment over the *length of finish* of the Lafite, and surprise about the *austerity* of the Latour. 'You are on the road to ruin,' Brian said happily.

And then one night, as the waiter poured the Haut-Brion, he said, 'I'm afraid, gentlemen, this is the last bottle.'

'Ah well,' Brian sighed, 'it couldn't last for ever.'

'Sad though. The *last* bottle.'

'One must learn to interpret the omens,' Brian said. 'Time to go home.'

PART VIII

London

I'm not sure when the penny finally dropped that Brian had no intention of making *Darkness Before Dawn*. It might have been a year or so after I began work, or even later. My suspicions were aroused when Stephen Vernon told me about money offers that had been made and ignored, but whether Brian was conscious or unconscious of his decision is difficult to know.

Perhaps at some stage along the way Brian realised he was unequal to the task, even with St Thérèse dragooned as co-producer. A project forever in development was possibly more valuable to him than a film in production. It gave focus to his life, provided conversation, and afforded a motive for foreign travel, and the opportunity to meet new people. More importantly, the subject matter involved him in a perpetual dialogue with God. The Box Office Blockbuster was a highly original form of prayer – a ticket to heaven.

I often thought that Brian envisaged eternity as a perpetual luncheon party attended by a revolving pool of guests drawn from the famous, the beautiful, the talented and the witty of all mankind. Gerald Hamilton would be there, of course, visiting with Oscar Wilde from the other place, and Noël Coward, and probably Voltaire and Leonardo. (On eternal Friday there might be the occasional saint or pope. And on Ladies' Night, St Thérèse and St Bridget would drop by, along with Moura Budberg, Nefertiti and Hermione Gingold.) As the champagne and the claret flowed – vintage Krug and Haut-Brion 1682 – I imagined Brian telling stories while God, a lovely old boy with a long white beard and a great sense of humour, laughed like a drain.

I saw Brian standing on a cloud explaining his decision to abandon terrestrial film-making to a group of young, good-looking male angels: 'The budgetary and technical restrictions on earth are simply too limiting for such an important spiritual work of art. And then one's audience is confined to the living, when really I want every soul from the beginning of time to have the chance to see it. Of course, Christopher would have liked a big première for *Darkness Before Dawn* at the Odeon, Leicester Square, with search-lights and all that – and a party afterwards at the Café Royal with lots of booze for his freeloading pals. But there is only one place for the première of a film of this importance and splendour – and that is here in Heaven. It will be an absolute triumph! A smash hit!'

Brian might have found the project rewarding as prayer, but financially it was a perpetual drain. It provided no income, but demanded constant outgoings – even without paying the writer. His finances drifted inexorably into a state as parlous as my own. We would sit in the Turk's Head swapping horror stories. 'Do you know,' Brian said, 'I had a letter from the Post Office the other day threatening to cut off my phone?'

'Outrageous!'

'They overcharge so much for phone calls, is it any wonder I am unable to pay? However, I have dealt with it satisfactorily.'

'What did you do? Give them the old cheque's-in-the-post routine?'

'No, no. I threatened to commit suicide.'

'Fantastic!' I said in unabashed admiration. 'That's telling them!'

'I called them up and spoke to this nice West Indian woman – I do love the accent, so warm and reassuring – and asked the name of the man in charge of things. A Mr Phelps, apparently. Then I told her that I was old and ill and needed the phone as a matter of life and death. And that if they cut it off I would kill myself after posting a note to the *Daily Mirror* saying that I had been driven to such desperate measures because of the threats of their man Phelps. I was assured by this nice lady – after brief, muffled consultation on the other end of the line – that the phone would remain on.'

Changing the subject, I wondered idly how many champagne breakfasts the old-age pension was good for. 'I don't know,' Brian said. 'How much is the old-age pension?'

'How would I know? You tell me.'

It came out that Brian had never collected it. 'It didn't seem right. I mean, it's for poor old men in council houses without a pot to piss in.'

'No, Bri – it's for everybody over sixty-five. You've paid in and have a right to collect. Think of all the tax the bastards have leeched out of you over the years. And you are a poor old man without a pot to piss in.'

'Brutal, but true,' Brian said nodding, not in the least upset. 'I am a poor old bastard without a pot to piss in – although I do not live in a council house.'

'But you are forced to reside in subsidised housing. You could probably get Social Security to pay the rent. And you have seventeen years of old-age pension out there to claim. A bloody fortune!'

'My, Christopher, how you cheer me up!'

I wrote letters to the authorities outlining an old man's despair over not receiving his old-age pension, and was careful to mention his suicidal disposition. I was promised urgent attention. In due course Brian was signed up for the pension, while his claim for back payment was researched. Belgravia's most recent OAP reacted in character. 'Let's celebrate! A Slap-Up at Wheeler's?'

'Bri, you're broke! It will take time before you get any of this cash.'

'That's all right. The manager lets me sign the bill.'

At the nadir of Brian's financial woes, as he would later explain, St Thérèse ground out a miracle. Or rather, his friends Stephen and Ursula Vernon discreetly persuaded the Grosvenor Estate to propose a generous deal on the Kinnerton Street house. Although Brian had lived there long enough to be a sitting tenant, and could not be evicted, he had no lease so could have been charged rent at a market rate. The estate, however, now suggested that if he gave up any claim on the house, they would give him £80,000 and a written agreement that he could remain for the rest of his life at the rent of three pounds a week. This was a good deal by any standards.

Brian chose to look the gift horse in the mouth – in fact, to go over its teeth one by one. 'You can see how these dukes make their money. A large four-bedroom house in the smart end of one of the most fashionable streets in Belgravia must be worth more than £80,000. Why, only the other day I read in the *Standard* that property prices in London are soaring.'

'All that is true. But you do not own the house. You rent it. For three pounds a week.'

'I am a sitting tenant (absurd term!) which means that if I went to court I could force the estate to sell me a lease on the house. I have a right to buy.'

'Maybe, but you would need money. A substantial down-payment at least, and then an enormous mortgage. You don't have the cash for the deposit and no mortgage company is going to lend a small fortune to a broke old bastard without a pot to piss in. This deal gives you the security of a roof over your head for the rest of your life at three pounds a week, and gives you a nest egg of £80,000. Take it! Quick! Before they sober up.'

'You don't think I should hold out for £100,000?'

'What do you mean – hold out? What's in it for them? The

Grosvenor Estate is a tough outfit. I bet there are people in the office strongly opposed to the whole idea of handing over a large amount of money for a house they're eventually going to get back anyway. The only reason you have this offer, if you ask me, is because of Lady Ursula. In the circumstances, to ask for more would be provocative – greedy even.'

'Greedy? I'm an elderly gentleman looking for a means of support. I have not, perhaps, managed my money over the years as well as I might. I will talk to my solicitor.'

His solicitor, if indeed he had one, seems to have agreed with my analysis and Brian duly accepted the arrangement. He became uncharacteristically careful with money in the weeks before the cheque arrived, delivering various homilies to himself on prudence and wise investing. 'I'm going to be most careful with this money. A large sum, it must be invested wisely. Some bond that will give me an income.'

'Good idea.'

'I had invested the money my sister left me, you know, which provided a small income for many years. Unfortunately, when it had to be renewed and reinvested I foolishly took the capital and squandered it. Went a bit mad, if truth be told – cracked under the strain of living for years within a fixed income. I do not intend to make the same mistake again.'

The cheque arrived and Brian did not give in to temptation. There were no large champagne parties or expensive world trips, not even long, boozy lunches. On the contrary, he began to exhibit peculiar signs of frugality. One day I went to meet him in the Wilton Arms and found him sitting at the bar beside a young man, signing a large stack of papers. 'Just finishing off a little business.' He briefly explained the investment he had chosen – an annuity. At the age of eighty-two he was investing all his capital in an insurance scheme. It was an actuary's dream: to gamble high interest payments against the life of an old man with untold ailments, a weak heart, bad lungs, who took no exercise, drank too much, ate the richest foods, and who might reasonably be expected to die on the morrow.

'Bri, can I have a word?' I led him under protest to a corner of the pub where we could talk. The salesman watched us nervously.

'What is it?'

'Have you spoken to anybody about this? Are you sure this is the best thing to do?'

'This young man is an expert. He represents a reputable company. This is his profession.'

'He's a spiv! He's just selling policies that get him the most commission. It's ridiculous to tie up all your money like this.'

'Where else could I get such a high return? He has come around the house several evenings to explain things. And don't look so bloody clever – he's not like that.'

'Bri, you're buying an annuity at eighty-two years old!'

'Oh, I see. Think I'm going to drop dead, do you?'

'Of course not. But this wideboy is taking advantage of you.'

'Firstly, if I do drop dead don't think you're going to get any of my money. Secondly, I'll outlive the lot of you. I've buried three doctors in the last ten years.'

'Well, it's your business.'

'Thank you.' Brian returned to the bar and, to the enormous relief of the salesman, completed signing the contract. I joined them, severe and disapproving. The salesman quickly placed the signed papers in his briefcase, snapped it shut, and scurried away before his client could change his mind.

'I'm glad that's out of the way,' Brian said. 'Having the responsibility of investing all that money has quite cramped my style. It doesn't suit. It's made me positively parsimonious for the last couple of weeks. I've hardly been out. Perhaps that's why there are so many rich misers – forever calculating whether they can live off the interest on the interest. Now I can get back to living beyond my means. We must celebrate – the lump sum is in safe institutional hands. Let's squander the interest! Wheeler's?'

'I expect they've been wondering where you've been.'

'A lengthy and extravagant lunch is called for – I hope you've no pressing engagements. We'll kick off with a bottle of Krug.'

'It'll do.'

'A Dover sole, perhaps?'

'Very pleasant.'

'A bottle of good white Burgundy as an accompaniment, of course. And afterwards, no doubt, a little Marc de Bourgogne on your lemon sorbet? You love it so – it's a pleasure to watch your smiling face as you tuck in!' We rose from the bar and Brian put an arm around my shoulder as we walked out of the door together, and made our way down the street in high spirits. He was delighted to be relieved of the dreadful financial burden of holding on to a large sum of money. 'You have many qualities, Christopher,' Brian said kindly, 'but giving sound financial advice is not among them.'

He was right. The actuaries had bet on the wrong old war horse, and Brian would live for many years to benefit from his lunatic act of financial prescience.

It would be an understatement to say that Brian was casual in regard to his health – he was reckless and defiant, provoking the gods. He disregarded everything that was wrong with him, except for taking a large number of pills and puffing on his inhaler. But one damp December I discovered from his lodger that he had been walking up and down Kinnerton Street in the cold and wet, without hat, coat or umbrella, and contracted a chest condition that laid him low. He had pushed himself even beyond the limits of his granite endurance, and was confined to bed for a week or so.

I went to see him on Christmas Eve to wish him the season's greetings. I found him sitting in his winged chair in a dressing gown, passing the time with his doctor, a tall young man in an old, shapeless suit that somehow appeared elegant. The doctor had a manner that expressed a wry, tolerant view of human nature. 'Brian's been very ill. And while he's pretty weak still, he's going to be all right. I'd say he's been extremely lucky – this time.'

'A miracle,' Brian said. 'St Thérèse is very good at chest cases – it's her speciality. You've been very kind and helpful too, of course,' he added quickly, in case he hurt the doctor's feelings. 'I feel much better now. No need to come tomorrow.'

'I have no intention of coming tomorrow,' the doctor said. 'It's Christmas Day!'

'Is it?' Brian said. 'I didn't know.'

'I thought you said friends were bringing you lunch?'

'Did I? I can't quite remember. But that's right – somebody's going to bring me lunch. Turkey, no doubt – although I much prefer goose. But sick old geezers can't be choosers.'

The doctor indicated subtly that he wished to speak to me and I followed him into the hall. 'You're a good friend of Brian's – I've heard him speak of you. Will you talk to him? Walking up and down the street from pub to pub in the freezing rain without a hat and coat is frankly suicidal.'

'I'll have a go, doctor.'

'And then there's the drink . . .'

'He likes a drink.'

'And so do I – but I am not a sick man in my eighties taking a number of strong prescription medicines.'

'He'll just say he's buried—'

'—three doctors in the last ten years. Yes, I've heard that one.' The doctor had a twinkle in his eye. 'And I'm not so arrogant as to ignore the warning. But if he continues to expose himself to the elements he could catch pneumonia and it could kill him. It's simple common sense.'

'He doesn't much hold with common sense. He's Irish – he believes in magic. But of course you're right, and I'll talk to him.'

I tried. I really tried. I suggested placing a hat and coat on the banisters at the bottom of the stairs as a constant reminder to wrap up. 'I never wear hats. You know that!' I changed tack and suggested a large umbrella by the door. 'I always leave them behind in pubs and places. It would cost me a fortune.' I said the doctor had suggested he should watch his consumption of alcohol, because of all the tablets he was taking. 'Those bloody tablets! I take so many I rattle. And none of them do me as much good as a glass of champagne and a good old chinwag with yourself! Open a bottle! It's Christmas!'

Defeated, I fetched the champagne. We sat in the gloom in front of the electric fire. 'This is cosy,' Brian said, instantly and completely happy. 'We're good old friends, aren't we Christopher?'

'The best!'

'Funny, me forgetting Christmas. I must have been under the weather. Well, Happy Christmas!'

'Happy Christmas, Bri!'

Suddenly, and for the first time, Brian seemed old to me. Ridiculous as it must seem, up until that moment I had never thought of him as an old man. I knew his actual age, of course, and was aware of his frailty, but he seemed ageless and indestructible, a man basking in the perpetual protection of spirit guides and saints. My callous young mind had never entertained the idea that he might actually have moments of fear in regard to his own mortality, let alone that such a worldly character would have nowhere to go at Christmas.

When it was time to leave I went over to the winged chair, stooped and kissed Brian on the cheek. I don't think that I had ever kissed him before – and don't recall ever kissing him again. As I straightened, I looked into his face and those clear, blue Irish eyes. The roguery and sophistication had evaporated, replaced by a childlike openness that was kind and simple and pure. I was blessed with a look of the utmost gentleness. Saintly, would have been the word to describe it, had I been more Christian. As I hurried away into the cold, my heart was bursting.

I began to spend more and more time in America, and was away for as much as a year at a time, but always checked in with Brian when I returned home. At first, he enjoyed hearing about my adventures, and telling me of his own experiences in New York and Hollywood. But as time went by he seemed to lose interest. I suppose it was naïve of me to expect him to share in my excitement over the various new projects I had under way – a non-fiction book and a couple of commissions to write screenplays. After all, the Box Office Blockbuster and Big Bestseller were becalmed, and we both now tacitly understood that was the way things were likely to remain. As my career moved on, Brian instigated a process of rejection that I failed at first to understand or even recognise. But suddenly, I became exploited in the same way I had witnessed him plunder other of his rich or successful old friends. I had graduated from protégé to mark. I suppose it was a rite of passage, but it was hurtful and I resented it.

The rewards of working on the Box Office Blockbuster and Big Bestseller had not been pecuniary, but they were substantial. I learned a lot at the academy of Kinnerton Street, travelling the road with its dean and grand master. Could any young man – especially one as unschooled and wayward as myself – ever have stumbled upon a better tutor? I knew that I had been in the presence of a Great Spirit, and wanted to show my appreciation.

At first I enjoyed taking Brian out to expensive restaurants, and extravagantly repaying the largesse he had bestowed upon me, but he was not about to be grateful or gracious on these occasions, or even allow me the pleasure of being generous. He wanted it to hurt. He also became increasingly outrageous in demands for money. Once, he asked for a hundred pounds in front of a roomful of people, and when I wrote out a cheque said, as if I had spoilt his fun, 'It's too easy!'

On another occasion I was sitting in the front room when Ronnie the milkman passed silently in his electric float. Brian flung open the window. 'Ronnie! Just the man I want to see! Hollywood Harry's here and wants to pay the bill!'

'Nothing would give me greater pleasure,' I said through gritted teeth, and went outside into the street for a reckoning.

'Hello,' Ronnie said. 'Where you been? 'Ollywood?' He lowered his voice. 'It's eighty quid.'

'Eighty quid – for milk! I've never actually seen him touch the stuff.'

'I give him the odd fiver, like,' Ronnie said, shamefaced. 'When he's short and can't make the bank.'

'You're a nice man, Ronnie,' I said, writing a cheque. 'But you're a mug.'

'Like you, an' all!' Ronnie said with a wink. 'Let's face it, governor – he's a difficult bloke to say no to.'

This deliberate and shameless exploitation of old friends was not confined to me. Robin Maugham, Harry Clifton and Terence Young had all been stung in their time, in a manner that was deliberately designed to cause maximum affront. But the most extreme financial bludgeoning was visited upon Nic Head, an old friend who had been regarded almost as a son. 'I owed Brian a couple of hundred quid, and as I was about to go away told him I would pay him on my return. In the meantime I lent him my old vintage Bentley, my pride and joy, to use as he wished. I stayed away a couple of weeks longer than I originally planned and returned to find Brian had sold the Bentley. For two hundred quid!'

It became impossible to predict how our reunions would

go when I returned from Los Angeles to London. There were times when Brian seemed delighted to see me, and we would pick up our relationship as though it had never been interrupted. On other occasions he became difficult and strange, as if intent on sabotaging our friendship. I once arrived at the house to take him out to lunch and found him in the company of a sour, swarthy youth who oozed mute hostility. 'Mustapha,' Brian said. 'You don't mind if he joins us, do you?'

It was the last thing I wanted, but there seemed no gracious way to avoid it. The glowering and ill-humoured Mustapha, it turned out, was an Algerian currently employed as a dishwasher in some cheap tourist hotel in Victoria. He would have been depressing company at the best of times, but was a real wet blanket in the role of unwelcome guest at a reunion lunch. But as he seemed to be silent as statuary, and grunted rather than articulated, I hoped he could be ignored.

We made our way to Wheeler's and took a corner table, with Mustapha seated next to Brian. I ordered a good bottle of white Burgundy, a Chassagne-Montrachet – one of our favourites. 'That's right,' Brian said, 'push the boat out!' He turned to Mustapha. 'Have what you like! My friend is terribly rich.'

We ordered potted shrimps, followed by Dover sole, while Mustapha loudly voiced his disappointment at the lack of lamb. He did not like fish, he complained when told we were in a fish restaurant. He was eventually accommodated with something or other, although he continued to grumble and sulk as the meal progressed.

I am uncertain at what point during our lunch things began to go wrong – fairly early on, I would say. It was almost as if Brian had intended the entire thing to be some sort of punishment. Before lunch I had an appointment at the American embassy, and was wearing a suit and tie for the occasion, an ensemble that Brian seemed to think was worn to impress him.

'New suit?'

'Quite new.'

'Savile Row, I presume.' This was said with disdain.

'Anderson & Sheppard.'

'Ah,' Brian said, with condescension. 'I'm Huntsman, of course.' He meant that he had his suits made at the most expensive and august tailors on the Row, something I knew to be entirely untrue. He had a collection of jackets and suits from various Savile Row tailors, all of them at least twenty years old, but none of them were from Huntsman. I prepared for a strange and perverse time of it.

'Christopher is the best-*dressed* scriptwriter in Hollywood,' Brian said to Mustapha.

'That was Lee Marvin's putdown of Terence Young as a director, I seem to remember.'

'Do you ever come across Terence in Hollywood?'

'About three months ago I saw him in a swish restaurant with an eighteen-year-old starlet. He had a red Rolls convertible outside.'

'Rented, no doubt.'

'I went up to him and we embraced Hollywood-style. Threw our arms around each other and banged each other's backs, like Italians. I'm not sure he remembered who I was.'

'Toilet!' Mustapha declared, rising from his seat and heading determinedly towards the lavatory.

'Man of few words, Mustapha,' I said, 'but he does manage to communicate.'

'Wonderful chap!'

'Not the jolliest of companions. I thought you preferred Moroccans or Tunisians. These Algerians always seem such a dour lot.'

'Mustapha is very deep.'

'Ah.' I said that the name reminded me of a true story.

During the war the British Ambassador to Moscow received a Turkish colleague at the embassy. The man handed across his card and the diplomat was cheered, amidst the bleak misery of wartime Russia in winter, to read the inscription: Mustapha Kunt. 'Spelt with a K. The diplomat immediately wrote to a friend that in the hard times that were upon them they all felt like that, but lacked the courage to put it on their cards.'

'What an extraordinary coincidence! Mustapha's family name is spelt with a K – K-O-C-H. Pronounced Cock!' Brian raised his hand to his mouth, screwed up his eyes and began to chuckle. I joined in, and for a moment we slipped back into the comfortable world of old we had shared.

Mustapha returned from the lavatory and sat down without a word. Some harsh desert wind seemed to accompany him, blasting and desiccating everything in its path. Once again, the life went out of lunch. I ate without enthusiasm as Brian gulped wine. 'Waiter, another bottle,' he demanded.

'Christ, Bri, do you really think . . .?'

'Excellent Burgundy. Pity Mustapha is so devout he won't join us in a glass.'

'Yeccch,' Mustapha said, showing animation for the first time. 'No drink. Never.' For a moment it looked as if he was going to spit. 'Urgh!'

The only pleasure I took in the second bottle was the degree to which the consumption of alcohol irked Mustapha. Brian continued to throw back the wine recklessly, then rose unsteadily and made his way to the lavatory. Mustapha had picked distastefully at his food throughout the meal, suspiciously pushing fish around his plate with a fork, and pulling faces. A mountain of chocolate ice cream had cheered him temporarily, and I now watched as he scraped the last vestiges from his bowl. Neither one of us made any attempt to speak to the other. I asked for the bill, which with two bottles of expensive wine was hefty, and slipped a credit card on to the plate.

Brian returned and almost fell as he made his way to the table. He had a large pee stain a foot long down the right side of his trousers and was flushed a vivid vermilion. He sat down heavily, all but collapsing on to the chair. 'Waiter,' he called at his most imperious, 'open another bottle of wine and bring it here with the cork in it.'

'On the bill, sir?' The waiter gave me a questioning, sympathetic look.

'Of course, on the bill!' Brian snapped.

The wine was brought and Brian shoved the bottle into the left-hand pocket of his trousers. He stood and began to make his way out of the restaurant, and Mustapha followed. I duly signed the new credit card slip. The waiter nodded in the direction of Brian's departing form. 'He all right, sir?'

'Pray for us!'

Brian lurched down Kinnerton Street, stopping every twenty yards or so to catch his breath. He stood gasping for air, one hand resting on Mustapha's shoulder for support. I walked beside him, angry and depressed. Not a single word was exchanged in the twenty minutes it took to reach the house. When at last we arrived at the front door, he turned towards me and I thought he was going to thank me for lunch. 'You don't have a tenner on you, do you? I owe the milkman . . .'

I dug into my pocket and handed over a twenty-pound note. As Brian stepped through the front door, steadied by Mustapha, I turned on my heel and walked away.

And so it went. Up and down, and uncertain. The bad times were so deliberately perverse that there were occasions when I vowed never to subject myself to the considerable expense of being ill-treated by Brian again. And now when I returned from America, I did not always call. Little by little, the distance between us grew.

But I remember one magnificent occasion when all the

A refreshed, post-prandial Brian in happier times

elements of our early friendship fell effortlessly back into place. In Los Angeles, I had been living with the writer Mary Agnes Donoghue – who would become my wife – and somewhat nervously introduced her to Brian. Introductions always carried an element of danger, as you could never tell how he would react. ('You've got a nice pair,' he once said to a girlfriend I introduced. 'A very nice pair!') But Mary Agnes came from an Irish-American background, and even more importantly shared Brian's magical approach to the world. She told Brian she had watched his version of *A Christmas Carol* every Christmas Eve throughout her childhood in New York, and that it had assumed mythological proportions in her imagination. Brian nodded, and the friendship was set. He now became very well-behaved when we all went out together, and our relationship entered a new phase in which he adopted the persona of a dignified, grand old man.

When Mary Agnes's first film was being made, I took Brian out for lunch and told him it was turning out to be a miserable experience. The highly paid star was on drugs and proving to be impossible. We were walking down Kinnerton Street, beating the familiar path to the Turk's Head at the time. Brian stopped dead. For a moment I thought he was choking as he pushed a finger deep into his mouth and seemed to be ripping at it with his teeth. I then realised he was trying to dislodge a ring. He pulled off a triple gold and platinum Tiffany band, which he had worn ever since I had known him, and told me to give it to Mary Agnes. Pointing a finger like a pistol, he said, 'Tell her to tell those actors – "YOU DO WHAT I SAY!"'

Later, he organised a screening of *Playboy of the Western World* for Mary Agnes in a private cinema in South Audley Street. The invited audience was made up of the usual mix: grandees, writers, a couple of Guardsmen, an air steward, a lodger, a monk and Brian's confessor from the Brompton Oratory. Afterwards, we went on to Kinnerton Street to find a feast laid on: half-kilo tins of caviar on ice, a whole poached salmon in aspic, cold salads, and innumerable bottles of champagne and wine. Brian stood in front of his winged chair, fingering a button on his jacket, waiting for silence in which to make a formal announcement. 'I would just like to say – everything you see before you for this Slap-Up Feed is stolen.' There was laughter and applause. No doubt some of the guests thought he was joking. I knew he wasn't. One by one, Brian singled out the various light-fingered donors for praise: the filched salmon came from the lodger, a restaurant employee; the caviar from the air steward; the champagne had been liberated from the overpriced cellar of the Savoy. Each of the men responsible took a bow.

One of the guests was Sarah Churchill, the most wild of Winston's children and the favourite. At the beginning of lunch she seemed dusty and brittle, but after two glasses of champagne she sparkled. The years fell away and she became a high-spirited young girl, displaying the type of impetuous behaviour that had landed her in so much trouble over the years. She leapt on to the coffee table, held her champagne glass high, and offered a toast. 'I've just come back from Russia, and this is how the Russians – who are wonderful – drink a toast. Back in one! *Na vashe zdorovie!*'

We all threw a glass of champagne back in one in the manner of the wonderful Russians. It was a rollicking lunch, and still going full bore at three o'clock when the doorbell rang. By force of old habit, I made my way to open it. A small man in glasses stood outside, clutching an attaché case. 'I have an appointment with Mr Hurst,' he said apologetically, peering in the direction of the convivial uproar. 'This is the right address? I'm from Social Security.'

'One moment, please.' I closed the door and went to fetch Brian, gesturing to him wildly from the corridor. 'Christ, Bri – it's a man from Social Security. Says he has an appointment.'

'My God, I completely forgot! How awkward! Not the best time to beg for supplementary benefit.'

'Want me to get rid of him?'

'No, no. Terribly difficult to get an appointment with these people, you know. They are modern-day pashas with millions at their fingertips. They have allowances for everything if you play your cards right – carpets, central heating, you name it. I'm up for a rent allowance. A supplementary, they call it. No, don't send him away – I'll talk to him. Try and shut them up a bit in there if you can.'

'Okay. Remember – poor-old-geezer-without-a-pot-to-piss-in mode.'

Before re-entering the party, I watched Brian walk down the corridor towards the front door. No great actor – classical, method or instinctive – could have done a better or faster job of getting into character. With every step, he shed aspects of the persona of the confidant, sophisticated, *bon viveur* and little by little adopted the characteristics of impoverished old age. It was masterful. As Brian opened the front door, the man from the Social was greeted by a pathetic, geriatric shell of shuffling misery.

I tried to subdue the revellers, but without much success. A couple of the heartier laughers pulled back a little, but the low roar of alcohol-assisted merriment was impossible to suppress. I stood listening carefully for the Social Security man to leave, and went back into the corridor as soon as I heard the front door close. 'How did it go?'

'All right – I think. I took him upstairs to the least decorated bedroom at the back – the dark one with the water stain on the ceiling and the musty smell. I think he was suitably depressed. Told him you were my nephew holding his wedding reception here. Said your friends had got a bit out of hand and quite worn me out.'

'A wedding reception – on a Wednesday afternoon?'

'He did look a bit sceptical.'

'As well he might – with Sarah doing Cossack dances on the coffee table among all the liberated champagne and caviar.'

'Yes, I thought it wise not to let him get a glimpse of the revels. Perhaps I should have introduced him. "Silence everyone, I want you to meet Mr Smith from Social Security. He's here about the supplementary. The old-age pensioner's caviar allowance."'

We both began to laugh. We laughed until tears came. We laughed so hard we had to lean on one another for support. 'You have to laugh!' Brian said.

I nodded, wiping my eyes.

'Dear, dear, the things that happen,' Brian said, regaining his breath before we went back into the front room. He shot me a conspiratorial look and winked. 'We've had a few laughs over the years, haven't we, Christopher?'

I was away in America when the British Film Institute organised a ninetieth birthday party for Brian. The surviving theatrical knights and knights-to-be he had directed duly showed up – Roger Moore, Donald Sinden and Alec Guinness. Physically, Brian was wasted and gaunt, and mentally he was pretty far gone. Senility is a particularly cruel fate for a lifelong wit and raconteur. Without travel or daily gossip, Brian was starved of new material and began to repeat stories to me that I had not only heard several times before, but had taped, read in transcription and written up. 'Did I tell you when I had jaundice in Cairo . . .?'

'Did you ever! The Daffodil of B11.'

Brian nodded, and fell silent. Ten minutes later he said, 'I was in hospital in Cairo during the First World War, bright yellow with jaundice . . .'

He began to show up uninvited two or three times a week at our friend Valerie's flat behind the Nag's Head, expecting to be fed. 'He did not want to eat whatever I might have prepared for myself, but demanded soup or scrambled eggs. And it didn't matter if I had friends, or was having a dinner party, he would just sit down and join in. Much as I loved Brian, I began to find it very trying.'

And then, on a trip back to London from America, I called Kinnerton Street and found the phone cut off. Alarmed, I went round to the house. A shifty, evil-looking character opened the front door a crack and became defensive when I asked for Brian. The place looked as if it had been cleaned out and abandoned. 'He's in the hospital,' the man said. 'I'm sort of looking after the house. Part-time, like.'

'Which hospital?'

'Dunno. One of them round here.'

I called Brian's lifelong friend Francis Crowdie to see if he knew what had happened. (Francis had been employed by the World Service of the BBC because of his crystal-clear and beautiful diction, and used to broadcast to Eastern European countries behind the Iron Curtain. 'Imagine – all those Communists over there sound just like Francis when they speak English,' Brian once said. 'Pound-noteish and frightfully posh. Mustn't it be strange?') The plummy tones of the old BBC rang out as Francis put me in the picture: 'Brian has finally achieved senility. He's in a ward in a hospital in Chelsea and had the cheek to write me down as his next of kin. I told them, "I am neither next, nor kin".'

I described my encounter with the man at the door in Kinnerton Street. 'The place has been looted and ransacked by rent boys and ruffians,' Francis said in exasperation. 'I went round as soon as I heard Brian had been taken to hospital but was already too late. He had given the keys to some dreadful person. They've taken everything!'

'Does he recognise people?'

'Sometimes. He seems to recognise me most of the time. Other people he's known for years he stares at blankly. Of course, you never know with Brian. Maybe they always bored him and this is his revenge. He's occasionally lucid. Last time I was there he was convinced we were in Morocco. I told him, "We are not in Morocco!" Most of the time he seems to think he's resting in between making films at Pinewood. He's perfectly content. Quite untroubled. Happy as a lark.'

I went to visit him in a large public ward in St Stephen's Hospital in Chelsea, and marched past his bed, half-knowing that the frail and wasted sleeping figure was Brian, but not wanting to know. But how could I have missed the sumptuous silk dressing gown and embroidered black-and-gold Moroccan slippers? I was led back by a nurse, and he woke with a start. Almost immediately, the shell was infused with the spirit of the old Brian. The pale blue Irish eyes twinkled: 'Christopher!'

I sat beside him, hoping he did not notice the effect the sight of him had on me. After I regained my composure, I told him a joke and related some racy Hollywood gossip. 'Where do you get all this stuff?' He became confused when I reminded him that I had been living in Los Angeles on and off for more than a decade. 'So that's where you've been!'

'How long have you been here?'

'Oh ages! I've lived here for years and years!'

'I meant, here – in hospital.'

'Oh, I'm not in hospital,' he said confidently. Suddenly, he was overcome with doubt. 'Am I?' He became a lost and muddled child, and his voice took on a tone that was heart-breaking. 'Am I?'

We were in the geriatric ward among a dozen old men in advanced states of decay and despair. No one was expected to come out of this awful place alive. In the next bed a man lay dying, skeletal and bloodless, while his wife sat bolt upright in a chair beside him. It was a silent vigil in which the couple said nothing to one another, a hopeless attendance on death.

'Poor chap,' Brian whispered. 'He hasn't got long. His wife comes in every day, you know. And just sits.'

Brian rose from his bed to go to the bathroom, making a performance of brushing his long white hair and tying the sash around his gorgeous dressing gown. As he passed the foot of the neighbouring bed he paused beside the woman's chair. 'Madame,' he announced grandly, 'it has been my privilege over the past few days to observe you closely. You are one of the most dignified and beautiful women I have ever seen.' He turned to the old man. 'You, sir, are a very lucky man.'

He moved on. The woman, so forlorn and without hope a moment earlier, now glowed like a young girl. And the old man resigned and close to death, turned to her with pride and love in his eyes. They had been blessed.

Oh Brian, I thought, I'm going to miss you!

After an hour or so I rose to leave. 'What an interesting day,' Brian said. 'So much has happened. And when it doesn't, no matter. I just sit here quietly and rest.'

I asked if there was anything he needed. He thought for a

while, shook his head – and then suddenly cried, 'Socks! I'd love a pair of socks.'

The following day I went to Liberty's on Regent Street and bought a selection of luxurious cashmere socks in a variety of wild colours – red, yellow, purple, blue, dark green – and even a fabulous pair with pink candy stripes that I knew would make him laugh. When I took them to the hospital I was disappointed to find Brian surrounded by a dozen pairs of socks.

'Coals to Newcastle,' I said, handing him my contribution. 'Where on earth did all these socks come from?'

'I really don't know.' He seemed puzzled. 'You know, I think I must have prayed for them. I did want a pair of socks.'

'Ah, that would be St Thérèse, then. Another miracle ground out in the back room.'

'The miracle of the socks!' Brian chuckled as he took mine out of their bag, and rubbed the soft cashmere sensuously against his face. 'Oh, these are wonderful!' He gestured towards an uninspiring pair of grey socks on the bedside table, and his voice took on something of its old, wicked bite. 'Much better than those bloody things! I'll see they're given to the deserving poor.'

As I sat down, he called out to a passing nurse. 'Bring us a bottle of champagne, will you?'

'You'll have your cocoa with the rest of them.'

'Cocoa then,' he replied cheerfully. He turned to me. 'Cocoa all right?'

'Cocoa's fine.'

We chatted quietly until the nurse returned with the cocoa. 'I'm not supposed to bring visitors drinks,' she complained, 'but as it's you, Brian.'

'They're marvellous here!' He made it sound as if he were talking about the staff at the Ritz. 'Marvellous!' We sipped the hot drinks. 'This cocoa's nice, isn't it?'

'Very nice, Bri.'

As the nurse passed by again he called out, 'My friend thinks the cocoa's very nice.'

'Does he, now?' the nurse said, winking at me. 'That's good.'

Every now and again, Brian would stop a nurse and ask, 'What happens next?' He looked puzzled. 'They all seem so busy – where are they all going?'

We cradled our mugs of cocoa in our hands, saying nothing. I could not speak and once again hoped he did not see the tears in my eyes. It would not be long now. Brian was drifting gently from one magical state to another. The cocoa was wonderful and I knew it would never taste so good again.

PART IX

End

Brian Desmond Hurst died on 26 September 1986, in a nursing home called the Delaware, off the Harrow Road, and was cremated in the West London Crematorium. The obituaries were respectful and shot through with inaccuracies and mistakes, as was only right and proper for a man who had invented himself. *The Times* reported that he had been educated at Westminster, some confabulation Brian must have once put about and long since forgotten. In a sly, final sentence couched in the code of the day, the paper informed its readers of his sexual nature: 'He never married.'

None of the personal effects from Kinnerton Street survived. Everything was stolen – the first editions of T. E. Lawrence and Charles Doughty's *Arabia Deserta*, the painting of St Bridget, the portrait of Brian from the 1950s which hung on the stairs, the dubious Monet, and the gift-shop bust of Nefertiti. I doubt if Brian would have minded very much.

His nephew travelled from Ulster to pay for the funeral arrangements – and take care of the more insistent creditors. (As usual, the current Kinnerton Street milkman was owed money: 'Funny, I knew Bri wouldn't let me down and somebody would show up to pay.') There had been a time when Brian's Belfast relations had expectations, fuelled by promises – the house in Kinnerton Street, the Monet, various treasures, and unknown amounts of cash. But few delusions remained in the end. They had grown to love him, and had been kind and generous to him when he was lonely and most needed them. His ashes were taken back to Ireland,

and scattered on the grave of his brother Robert, at Dundonald cemetery in Belfast.

Contact with his family had been re-established when Brian was filming *Playboy* in Ireland, and had never since been broken. He expressed a proprietary, familial affection for his great-niece and nephew, and was proud of their achievements – Marion, active in Ulster politics, became the Mayor of Bangor; Robert became a squadron-leader in the Royal Air Force. As Brian's London circle of friends died off and narrowed, he began to rely increasingly on the kindness of his family. In his final years, he had often gone to Belfast to spend holidays and Christmas, and his last role as *magnifico* was played out in Bangor, as Santa Claus in crimson robes and a Big White Beard. *A triumph!*

Today, Brian is almost entirely forgotten. When I placed an advertisement in the Belfast press in an attempt to locate family members, it generated a news story on just *how* forgotten. A banner on the front of the Belfast *News Letter* advertised a double-page feature article with the question: HAS ANYONE HEARD OF BRIAN DESMOND HURST? The piece described him as 'Ulster's Best Kept Secret'. Similarly, when the film critic of the London *Evening Standard* recently wrote up a National Film Theatre showing of a 1947 'Golden Oldie' – *Hungry Hill*, starring Margaret Lockwood and Dennis Price, with the film debut of a smouldering Siobhan McKenna – he wrote: 'Not everyone remembers Brian Desmond Hurst. Very few, I'd say.'

The truth is that Brian outlived his reputation. When he died at the age of ninety-one he had not made a film in more than twenty years. The critics, actors and directors who rated his talent were mostly dead, and the body of work left behind was such a mixed bag it was hard to categorise. The variety and range of the output made him impossible to pigeonhole and blurred his individuality as a filmmaker. He was never associated with a particular genre, or affiliated with a school or group, and refused to be taken *too* seriously. He was a talented director, who saw film as a personal adventure, and the medium perfectly suited his operatic instinct and picnic ways, while enabling him to make the large amounts of money he needed, for he found life expensive.

I had always assumed that Brian's ashes had been scattered on Howth Head, north of Dublin, in the vicinity of those of his beloved sister, Patricia. He had loved his brother, Robert, but it was an irony for him to end up in Dundonald. In many ways this middle-class suburb of Belfast represented everything he was not. He even invoked the name, when he wanted to accuse fellow expatriates from Belfast of being suburban: '*Very* Dundonald.'

It therefore seemed right, as I drew close to completing this memoir, to take a couple of handfuls of soil from his brother's grave in Belfast, and carry them south across the border and scatter them at Howth Head, to be with Patricia. (When the idea first occurred to me, I heard the sceptical voice of Brian: 'Only took you twenty years to think of it.')

My plan was to follow in Brian's footsteps, when he had been driven by Harry Clifton's valet, Dodge, to Howth Head, with two dozen roses and champagne, to scatter his sister's ashes. I travelled to Belfast and was directed to the Dundonald grave by Brian's great niece and nephew, Marion and Robert. I filled a champagne glass with earth and marble chips from the foot of the grave, and took the train to Dublin and checked into the Shelbourne hotel. That evening I walked around St Stephen's Green, and through the city, thinking of my old friend. I dropped into a pub for a drink, and as I stood patiently awaiting the delivery of a slow pint of Guinness, a man standing a little way along the bar smiled and caught my eye.

He was a skinny fellow, with high rosy cheeks, and eyes that danced with mischief at the pleasure of being alive. A cheap, formless suit hung from him, and his shirt was of a dazzling pattern of tiny blue arrows. The tie was flame red with a knot the size of a fist. He began to speak: 'Riverrun past Eve and Adam's from swerve of shore to bend of bay, brings us by a commodius vicus of recirculation back to Howth Castle and environs.'

As a man with a champagne glass full of earth taken from a Dundonald grave on a mission to Howth Head to scatter it in memory of the Empress of Ireland, the words struck me as a Brian-like Irish incantation and portent. 'I'm off to Howth in the morning.' I exaggerated a little: 'To scatter an old friend's ashes.'

'When a frond was a friend inneed to carry, as earwigs do their dead,' the man said, 'their soil to the earthball where indeeth we shall calm decline, our legacy unknown.'

'*Finnegans Wake*?'

'Taken from the sacred text itself,' the man said happily, 'and the glory is that this night it did not fall on deaf ears. Did *not*!'

I smiled to myself, as I remembered a clumsy conversation I had with Brian about the book thirty years earlier. '*Finnegans Wake* is a load of bollocks, isn't it?' God knows what possessed me to be so recklessly provocative, but it was a genuine question arrived at honestly. The book confounded me. Gobbledegook. Gibberish. Unbridled, incontinent, non-stop, exhausting, professional Irishness – meaningless and impossible.

Brian did not answer at first. At length, he said, 'That is your studied opinion, is it? That is your penetrating insight and considered intellectual assessment of one of the great books to have been produced by one of the greatest literary geniuses ever to have come from a race of great literary geniuses? *A load of bollocks?*'

'Well, the book doesn't make any sense,' I said, backtracking in the face of Brian's evident anger. 'You can't *read* it. It's a formless loop of puns and wordplay – language without rules, words spewed out for their sound. If all literature was like that nobody would ever read. I mean, *okay*, Joyce is a great writer – *Dubliners*, and all that – but don't you think even *Ulysses* is overrated? It's just a big literary experiment. Again, you can't really *read* it for pleasure, you have to struggle through it – fight the bloody thing.'

There was another extended silence. 'It is generous of you to allow that Joyce has stature as a writer. However, we now move from the brute assessment of *Finnegans Wake* – a difficult but sublime work – to the philistine dismissal of *Ulysses*, one of the greatest and most influential novels of the twentieth century.' Brian took a deep breath. 'You are *wrong*. Ignorantly, unimaginatively, enormously, Anglo-Saxonly *wrong*! *Finnegans Wake* is music. It is song and laughter. It is enormously witty and madly clever. It is a great Irish writer's ecstatic expression of joy in the use of language. It is the endless dream of Ireland and all her history. A book for angels.'

The subject was dropped, and I never uttered heresies about James Joyce again. However, further attempts at the books in question left me brow-furrowed as ever. Must be an Irish thing, some sort of Gaelic code, I thought, and left it at that. Joyce and his books remained closed for more than thirty years.

'Know any more of *Finnegans Wake*?' I asked the man in the pub.

'*Reams* of it. Page upon page. Chapter and verse. I drive people bloody mad with the recitation of the bottomless book. I cannot be stopped. I'm a man obsessed with the beauty of the writing and the sound of the words. And the humour and the play. Driven I am, seduced and bewitched. I don't read the papers. I do *not*! Neither do I watch the television. You will not find me beside the wireless of an evening listening to the football results. Never! It's *Finnegans Wake* that takes up my leisure hours – the reading of it and the reciting of it. I *wallow* in it. Rejoice in it, I do. Shout it out it in the bath.'

'He's not joking,' another drinker at the bar said. 'He knows more of that book than the Holy Father in Rome knows the Bible. And that's God's truth!'

Thus prompted, the man found voice: 'Renove that bible. In spite of all that science could boot or art could eke. Bolt the grinden. Cave and can em. Single wrecks for the weak, double axe for the mail, and quick queck quack for the radiose. You will never have post in your pocket unless you have brasse on your plate. Mind the monks and their Grasps. Scrape your souls. Commit no miracles. Post pine no bills. Practise preaching. Think in your stomach. Import through the nose. Let earwigger's wivable teach you the dance.'

The words rolled out, natural and clear, and I listened with new ears and understanding to this high falutin', Gaelic literary rap. Enlightenment had finally come. Passages spoken aloud from *Finnegans Wake* in an Irish accent, by someone who loved the prose enough to commit wedges of it to memory, released its power. The mysteries and wonder of the book had been unlocked, not by a literary intellectual, but a half-tight man in a cheap suit standing at the bar of a Dublin pub. It was as if Brian had taken me by the elbow, and guided me into this particular tavern to receive a final Celtic benediction.

I explained to the man the revelation that his passionate recitation had brought about, and told of my previous scepticism and bewilderment. (I could hear Brian: 'My friend is English and a bit thick, but he gets there in the end.') The man was exhilarated at the news of my conversion, a mood consolidated by the offer of a drink. 'A pint would keep the whistle whetted,' he said. 'We will drink side by side beside the Liffey, and the sloothering slide of her, giddygaddy, grannyma, gossipaceous Annalivia.'

It helped to be in a pub with a drink in the hand – after all, the hero of the book, the sleeping, dreaming, aptly named Mr Porter (a.k.a. Humphrey Chimpden Earwicker) is a publican, landlord of the Bristol, city of my birth. But there is only so much genius a man can absorb over a pint, or even two. Unwilling to hear the whole of *Finnegans Wake* in a single evening, I made to move.

'Seen you off, has he?' the other drinker said. 'He never shuts up. It's the *Finnegans Wake* morning, noon and bloody night.'

'I will not shut up! My voice will *not* be stilled. No, not even by the intermisunderstanding minds of the anticollaborators. There are those who have threatened to *shoot* me, so they have. But with a bullet in the brain and another in the heart, and my torso riddled with the machine-gun fire, I would continue.' He lowered his voice and gestured towards the fellow drinkers surrounding us. 'Sometimes, when drink loosens the soul in them, and they feel close to the real man inside, I see them get carried away and laugh and cry with it.'

As I nodded and smiled, and backed away towards the door, he was off again: 'Big the dog the dig the bog the bagger the dugger the begadag degabug, this the quemquem that the quum, two hoots or three jeers for the grape, vine and brew . . .'

The following morning I prepared for the ceremony. I had ordered two dozen yellow roses to be delivered to the hotel (without Brian by my side I had no faith that magical intervention would provide them en route), and bought a magnum of champagne (the man in the wine shop apologised for not having Krug, and offered me Roederer instead – 'It'll do,' I said). A small packet of smoked salmon sandwiches and a wedge of lemon completed my sacramental necessities, and I set off for Howth Head.

This was James Joyce country again, where Molly Bloom in *Ulysses* had gone with her lover in his grey tweed suit and straw hat, and made hot love among the earwigs hidden under the wild ferns. Joyce described the bay beneath the sheer cliffs and open moor – purple by the Lion's Head, green by Drumleck, and yellowgreen towards Sutton – and wrote of the heather on fire, and a nanny goat walking sure-footed and dropping raisins, and the silence except for the buzzing of flies.

At the highest point of Howth Head, I passed a sign marked DANGEROUS CLIFFS and followed the path along the top of them, amazed that a place so close to the city remained this wild and empty. It had been raining lightly when I set out, but it now stopped and began to clear until all around me the sky, cliffs and sea were layered and washed in myriad hues of grey and green and blue. I left the path, and began a perilous descent to the edge of the cliffs, down through yellow blossoming gorse and white outcrops of rock. I found what I considered to be a suitable place and made ready for the ritual. Below the precarious perch of my cliff-top eyrie was a sheer drop of hundreds of feet, where gulls screeched and wheeled over rocks and ocean.

A yacht went by under power, a plane turned lazily towards Dublin airport, and a ferry emerged from the harbour and moved methodically across the flat sea towards Scotland. In the far distance low white clouds draped the hills like smoke. The setting was near perfect, a day touched with Brian's magic.

('Advice to a writer of your temperament,' I heard him whisper in my ear. 'Keep the purple to an *absolute* minimum.')

I laid the roses among the rocks, opened the magnum, and unwrapped the champagne glass from its protective bubble-wrap – '*Bubble-wrap* – how *dreadful*!' I scattered the earth and marble chips among the yellow roses, and doused them generously with champagne. I washed the graveyard earth from the glass with more champagne, and filled it for a silent toast to my old friend.

I took the smoked salmon sandwiches from their tinfoil, squeezed lemon on to them, and began to eat. High above on the cliff path a man came into view with a dog running ahead of him. He looked down and saw me, and I must have made a strange spectacle – crouched among the rocks at the very edge of the cliffs, with two dozen yellow roses at my feet and a magnum of champagne on my knee, eating a sandwich. Unperturbed, the man called down as he passed, 'Splendid spot for a bite of lunch!'

The champagne and the smoked salmon sandwiches tasted good, and I drifted into a reverie and summoned ghosts. I remembered the friends I had loved and lost over the years, and drank a toast to each of them: Geoffrey, the first to die, an old Cotswold painter neglected by his muse, with the face of a farmer and the voice of a duke, who dropped dead while drawing a nude model, a local bus conductor's wife who charged ten shillings an hour for topless, more for the altogether; Tony, one of the funniest men I have ever known, a hard drinker who developed sclerosis of the liver and went around the world in search of a Holy Man to cure him, and returned from a remote island in Indonesia having found a shaman who told him to drink only Arak; Craig, lion-hearted veteran of the secret war in Laos, who loved to fly, and returning from an air show in a vintage plane with all the dangerous stunts safely behind him, crashed and died when the engine cut out; Allen, cheerful and brave in the face of a long and painful illness, whose last words when his feeding tube became dislodged were a joke, as he called for the chef of his favourite restaurant. And my big brother John, in pyjamas and dressing gown, clutching a copy of *Cold Comfort Farm*, felled suddenly by an aneurism.

The ghosts gathered around me . . . Bob and Celia and Franco, Uffe and Hank. One by one, I drank to their memory, and the friendship we had shared. An indulgent and comfortable melancholy crept over me as I remembered old times with these great friends. It was a pleasant couple of hours of gentle sadness I spent, perched up there on the cliffs above Howth, among the good company of the dead.

I refilled the glass for one final toast, and tipped the remainder of the champagne over the roses. It was difficult to find suitable words. I was mildly drunk, and somewhat mawkish – a mood that would not do for Brian. The emotional heart-to-heart had never been the way it was with us. We'd downed many a Great Big Glass of Wine together, and enjoyed our share of Slap-Up Feeds. We'd had a few laughs over the years . . . been good old friends. The best.

I raised my glass: 'I doubt if you noticed, or much cared, but I loved you, Brian Desmond Hurst – you magnificent old Irish bugger.'

NOTE TO THE READER

In accordance with the house style that any memoir of Brian is bound to take on, I have sometimes sacrificed the veracity of time and place better to serve the story. We went to Ireland three times, and Tangier and Malta twice each, and spent a dreadful week on Gibraltar . . . I have merged these various journeys into single episodes as little purpose is served by sticking to a strict chronological order.

The events and conversations are reconstructed as accurately as possible, incredible though many of them may seem. I have dipped into Brian's unpublished autobiography, *Travelling the Road*, for numerous anecdotes. I still retain a dozen or so tapes of Brian recounting anecdotes for the Big Bestseller, but, alas, it is impossible to reproduce the subtle charm of their telling on the page.

I also kept a journal throughout the period – although it is infuriatingly vague and incomplete, while painting an embarrassing picture of the author as a wild and callow youth. At the time I was mostly concerned with other things. However, as an *aide-mémoire* and timeline it has proved invaluable. Brian's great-niece and nephew, Marion Smith and Robert Hurst, kindly showed me around Belfast and dug out old family photographs. I would like to thank Valerie Martin, who transcribed the original tapes with Brian, supplied several photos, and reminded me of various incidents.

A number of authors have proved very useful. For a historical insight into the relentless pursuit of Guardsmen, I have drawn on *My Father and Myself* by J. R. Ackerley. Gerald Hamilton wrote about himself extensively in three autobiographies: *As Young as Sophocles*, *Mr Norris and I* and *The Way It Was With Me*. As might be expected, these are largely self-serving volumes, and – without the personality of Gerald to deliver the stories – they lack colour. He comes to life in Christopher Isherwood's novel *Mr Norris Changes Trains*; Isherwood also wrote about his real-life relationship with Gerald Hamilton in *Christopher and His Kind*. For more of both the serious and hilarious side of Kenneth Williams, I recommend his *Letters* and *Diaries*. For aficionados of the peculiar, Harry Clifton's mother Violet wrote a strange book in a high, poetic style verging on the biblical to commemorate her extraordinary husband. *The Book of Talbot* is a chronicle of passion, the tone of which is best conveyed by the dedication: 'To God for Talbot'. Roy Ward Baker, who was to direct *Darkness Before Dawn*, has written his own memoirs, *Director's Cut*. William McQuitty, who worked with Brian as assistant director and later as his producer, has also written an autobiography, *A Life to Remember*.

Moura Budberg appears in numerous books, but the one that goes furthest in sorting through the tangle of truth and untruth in her life is Andrea Lynn's *Shadow Lovers*. Her daughter, Tania Alexander, wrote defensively of her mother in *Tania: Memories of a Lost World*. Nina Berberova, the Russian writer, recorded her disillusion with her friend in *The Italics Are Mine*. Her biography of Moura, written in Russian, is translated only into French, *Histoire de la Baronne Boudberg*.

There are many books on the Gallipoli campaign, but the classic is *Gallipoli* by Alan Moorehead. Compton Mackenzie's *Gallipoli Memoirs* gives a vivid, eyewitness account and sense of the period, while the tragedy and grandeur of the campaign is captured in *Gallipoli Diary*, the fascinating personal diaries of that most civilised of soldiers, General Sir Ian Hamilton. For dates and details of the movement of the Royal Irish Rifles, I am indebted to Ray Westlake's *British Regiments at Gallipoli*.

I am grateful to Tom Dewe Mathews for early research into Brian's film career, and to Byron Rogers for biographical details on Major Donald Neville-Willing, contained in a profile published in the *Telegraph Magazine*. Betty 'Joe' Carstairs – like Brian – lived to be so old as to be practically forgotten. However, her eccentric life provoked the interest of a writer on the *Daily Telegraph*, resulting in a charming biography by Kate Summerscale, *The Queen of Whale Cay*. My thanks also to Edwina Barstow for picture research and Permissions.

My personal memoir of Brian has not attempted a detailed description, analysis or serious evaluation of his films. *Empress* is not that sort of book, and besides, I am too much of a fan to do a decent job. But it should be done, and I hope that this book might inspire some serious student of film (preferably Irish) to write a proper study. Brian executed a large body of work, and half a dozen or so of his films have withstood the test of time.

I owe an enormous debt of gratitude to Mark Lucas, my agent and friend, who has encouraged me to write this book for as long as I have known him. It only took me twenty years to take the plunge. I would also like to thank my editor, Andrew Gordon, for agreeing to publish a book about a man the world has forgotten. His enthusiasm and commitment from beginning to end have been a writer's tonic.

Most of all I would like to thank Mary Agnes Donoghue. This is the third book she has supported from the outset, read closely, and to which she has contributed editorial insight. She has saved the reader from the worst of the purple, and the more tortured of the metaphors; and she has saved the author from himself.